DAVID LLEWELYN

INVIS
GOLD
IN ASIA

CREATING WEALTH THROUGH INTELLECTUAL PROPERTY

mc Marshall Cavendish Business

Project editor: Lee Mei Lin
Design by Benson Tan / Cover by OpalWorks Co Ltd

Published by Marshall Cavendish Business
An imprint of Marshall Cavendish International (Asia) Pte Ltd
1 New Industrial Road, Singapore 536196

Other Marshall Cavendish Offices
Marshall Cavendish Ltd. PO Box 65829, London EC1P 1NY, UK • Marshall Cavendish Corporation. 99 White Plains Road, Tarrytown NY 10591-9001, USA • Marshall Cavendish International (Thailand) Co Ltd. 253 Asoke, 12th Flr, Sukhumvit 21 Road, Klongtoey Nua, Wattana, Bangkok 10110, Thailand • Marshall Cavendish (Malaysia) Sdn Bhd, Times Subang, Lot 46, Subang Hi-Tech Industrial Park, Batu Tiga, 40000 Shah Alam, Selangor Darul Ehsan, Malaysia

Llewelyn, David.
Invisible gold in Asia : creating wealth through intellectual property /
David Llewelyn. – Singapore : Marshall Cavendish Business, c2010.
p. cm.
Includes bibliographical references and index.
ISBN-13 : 978-981-261-890-0

1. Intellectual property – Asia. 2. Industrial property – Asia. I. Title.

KNC370
346.5048 – dc22 OCN646764002

Printed in Singapore by Fabulous Printers Pte Ltd

INVISIBLE GOLD IN ASIA

“Don’t make the mistake of thinking something is valuable merely because you can measure it. It is far better to work out what you value and then see if you can measure it.”

Acknowledgements

I have been very fortunate to benefit both from being taught by some of the best brains in the intellectual property (IP) law field around the world and from working with outstanding individuals in a variety of businesses and institutions that recognise the importance of IP rights.

In the first category are Professor Gerald Dworkin (who first taught me IP law at Southampton University, was then a colleague at Queen Mary College London and subsequently my predecessor both as Professor at King's College London and as Director of the IP Academy Singapore); Professor Bill Cornish (who recruited me more than 30 years ago as research fellow to the Max Planck Institute for IP Law in Munich, then asked me to teach IP law with him on the University of London Master of Laws programme at LSE and much later invited me to join him as co-author of his groundbreaking textbook on the subject); Professor Dieter Stauder at the Max Planck Institute (who taught me a lot both about IP laws other than those of England and about life); Robert Swift of Linklaters (who taught me to use one word where previously I had used five); Lord Justice Jacob (who got me my job at Linklaters and has been an inspiration and irritation ever since); Professor Jim Lahore (with whom I taught for many years at Queen Mary College London and who instilled in me a sense of the absurd side of IP); and the late Professor Sir Hugh Laddie (who, particularly in the last three years of his life when we lectured and laughed together a lot, reminded me of the importance of combining an enquiring mind with a respect for others' views).

In the second are John Runeckles (the best commercial IP lawyer and analyst of a horse race I have known); Hugh Brett (one of the most knowledgeable and open-minded of IP lawyers); Dimitrios Drivas and Bob Raskopf (who, along with David Eisenberg in London, taught me that US lawyers can have a sense of humour but can't drink); Professor John Phillips and Dr Tanya Aplin of King's College London; Professor Spyros Maniatis, Director of the Centre for Commercial Law Studies at Queen Mary College London; Professor Hugh Hansen, father of the always excellent Annual Fordham International IP conference in New York; Jeremy Hemans and Sharon Snodgrass of the IP investment and strategy company IPR-X; Ho Cheng Huat and Rose Ramli of the IP Academy Singapore; Chan Lai Fung, Permanent Secretary at the Ministry of Law in Singapore; and Professors Johannes Chan and Lim Chin Leng of the Hong Kong University Faculty of Law.

In a category of her own is my former Deputy Director at the IP Academy Singapore and now observer of the Hong Kong scene, Lyn Ng, who is not only immensely talented in any area she deigns to touch but knows more about restaurants around the world than anyone else.

I would also like to thank for her help, and support when I got fed up, my research assistant for the past nine months, Beverley Koranteng-Aitkins: she's learnt a lot and so have I.

To Low Chee Wah I owe the introduction to my publisher Marshall Cavendish and Chris Newson, who immediately "got it" about the importance of IP and the need to make it more accessible. In turn, the accessibility of this book, such as it is, has been improved greatly through the efforts of his colleague Lee Mei Lin and my editor, Emilyn Tan.

However, despite the help of all these people and many more, there will be mistakes in what follows and those mistakes are my fault alone. Corrections and comments will be gratefully received at gidavid.llewelyn@gmail.com.

Last but first in importance, I must thank the three Cs: my wife Carolyn, daughter Cerys and secretary "computer says no" Carol, without whom this would not have seen the light of day; and my parents, for leaving me to do my own thing.

Singapore
July 2010

Contents

Introduction

Intellectual Property Rights, or IPRs, is the much-used and abused term for "Invisible Gold". Patents, copyrights and brands are the best known but there are many other varieties. From music to telecoms, from seeds to trees, IPRs protect the services and products demanded by the globalised world and are the must-have currency of the Knowledge Economy.

Everywhere, IPRs are becoming more important—and not just because of the scourge of piracy and counterfeiting that makes the headlines. Although you wouldn't guess it from most media coverage in Asia, there is the positive side of IPRs too: the encouragement and protection of creativity and innovation through which businesses and economies grow and thrive.

It is time for that positive aspect of IPRs to come to the fore in Asia. It is only in this way that businesses and economies can move away from the destructive drive for cheaper and cheaper prices and, instead, move up the added-value curve. As Chen Hong, General Manager of Chinese TV maker SVA Group, predicted in 2004 before the company plunged into losses: "We must invest and develop new products. If we focus on price alone, we don't have a future."

Governments all around Asia have come to realise that a nation's comparative advantage in the regional and global trade of the 21st century lies in the price premiums—the "added value"—that its creative and innovative businesses can command both at home and abroad. In his 2010 New Year message, Singapore Prime Minister Lee Hsien Loong called on his country's businesses to engage in "relentless innovation" and the creation of added value. It is the added value that IPRs protect.

It's cold out there

At the business level in Asian countries, IPRs provide much-needed shelter from the chill winds of local and foreign competition that now blow through economies previously protected by entrenched interests and trade barriers. In all Asian members of the World Trade Organisation, local businesses and even industries can no longer be nurtured through subsidies and overt preference. Alternative, but legal, obstacles to competition like IPRs must be built up and exploited.

There is a thirst to learn about these rights, about how businesses can use (and sometimes abuse) them to get ahead of the competition. At a governmental level, policymakers struggle to fit their own diverse economies with the rules of the IPR game written over the past couple of decades. As we will see, some of those rules seem to have been written to favour countries and businesses that have played the game for many years—who already have their reserves of Invisible Gold—and to maintain the competitive advantage of the IPR "haves" over the "have-nots". That is a problem for the future. What we will try and do is explain how to play the game by the existing rules, which are not going to change soon.

So, let's try and slake that thirst, whilst bearing in mind throughout the sage warning from Professor McMillan in his history of markets, *Reinventing the Bazaar*: "Intellectual property elicits fervent opinions: some say it is an oxymoron; others say the current rules are immutable. Neither view is correct. Because intellectual property involves mutually incompatible aims—rewarding the innovator versus allowing full usage of ideas—there is no universally ideal degree of intellectual property protection. Whether it should be strong or weak varies with the circumstances."

It's vital to appreciate at the outset that, globally, there are two markets for IPRs: the one in the USA and the one in the rest of the world. Contrary to the belief of many, in the IPR field (as in many others), what happens in the USA is very different to what happens everywhere else. IPRs and their protection are more of an integral and everyday part of business life in the USA than in any other country.

Some other countries share many of its characteristics: Australia and New Zealand, Britain, Canada, Finland, France, Germany, Ireland, Italy, South Africa, the Benelux and Scandinavian countries are all developed IPR markets. But it's still a mistake even there to rely on a view that what can be done in Baltimore can be done in Berlin or Bergen.

Then, when you get to Beijing, Bangkok or Bangalore, the differences are vast. Unlike Thomas Friedman's globalised world, the IP world is most definitely not flat. Instead, it is characterised by huge but subtle cultural undulations, by language differences and other barriers, and by deep trenches dug at national borders.

What's coming?

Part One of the book tries to explain to the non-specialist what IPRs are and to put them into their business context, using Asian examples wherever relevant. It also seeks to dispel some of the headline-seeking myths about IPRs.

Part Two looks at the IPR landscape around Asia today. The term "Asia" was originally a Western concept used to describe the eastern part of the land mass of Eurasia separated from Europe by the Ural Mountains—or, as the ancient Greeks would have said, "everything east of Greece". It incorporates a number of regions and peoples from vastly varied civilisations. It is likely that the peoples of ancient Asia themselves, such as the Chinese, Indians, Japanese, Persians and Arabs, did not conceive the idea of Asia because they did not view themselves collectively in the way Europeans did.

Given its size and diversity, it is often not clear today what countries are included in Asia. The term is sometimes used to refer to the Asia-Pacific region, which does not include Turkey, the Middle East, Central Asia or Russia but does include islands in the Pacific Ocean—a number of which may also be considered part of Australasia. Other descriptions of what is happening in Asia refer only to the countries in the West-centric term "Far East", to those in Southeast Asia or even to the countries of the Indian subcontinent.

"It's vital to appreciate at the outset that, globally, there are two markets for IPRs: the one in the USA and the one in the rest of the world."

In this book the author has taken a more limited view and looks at the ASEAN countries (Brunei Darussalam, Cambodia, Indonesia, Laos, Malaysia, Myanmar, the Philippines, Singapore, Thailand and Vietnam), plus China, Japan, the Republic of Korea, Taiwan and India, together with the other countries on the Indian subcontinent.

Asia

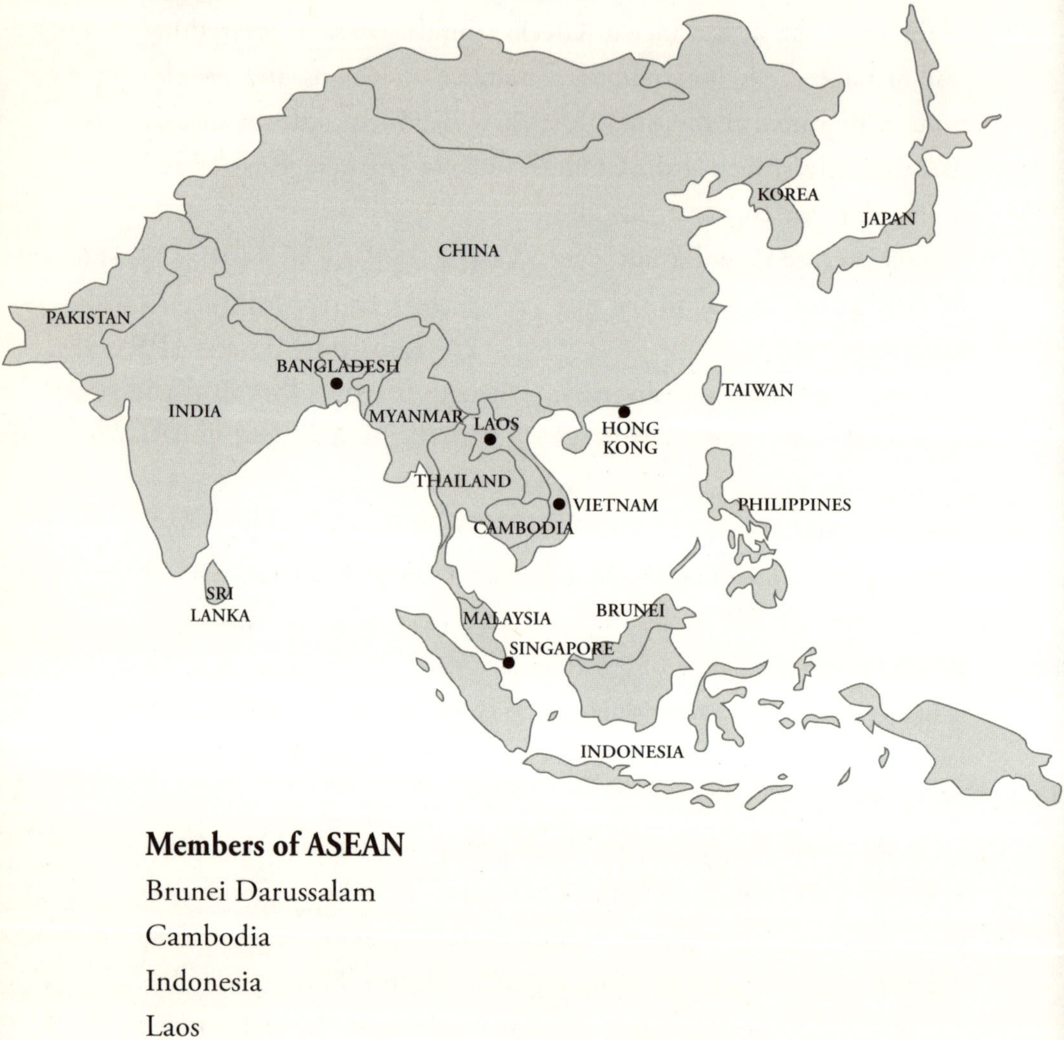

Members of ASEAN

Brunei Darussalam

Cambodia

Indonesia

Laos

Malaysia

Myanmar

Philippines

Singapore

Thailand

Vietnam

PART ONE

What Are Intellectual Property Rights?

01 Invisible Gold: what it is (and what it is not)

Patents, trade secrets, trademarks, publicity rights, domain names, geographical indications, copyright, design rights … the list goes on. These IPRs are the "Invisible Gold" at the heart of most successful businesses in the 21st century. But it is shrouded in mystery and in jargon, even though it affects us all.

Even the catch-all description "Intellectual Property Rights" is dangerously seductive and suggests misleadingly that there is a holistic coherence to these rights—that they can be dealt with in the same way. They can't:

- some are registered, others are not;
- some protect creativity, others do not;
- some last a short period, others for more than a century.

Let's try to shine some light on what IPRs are and how they work, starting with the most expensive and best-known: the patent, on which the pharmaceutical and electronics industries, as well as many others, rely to protect their innovations.

Then comes the trademark, or the brand, which lies behind the success of global powerhouses such as L'Oréal, Sony and Unilever.

The third of the principal IPRs is copyright, on which the success of the entertainment and software industries is based, but which is threatened by the digital revolution—and the ease of copying this has brought with it.

THE PATENT

What it is: A **patent** is a right granted by the State, in response to an application by the inventor, covering a novel product or process. The invention is novel if it has not been revealed or published before *anywhere in the world*—although this raises the interesting problem for the US Patent and Trademark Office, for example, as to how it can search the 25 per cent of the world's technology not even translated into a language its examiners can understand. In China, a patent law change in October 2009 introduced this worldwide novelty standard to replace the far less onerous China-wide standard that previously had led to the grant in that country of many patents with little, if any, inventive merit. One expert was quoted as saying that you could apply to patent a wheel in China and get it through under the old standard.

In some countries, again including China, what we are talking about is an invention patent, as opposed to a design patent or a utility patent, which you can also obtain there. But more on that later.

A patent lasts for 20 years in most countries, provided you pay your renewal fees. In Hong Kong, however, there is a short-term patent that can last for up to eight years, in addition to the standard 20-year patent (which must be based on a patent already granted by either the UK IP Office in Wales, the European Patent Office in Munich or the State IP Office in Beijing).

Remember that patents protect inventions, and an invention is not the same thing as a discovery. In the words of a 19th-century English judge:

> "When Volta discovered the effect of an electric current from the battery on a frog's leg he made a great discovery, but no patentable invention. A patentee must do more than add knowledge to what previously existed; he must make some addition, not only to knowledge, but to previously known inventions … to produce either a new or useful thing or result, or a new method of producing an old thing or result."

A patent is a genuine monopoly right, so it doesn't matter if someone else quite independently comes up with the same invention without knowing anything about your patent. As patent owner, you will usually have the right to stop them (only in the country that you have the patent) by going to court and asking for an injunction, if your patent claims cover their invention. Don't think that anyone—the State, for example—is going to do it for you. You will have to dig deep into your own pockets and spend lots of your own time enforcing and defending your patent if you want to stop infringers.

Be careful of the quirks in different countries. Even if you have a patent it may not be enough. In this area, as in many others, it is not safe to assume that other countries are the same as yours.

Patents can cover the brilliant and the banal—the new lifesaving drug or the new corkscrew. The majority of patents cover the incremental improvement but there are many examples where they add "the fuel of interest to the fire of genius", to use Abraham Lincoln's words. Usually, the profit motive is there, too.

Warnings such as "patented worldwide", "worldwide patents obtained" are just that—warnings. They have no legal significance and are rarely even true. In 2004, of the 5.4 million patents in force worldwide, 81 per cent were granted in just six countries: the USA,

Japan, the United Kingdom, Germany, the Republic of Korea and France. But the warnings can frighten the ignorant, or even impress bankers.

If you do go through the expense of getting a US patent, it's important to remember when selling products in the United States that a failure to mark the goods with the US patent number means the patent owner would be unable to claim damages in an infringement action until the infringer is actually notified of the infringement, and only for the period of infringement after receiving the notification.

> "You will have to dig deep into your own pockets and spend lots of your own time enforcing and defending your patent if you want to stop infringers."

Today the majority of patents are the product of teams; the individual inventor of the 17th, 18th and 19th centuries has largely been replaced by the research labs of large corporations. Most invention is incremental—the small step, rather than the "Eureka!" invention that puts swathes of people out of work or creates vast new job opportunities.

The patent is the most expensive IPR to obtain, and the more countries in which you want protection the more expensive it becomes. But, remarkably, the majority of granted patents is not put to use in any way (in Europe, some 30 per cent). They are not commercialised; they are the acorns that do not become oak trees. The ones that do can make and break fortunes—from ring-pulls to roentgen rays, or, as we know them, X-rays.

In many areas of business, patenting activity is a critical measure of success. For example, in 2005, 12 of the top 20 patent applicants in Germany were automobile or automobile component companies, reflecting the importance of that sector to the German economy. The applicants ranged from the well-known Audi, BMW, DaimlerChrysler, Bosch and Siemens to the less well-known Denso of Japan, INA-Schaeffler and Behr (which makes air-conditioning for cars and engine cooling systems).

Costly strands

US pharmaceutical giant Merck has lost two appeals (first in the Beijing No. 1 Intermediate Court, then the Beijing High Court) against a decision of the State Intellectual Property Office (SIPO) in China to take away one of its patents. This patent had been granted by SIPO in 2002 covering a process to make finasteride, a drug to treat hair loss.

“In 2004, of the 5.4 million patents in force worldwide, 81 per cent were granted in just six countries: the USA, Japan, the UK, Germany, Korea and France.”

In 2004, Henan Topfond Pharmaceutical, Ltd obtained approval from the State Food and Drug Administration to manufacture finasteride. Shortly before starting to make and distribute the product, Topfond discovered that Merck had been granted its patent, having applied for it as long ago as 1994. The Chinese company asked SIPO to take away the patent (in legal jargon, to invalidate it) because Merck had never marketed the drug in China. Topfond said this meant the patented invention had no “practical applicability”, which is required in Chinese laws. SIPO agreed with Topfond and invalidated Merck’s patent. As surprised about this as many foreign commentators, Merck kept fighting but at the end of 2008 failed in its second attempt to overturn that decision in the courts.

What's related

i. Trade secret

Often closely allied with the patent but valuable in itself is the **trade secret.** A trade secret or **confidential information** is information belonging to an individual or business that has a sufficient element of secrecy or confidentiality, such that the law will protect it and not allow its disclosure to others without consent. There is no need to register.

It was a hugely valuable trade secret—Formula X for its cola drink—that led the Coca-Cola Company to withdraw from India back in the 1970s rather than reveal it to the authorities. The secret formula still resides in a safe in the corporation's headquarters in Atlanta, Georgia, accessible only by the corporation's most senior officers.

When a former employee who had worked for 14 years with oil-based inks at Korea's Monami joined competitor Microceramic, Monami successfully sued in the Seoul District Court to prevent Microceramic from using its trade secrets about how to make ink. Monami was able to show that its former employee had in his mind particular trade secrets that would help his new employer get its product on the market much quicker than if it had to do the research itself from scratch.

On the other hand, in Australia the court refused to protect as a trade secret an idea as general as "a programme on millionaires with interviews, with some explaining the secrets of their success". The information or idea must be clearly described and obviously secret.

To establish a claim you must show that the occasion of communication was confidential (or the circumstances show that both sides would have accepted it was, if they had been asked at the time)—that what you say is "secret" can be clearly described and shown to not be known generally.

Storm the Wall

In October 2009 at the Shijiazhuang court, the Great Wall car company took the offensive in an action being brought against it by Fiat for copyright infringement, by bringing a bizarre counterclaim for breach of trade secrets—or industrial espionage. According to press reports, the Chinese company based its claim on Fiat's reliance on unauthorised photographs of Great Wall's Baoding production facilities for its GW Peri car, which looks very similar to the Fiat Panda. Fiat had the photos taken for use in its Chinese action against Great Wall for infringement of copyright, in which it had already succeeded in Italy, but Great Wall argued that the photos contain trade secrets. "Chinese companies that infringe intellectual property rights are increasingly adopting a strategy of claiming that investigations to gather evidence of their infringement actually constitute acts of industrial espionage," Elliot Papageorgiou, a partner at Rouse Legal, was quoted as saying.

ii. Know-how

Another related term is **know-how** (which is often very valuable commercially), but not all know-how will be protected as a trade secret.

Often, businesses try to protect trade secrets by requiring employees to sign an agreement stating they will not compete after they leave the employment, but in some countries such contracts are not allowed. For example, a new labour contract law in China, which came into force in January 2008, specifies that *only* senior management and employees with access to critical trade secrets can be required to enter into agreements that prevent them from moving to a competitor for a maximum period of two years after they leave the business. After all, a lot of a person's know-how is general skill and expertise, the use of which the law will generally not allow to be restrained. Otherwise how would an employee ever move jobs?

Different laws provide different answers to that question. It has been argued, for example, that one of the reasons for the huge success of Silicon Valley is the fact that California law does not allow post-employment restrictions on competition, however short they may be. On the other hand, Hong Kong law allows lengthy non-compete provisions in contracts.

"A lot of a person's know-how is general skill and expertise, the use of which the law will generally not allow to be restrained."

After the US arm of Thai Union seafood company, which owns the Chicken of the Sea tuna brand, employed two former executives of another US seafood company, Contessa Premium Foods, at the beginning of 2006, they got embroiled in a vicious legal fight in California. Contessa alleged Thai Union had conspired with its employees to steal Contessa's trade secrets, including its customer lists. After a six-week trial in Los Angeles, the court awarded Contessa more than US$4 million in damages.

In the September 2009 Prospectus for its American Depositary Shares, Shanda Games, one of China's leading online game companies, acknowledged in the Risk Factors section the dangers posed by such litigation:

> "Some of our employees were previously employed at other companies, including some of our current and potential competitors. To the extent these employees or any employees we may employ in the future are involved in research that is

> similar to the research that they performed at their former employers, our competitors may file lawsuits or initiate proceedings against us alleging that these employees violated the ... trade secret rights of their former employers. ... [This] could be costly and divert financial and management resources."

Whatever the country in which they are trading, businesses need to be very careful in this area.

THE TRADEMARK

What it is: A trademark (sometimes called a **brand**) is any sign used to differentiate the products or services (sometimes called a **service mark**, although the law still treats them as trademarks) of one business from those of others.

Sometimes a trademark is the same as the name of the company making the product it's used on, like the Seiko trademark for watches made by the Seiko-Hattori Company (which changed its name from K. Hattori and Company when its Seiko trademark became more well-known than the company). More frequently, the trademark is owned by a business the man in the street has never heard of. For example—and staying with Japan—the retailing trademark Uniqlo is just one of the brands used by Fast Retailing Company, which only the most avid readers of the business pages have heard of. Its portfolio of brands also includes Comptoir des Cottoniers, Princesse tam.tam and g.u.

Trademarks may be registered at the country's trademark office. This is usually part of the Intellectual Property Office where patents and designs are applied for (as in Singapore, IPOS; or Korea, KIPO), although not in China, where it is part of the State Administration for Industry and Commerce (SAIC).

Trademark registrations, like all other registered IPRs, are only protected in the country in which they are registered. This even applies in the Special Administrative Regions of Hong Kong and Macau, which have their own IPR systems. These are quite different to that in the rest of China. A trademark registered in the PRC doesn't cover either Macau or Hong Kong or vice versa. In October 2009 *China Daily* reported on the problems encountered in this respect by Taiwanese company Yunghe International Development. In February 2009 it was told that its soybean milk trademark, Yunghe, recognised in 2005 as a Top China Brand, had been registered for soybean products in Hong Kong by a mainland Chinese named Zheng, who had been a shareholder in one of Yunghe's former partners in the PRC that had hoped to be given a franchise. Even though Yunghe had already registered its trademark in Hong Kong for catering services, it was only after lengthy (and, no doubt, not inexpensive) submissions by Yunghe's lawyers to the Hong Kong IP Department that the trademark was transferred to its rightful Taiwanese owner.

"Trademark registrations, like all other registered IPRs, are only protected in the country in which they are registered."

In short, a trademark can be:

- a **word** ("Panasonic", "Singha" and "Parachute", the last being Marico's trademark for its packaged coconut hair oil that has made the transition from a successful domestic Indian brand to selling in over 20 other countries);
- a **combination of words** ("Tiger Balm" or "Thums Up");
- a **logo** (the Singapore Airlines Silver Kris or Apple Computer's apple. The Apple logo was infringed in China in 2008 when a

drawing of an apple with two wings was used by a Shenzhen company as its logo, and the Intermediate People's Court in Shenyang ordered it to pay RMB400,000 to the American computer giant);

- a **colour** (the shade of green registered by BP in Singapore for containers for liquid petroleum gas);
- a **number** (in South Africa, "46664", the Robben Island prisoner number given to Nelson Mandela during his 27-year incarceration);
- the **shape** of goods (the shape of the Coca-Cola contour bottle registered in Japan, or in India the shape of the Zippo cigarette lighter and the Mini Maglite torch);
- and even—in some countries—a **sound** (as in Singapore, "of a human voice yodelling the word 'Yahoo!' " and "a five-tone audio progression of the notes D-flat, D-flat, G, D-flat and A-flat", registered by Yahoo Inc and Intel Corp, respectively).

What's related

i. Unfair competition

In many countries such as Malaysia and India, even without registration a trademark or name *may* also be protected against confusion, if it has previously been used in the market (in what's called a **passing off** or **unfair competition** action, depending on which country you are in).

After one of India's largest companies, Larsen & Toubro—or L&T as it's often called—found another business using the trademarks LNT and Elente on their miniature circuit-breaker products, it sued them for passing off, arguing that people would think the products were connected in some way with the well-known L&T. The Delhi court agreed to break the circuit and told the loser that he could only use his full name Lachmi Narain Trades and not the confusing acronyms. In China a local trader was stopped by the court from using the Internet domain name www.ikea.com.cn after the Swedish Ikea company complained that it was an act of unfair competition to do so.

When in July 2005 Novelty Pte Ltd started a development of terraced houses in Singapore and decided to call it Amanusa, it was sued for passing off by the well-known Amanresorts group, which ran a number of luxury boutique resorts around Asia including the Amanusa resort in Bali. Amanresorts succeeded in its legal action even though it didn't have a resort in Singapore, the court noting that some 1,382 Singaporeans had spent time at the Bali resort between 1995 and 2005. Perhaps, thought the court, people will think that there is some sort of a connection between the luxury hotels and the terraced houses. On the other hand, when the Swiss owner of the Wienerwald chain of restaurants tried to stop a local firm of chartered accountants from using Wienerwald in the register of company names in Hong Kong, it failed because the court considered that the "goodwill" it had generated through its 420 restaurants in Europe, the USA and Japan "had not yet penetrated" Hong Kong.

The moral of that story is this: **if you can afford it, register your trademark in any country you might do business in, even if you are not doing so today.**

ii. Get-up

The passing off or unfair competition action can also protect the **get-up** (in English terminology) or **trade dress** (in American) of a product or a service—like the look of a Mexican fast-food restaurant called Two Pesos, which didn't like the way its décor and ambience was copied by its competitor Taco Cabana.

A few years ago in Hong Kong a local manufacturer, Jimmy's

Company, which had blatantly copied the get-up of an electric fan sold by fellow Hong Kong company Kemtron under the trademark Mistral, thought it could avoid legal problems by using its own trademark Koolaire on the copy fans. That way it hoped to remove any chance of consumers thinking wrongly that they were buying a Mistral fan. But by copying even the unusual shape of the fan's handle and feet, Jimmy's had gone too far and were stopped by the court from passing off.

If the handle and feet of Kemtron's fan had been standard rather than slightly unusual in shape, the claim for passing off by taking the get-up would not have succeeded. To copy is not necessarily to pass off. It depends on whether consumers will think there is a connection between the two products due to the copying.

As explained, the shape of a product or its packaging can also be registered as a trademark in many countries and it is far better to rely on that protection than the more uncertain protection provided by passing off or an action for unfair competition. When French luxury goods maker Hèrmes found a Korean manufacturer making copies of its famous Kelly and Birkin bags, it won its legal action in the Seoul Central District Court in 2008 for both trademark infringement and unfair competition.

Back to trademarks

Now for some golden rules with trademarks. **Transliterate, or lose it.** You must remember where you are. In China it is often not enough to just register a trademark like Starbucks. If you don't register the mark by which you are actually known—the Chinese version of your mark—someone else might go and register it. Then you will have the problem of trying to have the mark cancelled, which can take up to five years. In practice, many foreign companies are not prepared to embark on the lengthy and uncertain process of trying to have the mark cancelled. Instead, they just pay the blackmail money demanded by the local company to transfer the registration.

The US coffee shop chain found this out to its cost when it brought legal proceedings against the Shanghai Xingbake Coffee Bar Company in 2006. "Xing-ba-ke" is a Chinese transliteration of Starbucks. Even though it had already opened a coffee shop in Beijing, the US company had to sue the Shanghai look-alike chain, which was using not only the Xingbake trading name but also a logo very similar to Starbucks' distinctive green and black one, for trademark infringement and unfair competition. Although the Shanghai court awarded Starbucks the maximum permitted compensation of RMB500,000 and ordered the local company to change its name, the case shows the importance of registering logos and transliterations, as well as the mark you use in English-speaking countries.

As in so many other areas of business, **it pays to be culturally sensitive in the field of trademarks.** For example, some trademarks just do not work in particular countries. Although Yeo Hiap Seng is a top-selling food brand in a number of countries, the CEO of the Singapore company, Tjong Yik Min, told the *Straits Times* newspaper that its brand of soya bean milk didn't catch on in Thailand when it was introduced in 2001, possibly because "Yeo's" sounds too much like "horse urine" in Thai. The Japanese isotonic drink trademark Pocari Sweat sounds very odd to the Western ear too.

On the other hand, when German luxury car maker BMW moved into the Chinese market, it started to use as its trademark the transliteration 宝马 ("bǎomǎ", which today sounds very like the name of the 44th US President). This means "valued horse", which has a nice ring to Chinese ears. For the rugged Land Rover vehicle,

Ford (which acquired the business from BMW in 2000) uses the trademark 路虎 (lùhǔ, or "tiger of the road"), whereas French car company Citroën has registered the trademark 雪铁龙 (xuětǐelóng, or "snow-iron-dragon"). The trademark used by Coca-Cola in China, 可口可乐 ("ke-kou-ke-le", reflecting the four syllables of the "Coca-Cola" brand and fortunately meaning "delicious happiness"), was registered as a trademark in the country as long ago as 1928 (although the American company's cola drink was not sold in the PRC from its foundation in 1949 until 30 years later in January 1979, when the iconic Coke drink was again shipped into the country).

What it is not: Unlike the patent, a trademark is *not* a monopoly. It doesn't give its owner the right to stop other people from using it in any way. It only protects against confusion that results from another's use of the same or a similar mark on the same or similar goods or services the mark is registered for or has been used on. Marks are registered for particular goods or services only: "Tiger" for beer, "Tiger Balm" for medicinal products and "Tiger Airways" for airline services. These are all owned by different companies in Singapore, and co-exist happily.

The practice adopted by Wahaha (娃哈哈) is often best. The Hangzhou-based company registered the trademark Wahaha in China not only in the main classes of goods the company used it on, for example mineral water and fruit juices, but also in other classes for which it might later be used. To try and stop others coming too close to its well-known mark, the company also registered trademarks that may be confused with Wahaha, like Hawaha (哈娃哈) and Hahawa (哈哈娃).

In addition, in certain limited cases of well-known marks—particularly invented ones like Sony or Lenovo—the mark can even be relied on to protect against use of a similar one on dissimilar goods or services. For example, in 2006 in a legal action brought by Eastman Kodak, the owner of the well-known mark Kodak for films, the Suzhou Intermediate People's Court ordered a local business to stop its use of the trademark Kodak for elevators.

The importance of coming up with a good trademark cannot be underestimated. In his autobiography, the co-founder of Tokyo Tsuchin Kogyo Kabushiki Kaisha, the late Akio Morita, recollected that during his foreign trip outside Japan in 1953 he realised his company's name was not a good one to put on a product. It was a tongue twister nobody in the United States could pronounce. Even the English-language translation, Tokyo Telecommunications Engineering Company, was a mouthful, and the short-form Tokyo Teletech couldn't be used because there was an American company called Teletech. So Morita came up with "Sony" (more about this on the next page).

> "Unlike the patent, a trademark is not a monopoly. It doesn't give its owner the right to stop other people from using it in any way."

If registered, a trademark can last as long as the renewal fees are paid, generally every 10 years (but, unusually, seven in Macau), and as long as it doesn't become the description of the product on which it is used. This was a problem encountered by Sony when its Walkman product was so successful that in some countries "a walkman" became the description of a personal stereo system rather than a trademark used on a particular one made by Sony.

The ® symbol indicates that the trademark is registered (in some countries like Pakistan it is a criminal offence to use the symbol if the mark is not registered) but you don't have to use it, although it can help to warn people off. Similarly the ™ symbol can help frighten off the uninitiated but has no legal significance.

So Sony

Early in the life of the business that became global giant Sony, Morita struggled to find a memorable name or logo (symbol) for his company. First, he and fellow founder Masaru Ibuka rejected the choice of a symbol such as the Mercedes three-pointed star or the Rolls-Royce Spirit of Ecstasy. As he later recalled, deciding what it should be was far more difficult:

"The name would be our symbol, and therefore it should be short, no more than four or five characters. … We wanted a new name that could be recognised anywhere in the world, one that could be pronounced the same in any language. We made dozens and dozens of tries. Ibuka and I went through dictionaries looking for a bright name, and we came across the Latin word *sonus*, meaning 'sound'. The word itself seemed to have sound in it. Our business was full of sound, so we began to zero in on *sonus*. At that time in Japan borrowed English slang and nicknames were becoming popular and some people referred to bright young and cute boys as 'sonny', or 'sonny-boys', and, of course, 'sunny' and 'sonny' both had an optimistic and bright sound similar to the Latin root with which we were working. And we also thought of ourselves as 'sonny-boys' in those days. Unfortunately, the single word 'sonny' by itself would give us troubles in Japan because in the romanisation of our language, the word 'sonny' would be pronounced 'sohn-nee', which means to lose money. That was no way to launch a new product. We pondered this problem for a little while and the answer struck me one day: why not just drop one of the letters and make it 'Sony'? That was it!"

Later, Morita came to appreciate the importance of having come up with an invented brand name rather than using one that was less distinctive. A Japanese business started selling Sony chocolate and even registered it as a trademark for chocolate and snack foods. After a long court case, the electronics company won its claim for unfair competition because, in Morita's words, "No matter what dictionaries [the chocolate company's lawyers] went to they could not find the word 'Sony'. The name is unique, and it is ours."

Legend to Lenovo

Yang Yuanqing of China's Lianxiang computer company had the opposite problem in 2002 as he considered his company's Lianxiang trademark and its English-language equivalent, Legend. Unfortunately, the laudatory name "Legend" was unavailable as a trademark in many countries where such words cannot be registered. So, Yang took the major decision to change his company's trademark, taking the first two letters of the old one and adding the Latin word for "new"—*novo*—to it: Lenovo. He thought this appropriate as what he was trying to do was create "a new Lianxiang". As Ling Zhijun reports in *The Lenovo Affair*: "On 23rd April 2003, the 'Legend' banners that had waved over China for 14 years were changed simultaneously to 'LiangxiangLenovo'. ... Huge outdoor billboards announced the change, as well as golden time ads on TV. At least 200 million Chinese saw the nightly news broadcast, after which they saw the word 'legend' dissolve and melt into silvery watery [sic]. 'LianxiangLenovo' rose, surrounded by the brilliant rays of a sunrise. For eight weeks, the ad was broadcast for 30 seconds every day."

What's related

There are then three other IPRs that bear some similarities to trademarks.

i. Publicity right

A **publicity right** is a right given to celebrities under the laws of a few but not the majority of countries in Asia, such as China where it's known as a **portrait right.** The portrait right is, however, of limited scope. This can be seen from a legal case brought in the Haidian District People's Court in Beijing by famous Chinese athlete, Liu Xiang, against *LifeStyle* magazine.

Liu Xiang claimed that the magazine had infringed his portrait right by publishing his picture on its front cover above an advertisement for Zhong You, a department store, in a way that suggested he was endorsing the store. The court categorised portraits into those independent of and those that may be associated with a "significant public event", noting that the portrait right for the first is absolute but that for the latter it is subject to limitations. The court therefore decided that Liu Xiang's portrait right had not been infringed.

On appeal, the Beijing No. 1 Intermediate Court held that Liu Xiang's portrait right had been infringed as the design of the magazine's cover clearly suggested a connection between the athlete and Zhong You Department Store. The court also found that by making changes to the photograph of Liu Xiang, *LifeStyle* had not only ignored his portrait right but also breached advertising laws, which both expressly require a clear separation of advertisements from other content and prohibit advertisements likely to mislead consumers into thinking that they were in some way connected to the other, non-advertising content. The court awarded Liu Xiang RMB20,000 as damages, and ordered *LifeStyle* to issue a written apology to him in the magazine.

Sometimes celebrities, or their legal advisers, claim rights that in fact they don't have. In September 2002 the Nelson Mandela Foundation, relying rather dubiously on a trademark law, insisted that a local South African artist Yiul Damaso stop selling his paintings of Mandela represented, among other ways, as a Rastafarian. Art galleries around the country reportedly reacted by removing all paintings including any reference to the South African hero and former President. The country's *Mail & Guardian* newspaper expressed astonishment that even exhibitors at the World Summit on Sustainable Development crafts and art fair at Ubuntu Village were instructed by Foundation attorney Ishmail Ayob to remove all images of the former President. It quoted a bemused Jacob Khumalo, an unemployed artist from KwaZulu-Natal who was exhibiting at the fair, as saying: "Some of us painted the portraits from existing photographs to show our admiration for Madiba [Mandela]—nothing more. Yet now we are prevented from benefitting from the Earth Summit, because of this stupid law which nobody told us about."

In the same year, even though there was no real basis in law for doing so, Tamil superstar Rajnikant gave notice in Indian newspapers that anyone copying his style, and especially his actions and gestures in his latest film *Baba*, would be sued unless they got his permission, and paid.

ii. Domain names

A **domain name** is a contractual right to use a particular address on the World Wide Web (www.ipacademy.com.sg for the IP Academy Singapore or www.ipd.gov.hk for the IP Department of the Hong Kong SAR, for instance). The domain name itself belongs to the domain name registry and is not actually an intellectual property right. But it can give rise to IP disputes similar to trademark fights because of the global nature of the Internet and the fact that the domain name system is not product or service specific.

Family names such as McDonald or Ford that have become famous trademarks for particular goods or services are shared with tens of thousands of people around the world called McDonald or Ford, many of whom may like to have ford.com, mcdonalds.com.sg, or something like those as their domain name. Similarly, different businesses in different parts of the world may have identical names that they want to register as domain names. Provided there is no intention to mislead, there is nothing wrong with this.

But remember there is a world out there—something the *St Petersburg Times* from Florida forgot when its lawyers sent a letter to the *St Petersburg Times* in Russia demanding that it give up its domain name, www.sptimes.ru. The Russians pointed out firmly that their city had been around rather longer than the American one and perhaps the Florida newspaper should have its city's name changed!

iii. Geographical indication

A **geographical indication** (GI) is a right to prevent use of the indication by producers outside the geographical area.

For example, under Vietnamese law, only fish sauce made and bottled on the island of Phu Quoc, off the south-western province of Kien Giang, can bear the Phu Quoc name. Despite this, in 2005 Nguyen Thi Tinh, chairwoman of the Phu Quoc Fish Sauce Producers' Society, claimed that only six per cent of fish sauce carrying the Phu Quoc mark sold domestically was genuine.

In India over 60 GIs had been registered at the GI Registry in Chennai by the middle of 2008. Many were for textile products and handicrafts, such as Mysore silk, Kullu shawl and Kashmir pashmina, but also agricultural products such as Fazli mangoes, Mysore jasmine and Malabar peppers. Again, it's important to remember that the GI being protected in India may mean nothing if it's used in Sri Lanka or in Pakistan. Whether it's protected there depends on the law of Sri Lanka or of Pakistan.

A recent registration in India of Pisco liquor as a geographical indication illustrates well one of the problems in this area. Peru has been granted GI protection for this name used on brandy made from Pisquera grapes, but other countries claim justly that they make Pisco that is just as genuine as that made in Peru.

Native brandies were very popular with 17th-century Europeans. Through trial and error it was found that a local South American grape called Quebranta produced a pure, highly potent, aromatic brandy, which eventually became known by the name of the Peruvian port from which it was exported to grateful drinkers in Europe—Pisco. Peruvians feel a deep-seated national pride in pisco, which they make from the cream of the grape harvest and have been drinking at parties and rowdy peasant festivals for more than 400 years.

But pisco made in Chile has now found small export markets in the United States and Europe, largely because Peruvian exporters are hampered by hyper-inflation and an unfavourable exchange rate. A Peruvian official made the garbled claim in 2006: "Peru is planning action under international patent agreements—the same ones that guard copyrights over everything from computers to pharmaceuticals—to keep the pisco name exclusively for Peru." As happens so frequently when national sensitivities are concerned, this is nonsense but at least it indicates how sensitive people get about such important matters like drink and food.

According to Godofredo Gonzalez del Valle, whose family has

been making pisco in Peru for four generations, the distinctiveness of Peru's pisco comes from the stomp. "To make real pisco, you have to take your shoes off, crush the grapes and let it ferment in clay bottles. In Chile they make something called pisco, but it doesn't taste as it should."

Chilean pisco is sweeter and slightly weaker than Peruvian pisco. "Only Peru has the soil, the climate, and the tradition in making pisco that gives our drink a special taste, and which allows us to call it pisco," asserts Jaime Alvarez Calderon, who is in charge of Peru's multilateral economic negotiations office. Chileans disagree but certainly seem to have lost out in India.

The GIs most people will know are from their drinking of wines with an *appellation d'origine*.

THE COPYRIGHT

What it is: A **copyright** (or, in legal systems based on the Continental European model, an **author's right**) is a legal right that arises in works that are recorded—on paper, on film, on tape, on computer disk. It covers very broad subject matter, from doodles to Picasso paintings, from children's scrawls to sketches by world-famous architect I.M. Pei of the Bank of China Tower in Hong Kong, from TV programmes to Bollywood movies, from newspaper articles to Harry Potter books.

The aim of copyright is to encourage creativity and hence its importance for Asia. As Singapore's former UN Ambassador and now the widely-respected Dean of the Lee Kuan Yew School of Public Policy, Kishore Mahbubani wrote in his powerful recent book about the irresistible shift of global power to the East: "Asia is exploding because so many Asian minds, underused for centuries, are now exploding with creativity."

What it is not: What copyright does not protect is ideas or facts, which remain as free as air. What it protects is a work expressed in a particular way. When the horses and jockeys in the 3.40 race at Hong Kong's Happy Valley racecourse are set out in the race meeting programme bought by thousands of race-goers, complete with the colours worn by each jockey and details of the trainer and weight carried by each horse, this is a copyright work. As a consequence, if the *South China Morning Post* wants to publish the details of each race, it must pay Hong Kong Jockey Club for its permission to reproduce the copyright work.

> "The aim of copyright is to encourage creativity and hence its importance for Asia."

A copyright costs nothing to obtain and there is no need to use the © symbol. Except in a few countries such as Indonesia, there is no need, or possibility, to register. The copyright arises automatically when you put something on paper or other media. And you get the benefit of international conventions to obtain, again automatically and without payment, copyright in most countries of the world.

That's why copyright has become the most significant IP right for most businesses and why it presents so many opportunities for those who understand how to exploit these global bundles of rights. On the other hand, the flip-side is the huge challenge presented to rights-owners and their financial backers both by the dark and murky areas of commercial piracy, in which organised crime syndicates are frequently active, and by the young digital generation who have grown up believing that content is or should be free.

Today, copyright covers far more than its traditional subject matter of books, plays, music, engravings and sculpture. It also protects the products of technological advances, TV broadcasts, computer programs, sound recordings and databases. So, the copyright in a cartoon character, for example, can be exploited not only in its traditional forms such as in newspaper cartoon strips and in films but also on the Internet, mobile phones and in different distribution channels such as cable TV—all of them generating revenue based on ownership of copyright in the characters.

When ex-McKinsey partner Samir Patil bought long-established children's comic book brands Tinkle and Amar Chitra Katha (ACK) from publisher India Book House in 2007, it was not only the comic book market he was interested in but also the exciting opportunities to license the copyright in ACK's characters (such as shambolic jungle explorer Shikar Shambu) for use in these other media.

The duration of the copyright varies depending on its type, but as a general rule it has been getting longer and longer over recent years. Back in 1976 when the Hello Kitty character was created, the founder of its owner Sanrio, Shintaro Tsuji, was well aware that, unlike patent protection that expired after 15 (or sometimes slightly more and now usually 20) years, the cartoon cat's copyright protection lasted for at least 50 years in Japan. In many countries it lasts for the life of the author plus 70 years. Also, there may be a number of different copyrights in one product like a film (the copyright in the music, the screenplay, the film, the video, the DVD) but in most countries a written work such as a book, a menu or a computer program will now have copyright protection for the life of the author plus 50 or 70 years after.

Do remember, however, that although it may last for a long time (up to 120 or so years, depending on how long the author lives) copyright does expire. It is nonsense to suggest, as did some journalists in a 2007 midsummer media frenzy, that reproduction terracotta warriors found in Hamburg's Museum of Ethnology could be copyright infringements. There might have been fraud involved or it could even have been a breach of contract but copyright does not last 2,200 years. Anyone can copy a terracotta warrior and there is nothing another person can do to stop it.

That's the easy bit. Now come the "buts":

- But: **Copyright doesn't protect ideas, only the way they are expressed.** (Some very learned people object to this summary as not being completely accurate, but when has any statement in this hugely complicated area been 100 per cent true, except "It's impossible to generalise"?) Just as Fang Lijun has no monopoly over baldness in art, merely because Yue Minjun is well-known for featuring laughing people in his works does not mean he can stop another artist who adopts the same theme or idea. However, if that artist copies a substantial part of a particular painting by Yue featuring jocular men—say the *Portrait of the Artist and His Friends*, which sold in May 2007 at a Christie's, Hong Kong sale for HK$20.48 million—it is likely to be copyright infringement. Moving your unmade bed into your art gallery doesn't infringe Tracey Emin's rights, although if you suggest, falsely, that it's her messy bed, then you may be liable for passing off or unfair competition (depending on the country you are in)—another area of IP law. Similarly, there's nothing wrong legally with mimicking the distinctive style of Zhang Xiaogang, as long as you don't suggest that your haunting face with its bloodline is a work by him.
- But: Copyright is what is says it is—a right to stop unauthorised copying of a whole or a substantial part of a work such as a painting or sculpture. **It is not a monopoly right like a patent, which can be infringed unknowingly.** Two people can own

separate copyrights in a practically identical drawing of a view of the Great Wall or the Singapore Flyer; in fact, they may have sat next to each other when drawing it. Neither can stop the other exploiting their copyright as long as the later work was not copied from the earlier.

- But: Remember that most artwork borrows from or is inspired by others (another word is "steals" if you want to be emotive, as too many do in this field). Some artists admit the inspiration—the title *Le Dejeuner Sur L'herbe* is Yue Minjun's nod of acknowledgement to Edouard Manet's painting of the same name. Others don't like to acknowledge their sources, perhaps feeling it diminishes their artistic integrity in some way. If they are worried about copyright, however, they often don't need to be. **It's worth repeating that, for there to be copyright infringement, there must be a taking of a substantial part of another's work, and that doesn't mean the idea or the style.**
- But: Guarding your alleged rights too zealously may leave egg on your face if the fact that you yourself borrowed from an earlier work is pointed out by the hapless victim of your righteous indignation. All too frequently, copying is in the eye of the beholder, and a bit of restraint, of stepping back, is advisable before firing off threatening letters. After all, just because you have oversized dancing figures in your painting doesn't mean that Beryl Cook or Pan Dehai has infringed your copyright. They may have done it first or they may never have heard of you or even seen your work (so no chance of copying). Just because you're threatened with a copyright infringement suit does not mean you have infringed copyright. In this area, there is much unjustified sabre-rattling to see who blinks first.
- But: International copyright conventions mean that your local

Indonesian, Singaporean or Chinese copyright (depending on where you are when your work is created) is also automatically protected by a bundle of other national rights around the world, all of which last for the author's life plus at least another 50 years. It's protected but nobody is going to enforce it; that's up to you.

- But: If you're an employee when you create the artistic work, if it's within your job scope and you do it in your company time, copyright will probably belong to your employer. The flip-side: if you're engaging someone to create the work for you—say, to do a painting for your office—and you're paying, you need to make sure that you get a written transfer of the copyright if you want it. Otherwise it stays with the artist, and you don't want to have to track him or her down later when a postcard company wants to feature your painting.
- But: With the exception of J.M. Barrie's *Peter Pan* in Britain, which was given perpetual copyright in the UK to benefit the Great Ormond Street Hospital for Children, the copyright in works does expire, normally 50 or 70 years after the author's death.
- But: As long as it does last, that protection (like other IPRs) is national in its scope; there is no such thing as a global copyright. If your US, Indian or Chinese copyright work is being copied without your permission in the US, India or China, you must sue there or in all those places if it is being copied in them all. And that's not cheap.
- But: In countries following the Anglo-American legal tradition, like Hong Kong and India, copyright is a purely economic matter and follows the money. It can protect the banal (the railway timetable, the drawing of a finger on a ballot paper, the table of

horseracing results) to the sublime (the Fang Lijun painting or the Natsume Soseki novel). On ownership, the contract rules.

- **But:** You do have to register the copyright in the US (but almost nowhere else in the world) if you want to sue there and get the maximum damages and, very importantly, your attorney's costs. Two further notes of caution vis-à-vis that country: first, the law there gets far closer than anywhere else in the world to one of, "If it's worth copying it's worth protecting." Secondly, litigating is a national sport.
- **But:** Anywhere in the world copyright is a very powerful tool, and becoming more so as the digital world spreads. Despite the attendant problem that technology makes copying so easy, copyright in the bits and bytes of the digital world provides owners of content with the means to charge for access to many resources that were previously free. It even gives them the right to stop those selling electronic secateurs designed to cut through the technological fences—such as encryption surrounding online copyright material. The 1998 Digital Millennium Copyright Act in the US gave these and yet more far-reaching rights to copyright owners. (It is, however, fair to say that American courts have struggled with its interpretation since the law was passed hastily at the urging of powerful lobbyists.)

All in all, although it is by no means straightforward, copyright is of increasing significance in many areas. It is what it says it is: a right to prevent copying. It is not a monopoly right.

If I draw the view across the harbour from the old Star Ferry terminal in Hong Kong, I have copyright in my drawing. And so does everyone else who draws the same view. The right only allows each copyright owner to stop another person from *copying* his or her individual drawing, not creating their own drawing from exactly the same place as I or others sat at to draw mine and theirs, although it can also be used to stop indirect copies. Independent creation is an absolute defence against any legal action for copyright infringement ... although of course you may need to prove to the court that you hadn't seen what you are alleged to have copied.

Copyright and copy-wrong

Artists the world over demand it; artists the world over don't understand it ... What is copyright?

To take the law in India as an example, protection is given to artistic works—to graphic creations, photographs, sculptures (even the Frisbee was protected in this category) and collages irrespective of artistic quality; to works of architecture, including models of buildings; and to works of artistic craftsmanship (a Philippe Starck washbasin, for instance). If your works don't fall within these categories, you don't have copyright. Martin Creed's controversial Turner Prize-winning 2001 *Work No. 227: The light's going on and off*, where the artist used the Tate Gallery's existing light fittings, would not be protected by copyright, and neither would much performance art or piles of bricks. But a painting featuring bricks (or perhaps they are cobblestones), like works from the Tiananmen series by Ziang Xiaogang, would.

From the quick sketch of a bald man by a young student sitting in the back of a classroom and dreaming of being a future Fang Lijun to Microsoft's Windows 7 computer program, works recorded in some permanent way are protected by copyright for the life of the author and thereafter for at least 50 years (70 years in the case of the USA, UK and the European Union), without a need to register them or other formalities.

The digital dilemma

With the digital revolution and the viral spread of the Internet, copyright has been thrust into the legal limelight.

First, because of the ease of copying in the digital world and (especially with business models such as those of YouTube, which rely on free content and thereby much copyright infringement) the threat which that poses to copyright owners—what "technoscold" Andrew Keen describes, sensationally but inaccurately, in his thought-provoking book *The Cult of the Amateur* as "an industry-destroying, paradigm-shifting dismantling of 200 years of intellectual property law". Secondly, because to download is automatically to *copy* (onto a computer's hard-drive) and therefore needs the copyright owner's consent.

These two facts are what provide a huge opportunity for copyright owners if technology allows them to charge a fee to enter their digital vaults.

Just a word of explanation on that "automatically to copy" point, because it's critical to an understanding of what we are talking about. In the pre-digital world of paper books, vinyl gramophone records, audio and video tapes, borrowing a book, record or tape from a friend, either to see if you liked it or because you didn't have the money or inclination to buy it yourself, gave rise to no copyright issue. There was no "copy" made without permission of the copyright owner. You just read the book, played the record or ran the video on the video-recorder. There was no copyright infringement (or "piracy", in the emotive terminology peddled by the music and film companies and their expensive lobbyists).

Then along came the software revolution.

In February 1976, Bill Gates wrote his challenging "Open Letter to Hobbyists". He was bursting with pride about the "interpreter" program he and his two friends had written for the Altair microcomputer. But he complained that even though they had toiled almost round the clock for 60 days to write the program—and most of the following year debugging and documenting it—and despite thousands of copies changing hands, the royalties they had received up to that point amounted to something less than $2 an hour. Why? Because people were "stealing" his software, Gates complained, making copies and passing them around.

> "Copyright is the right to prevent copying. It is not a monopoly right."

Until then, writing software had been mostly either a cooperative venture among hobbyists or the preserve of big business with room-size mainframe computers. It was handled by committees, and an invoice for the work done might have read, "Software, $500,000". Now Gates was proposing a very different model—one much more like book publishing. "Who can afford to do professional work for nothing?" he asked. "Nothing would please me more than being able to hire 10 programmers and deluge the hobby market with good software."

But to do that he would have to collect a royalty on each copy of his programs that was sold, as did writers and recording artists. That meant "shrink-wrap" licensing of the software—creating a contractual mechanism that would place restraints on what buyers could do with their copies, and technical means of enforcing it to prevent those who had not paid for a copy from possessing one.

The licence revenues of the software industry are based on the technical fact that to load software onto a computer, to download from the Internet, to transfer digital files is to *copy* the bits and bytes onto your hard-drive (or whatever replaces it in the future). Thus, magically, to do that without getting permission from Microsoft or whoever else owns the copyright, is to infringe; it is to be called a copyright pirate. That technical consequence, combined with the phenomenal capability of the Internet to open up new markets of potential consumers, has handed to copyright owners unbounded possibilities, at the same time as presenting huge challenges.

Practically all software (even so-called open source) and the vast majority of things you download (music, articles, photos) are works protected by copyright belonging to someone, somewhere. Loading them onto your computer, downloading or transferring them without that person's or, more usually, corporation's permission, is copyright infringement. Although there are legal defences, they are far more limited than the man and woman in the street realises.

That is the "paradigm-shifting" change (to adopt Keen's consultant-speak) that the digital revolution has presented to copyright laws still essentially based on principles developed to protect the printers of 16th- and 17th-century England. At that time, finding and dealing with infringing book and pamphlet printers was a question of money and political connections. **Today, the ease and extent of unauthorised copying presents a critical challenge for social and economic policymakers all around the world.**

EVEN MORE RIGHTS

Other IPRs that don't fall easily into one of the main categories include:

Registered designs

Granted by the State, a **registered design** is a monopoly right (rather than a copyright, where independent creation doesn't infringe). It can last for up to 30 years in countries such as Pakistan, to protect novel designs like the shape of a vacuum cleaner or, in India (where the protection is for up to 15 years), even the cap for a Marico coconut oil bottle. In some countries such as China or the Republic of Korea, similar protection may be given by a **design patent**. In others such as China, a **utility patent** may also be available.

Some countries also give more limited protection to **unregistered designs.** Don't think that this only protects the pretty. The right may protect the most basic of industrial products such as prefabricated houses.

Fuss over fakes

In August 2006 Malaysian shoe designer Jimmy Choo (now separate from the Tamara Mellon-run company that bears his name) settled out of court for £80,000 (US$130,000) a registered design legal action against UK retailer New Look. New Look had copied some features of Choo's Bonbon shoes. In addition to paying the £80,000, they withdrew from sale 1,000 pairs of allegedly infringing shoes. Later in the year Marks & Spencer destroyed thousands of Jimmy Choo look-alike handbags as part of a confidential settlement, of course without admitting liability for design right infringement.

Compare that with the laid-back attitude towards low-priced plagiarism of Balenciaga designer Nicolas Ghesquière, of the celebrity-beloved and much-imitated Lariat handbag: "I'm OK with copying. It's all just a cycle, I guess"; and Miuccia Prada: "The high street, actually, is kind of good. The only thing is that you're always forced to do something new, something more. You are never allowed to enjoy anything

because it's always everywhere and then it's over, over, over in a very short time."

Semiconductor chip rights

A **semiconductor chip right** or a **mask-work right** is a right given to the creators of semiconductor chip layout designs by a few countries such as Pakistan. Described by Dutch commentator Kamperman Sanders as an example of "gunboat diplomacy", the right first saw the light of legislative day in the US in 1984, in response to furious lobbying by the likes of Intel, Motorola, AMD and National Semiconductor.

Plant or seed rights

A **plant breeder's right** or **plant patent** is a monopoly right granted in countries such as India and Thailand to protect novel plant varieties or seeds: flour made from protected corn would be an infringement. A similar right has been available in China to protect seed producers in that country since the 2000 Seed Law.

All this goes to show that there are many different types of intellectual property rights around the world and even within particular countries. **When developing new products or services, businesses must always be selective about which, if any, IPR is appropriate or best suited to the job they want it to do.**

As with all commercial decisions, that selection should be made on an informed basis and we need first of all to dispel some of the misconceptions that haunt too much of the debate about IPRs in Asia and elsewhere.

02 Ten dangerous misconceptions

As in any field that is a bit complicated and dominated by so-called experts, there is a lot of nonsense spoken in the Invisible Gold field —some through ignorance and confusion but also to bolster the arguments of one interest group or another. This chapter will try to correct some of the more common and dangerous misconceptions and, where appropriate, make suggestions about how these should be dealt with.

1. IP equals patents

A common mistake is to think that the only IPR is a patent. Indeed, many discussions take place in which IP and patents are used as synonyms. In fact, patents are not even half of the story. For the vast majority of businesses, especially in Asia, patents are irrelevant either due to the expense of obtaining them or because they are just inappropriate. Even in the USA, firms in a number of innovative industries (including semiconductors and precision instruments) rated patents as a relatively ineffective form of protection. Instead, they cited lead-time advantages, learning curves, complementary sales service and secrecy as generally more important sources of competitive advantage.

2. Having IPRs in your home market is enough

Another error is to look at IPRs with a purely national focus. Just because you have a trademark in Singapore or in Hong Kong means nothing once you go across the causeway to Malaysia or across the border into Guangdong. You must look at the position in each territory.

Not doing so was a mistake that cost the Beijing Wangzhihe Foodstuff Group a lot of time (two years and three months) and money (€10,000, or around RMB100,000) when it discovered at the beginning of 2007 that its German importer Okai Import Export GmbH had registered the Chinese company's trademark, Wangzhihe, in Germany. Although the Beijing company won its legal action against Okai for unfair competition in Germany, it could have avoided all the time and expense if it had registered the mark itself first.

On the other hand, as a result of international legal agreements every business will own some IPRs (particularly copyrights that do not require registration) in most countries of the world, although most don't realise it. Their IPRs lie there unrecognised and unexploited. An industry has grown up now under the grand-sounding title of Intellectual Asset Management, to help recognise, manage and exploit these rights but so far it has only scraped the surface of the huge untapped potential.

What's in a name?

When Konosuke Matsushita decided in the early 1960s to expand his eponymous company's small hi-fi exports to the United States, he realised both that his Japanese brand, National, belonged to another company in the US so he couldn't use it there, and that Americans found "Matsushita"

difficult to pronounce. As a result, his growing business adopted the trademark Panasonic for all the products it exported to North America. The story was completed only 47 years later, in October 2008, when Matsushita Electric changed its name to Panasonic Corporation and announced that its Japanese brand, National, would be dropped and replaced with Panasonic by 2010. (In China, the characters 松下电器 will continue to be used in view of their widespread recognition.)

3. IPRs protect, or restrict the flow of ideas

They don't, despite the firm views of many economists and others that they do. What they do—or may—protect is:

- the product or the process that embodies an idea (through patents);
- the brand or design which differentiates that product or that process (through trademark and design rights); and
- the way in which the idea is expressed, whether in a book, in software or in a drawing (through copyright).

It is inaccurate to say, as do McMillan and others, that IPRs restrict usage of ideas. What often can restrict the flow of ideas are contractual limitations on what employees or others can do or say. This is another book in itself, but in many areas of science, for example, exaggerated concerns that trade secrets might be revealed to competitors or patent protection prejudiced can lead to onerous (and frequently counterproductive) rules about what can and can't be said by researchers when attending conferences and other gatherings with their peers. Also, on the Internet, content owners often use technology to restrict access to what was previously free, despite what Internet prophet Chris Anderson claims in his 2009 bestseller, *Free: The Future of a Radical Price*: "If it's digital, sooner or later it's going to be free."

4. It's just a matter of copying what they do in the USA

In many parts of Asia, when discussing IPRs and how they can contribute to growth, there is a worrying tendency to think that because it works in the United States it will work there and that it's just a matter of adopting the American practice. It isn't, for all sorts of reasons.

The way the American legal system has developed, how litigation is an essential part of everyday business life and how it's paid for, the depth of the venture capital industry and its acceptance of risk, the longstanding links between academia and industry, the power of lobbyists in Washington and state capitals ... all these, and many other unique factors, have combined to make IP a part of the country's DNA to an extent that no other country gets close to.

What's good for America isn't necessarily good for Asian countries, which may have vastly different strengths and weaknesses or very different cultures in which to build an IP system appropriate for their own needs and aspirations.

Adapt by all means, but don't just adopt.

5. Getting the IPRs is the hard part

Complicated though it may seem, registering the trademark or being granted the patent is the easy part of playing the IP game. The hard part is to make IPRs an integral element of your business strategy, in your home market and when you start competing in other countries. Too often the businessman or woman sits back with a smug grin after proudly announcing, "I've got a patent/trademark/copyright [delete as applicable] protecting my product", expecting the world to beat a path to his or her door.

Instead, you should be thinking of the answers to questions such as:

- Why did you want a patent, a trademark, etc?
- Where else do you want one, having obtained it in your home market (in Japan, in China, in India, etc) and why?
- Can you afford it?
- When you get it, what are you going to do with it?
- Do you want to do it all yourself?
- In that foreign market you don't know, is it better to licence someone else to make the patented product or use the trademark and take a royalty on all their sales?
- What will you do if someone infringes the patent, trademark, etc?
- Can you afford litigation?

On the cost of enforcing patents in different countries, Vincent Zhong of Shenzhen-based flash memory company Netac noted in an interview with *Managing Intellectual Property* magazine: "In China, if you go for a case you can easily control the budget—around one or two million RMB. Overseas is almost out of control."

6. Getting IPRs can wait until you can afford it

Unfortunately, it's often then too late, either because you have to apply early (as with patents) or someone else got there first (as with many IPRs but particularly trademarks, designs and domain names). It costs far more to sort out a problem later than it does to anticipate and prevent the problem from happening.

This was a lesson learnt the hard way by Japanese company Ryohin

Kikaku (RK), which uses the trademark Muji. Muji is the abbreviation for *mujirushi ryôhin,* which can be translated as "unlabelled superior article" (so it's actually a trademark meaning "no brand"!), and has been used by RK since 1980. In 1984, RK registered Muji for clothes in Japan and in 1991 registered both Muji and Mujirushi Ryohin in Hong Kong. Unfortunately, when RK came to look at the China market in 1999, it found that the trademarks Muji and Mujirushi Ryohin had both already been registered in mainland China by Jet Best Investment (JBI), a Hong Kong company unrelated to RK, which had opened its first Muji store in 1995.

After a protracted process lasting nearly five years, in November 2005 the Chinese trademark office agreed to RK's request that it cancel JBI's marks, noting that JBI had even lied in their advertising by claiming that *their* trademarks were "Japanese brands". Even then the saga continued, and RK was stopped from using its trademarks while JBI appealed the decision to thc Beijing No. 1 Intermediate People's Court.

When this failed, JBI appealed yet again. Finally, at the end of 2007, the Beijing People's High Court decided, once and for all and without any further appeal possible, that the JBI trademarks should be cancelled. At long last, after seven years and spending a lot of money, RK could use its Muji trademark in China.

On the other hand, **an IP strategy must be sensible and recognise that businesses have limited budgets.** It's just as silly to allow the IP tail to wag the dog as it is to ignore the IP tail altogether. As Ryan Lee, the CEO and founder of Singapore company XM-1, says of those who copy his company's award-winning and patented X-Mini capsule speakers: "Many of them are too small to sue."

What every business can do is have someone *own* the IP part of the business strategy, in the same way as all businesses have someone who looks after the buildings or the factory. In that way the IP implications of all decisions will be considered even though they may have been outweighed by other perfectly sensible commercial considerations like cost.

7. IPRs are expensive, and only large businesses can afford them

Some IPRs (like patents) are expensive to obtain and to protect. Others cost nothing to obtain but arise automatically (like copyright in computer software, music or books); it's up to you to exploit and protect them. And there is a third category of IPRs that don't cost a lot but which you need to constantly nurture and safeguard because they are what separates you from your competitors (like trademarks, domain names and company names—all the legal rights that go into making a brand).

Again, it's about choosing the right IP strategy. Then it's about following and adapting it to take into account the ever-changing environment in which businesses operate today.

The governments of many Asian countries have done an excellent job in raising the profile of intellectual property and its importance in the knowledge economy of the 21st century. From primary schools to boardrooms, the likes of the IP Office of Singapore (IPOS) and the Hong Kong SAR IP Department have played the message loudly that IPRs are good and must be respected. They have encouraged businesses—often with grants and other financial incentives—to register trademarks, file for patents and designs, and to protect their copyright.

But … then what?

The small businessman who has spent his hard-earned cash to obtain a patent or a registered trademark needs to know what to do with it once he's got it. Until it's commercialised, turned into added value, it's just a number on a piece of paper that looks impressive on the wall alongside the educational certificates. It's a liability, not an asset. Often it comes as a shock to learn that nobody is going to turn that IPR into added value for him. Nobody is going to pay to protect it against infringement. All that is the IPR owner's job. And that job is a very difficult one. Far more fail than succeed, in all countries.

IPRs are commercial tools, useful or even invaluable in the hands of some, useless in the hands of others.

Realising the importance of helping businesses navigate their way effectively around the IP system, Thailand's National Innovation Agency (NIA) had a 2006 budget of THB400 million "to help Thai companies apply knowledge management to achieve innovation". Most other Asian countries have similar initiatives. In Singapore IPOS has an excellent programme for small- and medium-sized enterprises (SMEs) to learn about how to make money from IPRs.

The critical message should be that businesses need to be IP-aware, and savvy—not in an unthinking way but in a way that makes sense for them, with their resources and their budgets. There is no one-size-fits-all IP strategy. For some, IPRs are a waste of money; for others, they are their Invisible Gold.

8. IP infringement is theft

This is just an example of the misinformation and usurping of the language in which many IP owners—and particularly trade associations like the Business Software Alliance (BSA)—have indulged over recent years as the "war" on "IP theft" and "piracy" has been waged.

When another's IP right is infringed, it is not stolen—any more than a tenant who does not pay rent steals his landlord's apartment. The owner of the property, whether a trademark or an apartment, still has the property after the infringement or the non-payment, together with a right to sue for the lost income. Certainly, an IP infringement is a lost opportunity for the IP owner and should be discouraged strongly, but it is not theft. Nor does it help the debate on what is the very serious problem of counterfeiting and piracy to make such silly claims.

9. All IPRs are basically the same

They are not. Even though journalists use the terms "patent", "trademark" and "copyright" interchangeably, they are as different as football and American football, or basketball and netball. Some, like the patent and the registered design, are monopoly rights—only one person can have it. To infringe it, you don't even need to know about it. Others, like trademarks, are there to stop confusion and unfair trading behaviour. Copyright is what its name tells you—*a right to stop copying*. You can't copy what you don't know about.

One consequence of an undifferentiated view of IPRs is well expressed by Andrew Mertha in his study of piracy in China:

> "Patents fall under the science and technology *xitong* [or cluster], copyright falls under the propaganda and culture *xitong*, while trademarks fall under the finance and economics *xitong*," leading him to conclude that "the existence of SIPO notwithstanding, grouping patents, copyright, and trademarks together ... makes as much sense as placing molecular physics, pornography, and foreign investment within the same policy area."

10. You have a *right* to use your IPRs, and what's registered is valid

Owning an IPR does not give you the right to use it. It may infringe upon someone else's earlier and better right. For example, obtaining a patent does not give you the *right* to exercise the invention it covers. All it gives you is the right to stop *others* from doing things that fall within its scope. Similarly, if you create a drawing of the view across Hong Kong harbour by copying the drawing made by a person you are sitting next to, you own copyright in your drawing and can sue someone who copies it but the person whom, initially, you copied yours from can sue you too.

On the same lines, just because you have managed to get your patent granted or your trademark registered does not mean it will stand up to scrutiny if it's challenged. **There are many granted patents, registered designs and registered trademarks that are on the Register but shouldn't be.** After all, with the deluge of patent, design and trademark applications over recent years each application can only be examined quickly by the IP Office concerned before a decision is made if it should or should not go on the Register. Sometimes they get that decision wrong. From the other side of the coin, if you are threatened with a legal action by someone who says he or she has a patent/trademark/design, the first thing to do is get a good lawyer to check if it is a registration that can be attacked.

In October 2009 the *South China Morning Post* reported on a spat between the two cities of Jiangyou in Sichuan and Anlu in Hubei, over which was entitled to call itself the hometown of Li Bai, a Tang Dynasty poet. In 2003 Jiangyou had somehow managed to register as a trademark "the Hometown of Li Bai, the City of Chinese poems", but the State Administration of Industry and Commerce (SAIC)—which administers the trademark system—said quite correctly that it was not trademark infringement for Anlu to say in a TV commercial that it was Li Bai's hometown. Contrary to what some trademark owners think or threaten, owning a trademark does not give you the right to stop others from using it in any way.

Rogues and rupees?

In 2009 there was much media interest in India about how patent owner Somasundaram Ramkumar had succeeded using his Indian patent—which most commentators are confident should never have been granted—to prevent international phone companies like Samsung, Spice and Motorola from importing Dual SIM handsets into India. Never short of hyperbole, some journalists even described it as the Indian David taking on the multinational Goliaths. Unfortunately, the stones David was throwing were made of straw.

The Ramkumar litigation, remarkably, involved the customs authorities, the Madras High Court, the Gurgaon district court, the Punjab and Haryana High Court, the Central Excise Authorities, the Intellectual Property Appeal Board (IPAB) and the Delhi High Court. As a result it has become a *cause célèbre* in India—but not for the right reasons.

Even if Ramkumar loses ultimately—and all the signs are that he will—he has played the patent system superbly, and unscrupulously. His aim? To make as much money as he can from a very dubious patent. On the other hand (and there is often another side of the story in IP disputes), the small importers who ended up paying large sums—according to a local newspaper, as much as INR10 crore—just to avoid

being sued for infringement of his patent claims will end up very disgruntled. If they choose to throw good money after bad by taking him to court to try and recover the money they paid him under the mistaken belief that the patent was valid, they may succeed—although it is highly unlikely. However, the harm the false claims have caused to their businesses will never be fully compensated.

Ramkumar claimed to have applied to patent dual SIM technology in India in 2002, although the patent was only granted in 2008. Ramkumar then handed over the exploitation of his patent to Vikas Systems, in which he was a partner along with Messrs Diwakaran, Rajamani, Murugesan and James. The respected legal blog *SpicyIP* reported that the arrangement was that as patentee, Ramkumar would get 60 per cent of the patent royalties Vikas could extract from businesses threatened with patent infringement. The other partners would get 40 per cent between them.

But, from the outset Ramkumar faced a number of obstacles as every major phone company contested his right to his patent. Again, always remember that just because a patent has been granted does not mean it's valid. Indeed, most Indian legal experts agree that Ramkumar's patent is of very doubtful validity.

Taking the same view, in May 2009 Mathew Johns, the Mumbai Police Commissioner (Imports), announced he would release imports of mobile phones that had been blocked based on the claims in Ramkumar's patent. Johns' official report was unequivocal: " … it is clear that the claim made by Mr Ramkumar is vexatious because the impugned goods are covered by Prior Art declared by him and are not infringing the patent granted to him. Demurrage and other warehousing charges arising due to suspension of clearance are liquidated amounts and are to be borne by the Patent Holder."

Separately, Chennai Customs ruled in favour of Samsung and Hansum India, who were being prevented by Ramkumar from importing Dual SIM phones.

There is a postscript to this story. First the patent was contested. Then there was a murder. Most recently, *SpicyIP* (where, if you are interested, you can find details of the murder) has been threatened with a legal action against it. Ramkumar's lawyer Mr Ferdinand wrote to *SpicyIP* protesting his client's innocence and threatening "all legal action".

Unfortunately for Ferdinand, he seems to have picked the wrong target. In the blog, those behind *SpicyIP* responded firmly to the threats: "If Ferdinand thinks he can quell free speech through aggressive threats of initiating criminal action, he is sadly mistaken. This blog has always taken an 'issue'-based approach, critiqued ongoing IP cases and exposed flaws in the law wherever they existed. We value our freedom to continue with such reporting and we think it serves a public interest. Consequently we refuse to be intimidated and will staunchly defend our rights in this regard." Good for them.

03 A patchwork quilt of Invisible Gold

As we've seen, Invisible Gold can be found not only in patents but also in trademarks (registered and unregistered), trade secrets, copyright, design rights, geographical indications, database rights, semiconductor chip rights. The rights get more and more specific but they are all intellectual "property", even if invisible to the eye. But, although often bundled together, it is important to recognise that there are significant differences between the various rights that make up the patchwork quilt of Invisible Gold.

Frequently, the economic justification for a particular IP right (such as patents, where it is to provide an incentive to innovate) is beguilingly extended to other IP rights where it is not valid or relevant. So, providing an incentive to innovate is irrelevant as far as trademarks are concerned. The reason we have a trademark system is to allow businesses to build goodwill from selling readily identifiable products or services that consumers can repeat-purchase and to prevent other traders from causing confusion in the marketplace.

THE LONG AND LONGER

The length of time (in legal jargon, the "term") the particular IPR can last differs greatly, and even from country to country.

- Invention patents generally last for 20 years.
- Copyright for the life of the author plus 50 years (in China) or 70 years (in the likes of Singapore), designs for anything from three to 25 years.
- Trademarks can remain registered for as long as they are used, renewal fees are paid, and they don't become generic, like "escalator" or "tabloid", perhaps even "google" (which in many parts of the world has become a synonym for any search engine rather than, as it should be, the registered trademark of a particular search engine run by Google).

Consistent across most of the IP field, though, is that over recent years the terms of protection have become longer, usually as a result of effective lobbying by one industry group or another.

In all our interests, it should be necessary to justify monopolies and how long they last. Monopolies should not be extended without thought at the behest of this or that lobby group. IPRs are important to us all and to our well-being, both economic and cultural. They should be treated as important and evaluated coolly and constantly to ensure that they operate in the public interest. Fortunately, most still do, despite in recent years an all-too-prevalent lack of that cool evaluation, replaced instead by the heated "s/he who shouts loudest and longest" school of persuasion.

MUCH ADO ABOUT INNOVATION

"Innovation" is another buzzword. The Austrian economist Joseph Schumpeter defined it as "the commercialisation of inventions". It is often talked of in the same breath as research labs and patents, but again that's only one aspect of the many areas of business life in which IPRs are—or should be—important. Also, "innovation" often lies in the eye of the beholder. What is copying to one person (an R&D-based pharmaceutical company, for example) may well be innovation to another (a manufacturer of generic drugs that uses highly-efficient manufacturing processes).

In 2006 *Business Week* magazine compiled a list of the 10 companies with the most US patents in 2005 and compared it with the 10 who were considered in a poll to be the most innovative. In the former were six Asian companies (Canon, Matsushita, Samsung, Hitachi, Toshiba and Fujitsu) but in the latter, which was headed by Apple and 3M, only one (Sony) was Asian.

Numerically, and economically, there is no doubt that the vast majority of IPRs protect minor or incremental product or process improvements (through patents or utility models) or ways of differentiating products or services, both old and new (through brands or design rights).

An example from Thailand is provided by Aeroflex International Co, the leading locally-owned design patent owner, with four patents granted in Thailand between 2000 and 2006. In 1996 the company sold plastic sheets to truck manufacturers, which then formed them into bedliners for pickup trucks. In 1997 the company started making bedliners for Toyota, Isuzu, Nissan and other pickup truck makers. Then, in 1998, Aeroflex filed for a US patent covering a new type of bedliner that hooks onto the back of a truck without needing to be screwed down, eliminating an hour of metal drilling from the assembly line.

Despite the critical importance of incremental product or process improvements (witness Toyota's previously much-admired culture of continuous improvements or *kaizen*, which took a knock with the 2010 recall debacle), it is the very few radical or disruptive innovations which are mentioned most frequently in discussions about the money that can be made from intellectual property rights. It is these core, and usually patented, inventions that spawn whole new industries through what Schumpeter described as "the gales of creative destruction". Take, for example, the semiconductor chip. But these are the once-in-a-generation inventions and no sensible long-term IPR strategy can be based on them.

> "Numerically, and economically, there is no doubt that the vast majority of IPRs protect minor or incremental product or process improvements ... or ways of differentiating products or services, both old and new."

STEPPING STONES

The reality was well expressed by James Dyson, British inventor of the hugely successful Dual Cyclone vacuum cleaner now being manufactured in Malaysia. In his 1997 autobiography, he wrote:

> "The Japanese and the Koreans understand the importance of continuous active development, and of never letting up. They appreciate only too well that small step-by-step improvements add up, in the long term, to massive improvements which, in turn, generate patents, and thus ownership of technology."

Dyson's success with the Dual Cyclone came after its inventor had been ripped off in the USA with an earlier invention, the Ballbarrow (a wheelbarrow with a ball instead of the front wheel). Despite Dyson's sage advice to his business partners to avoid going to court in the USA—"the battle would be expensive, time-consuming and probably futile, since patent cases are very rarely won outright"—the board ignored him and wasted months and much money getting nowhere before kicking Dyson out of the company. With his next venture, Dyson had learnt his lesson and his eponymous company's Dual Cyclone vacuum cleaner was protected by patents, design rights and registered trademarks.

On the other hand, one should bear in mind the stark warnings put forward in Michael Porter's *Can Japan Compete?* (2000), in which he and his Japanese colleagues argued that, except in a handful of cases such as consumer electronics and cars "that carried the entire economy", continuous operational *inefficiency* took the place of strategy for Japanese companies in the 1980s and 1990s.

Coming back to that buzz word "innovation": it's astonishing how many self-styled gurus of innovation can speak for hours and write hundreds of pages without even mentioning IPRs. In the final analysis, IPRs of one form or another are what much innovation is about. Conversely, a lot of innovation in the services field cannot be protected by IPRs—except by brands, which competitors may be able to avoid easily. The innovation's value is manifested instead in incremental sales. Notwithstanding this, even in primarily service businesses, the mindset change which initiatives to encourage innovation and creativity bring about will usually provide competitive advantage. In the words of Singapore's Kenny Yap, Executive Chairman of ornamental fish company Qian Hu Corp and—arguably—the country's "Mr Fish": "Creativity and innovation are ways to set yourself apart from competitors."

For example, under the headline "Workers mobilised to innovate" on 29 September 2009, the *Financial Times* reported on how China Telecom had responded to the May 2008 restructuring of the country's telecoms industry by transforming itself into an innovation-led business. Through the Innovation Works programme introduced (with the help of IBM) at its research institute in Shanghai, the company offers incentives to its research staff to come up with improved or new services. As China Telecom evolves, there is little doubt those research staff will start developing products and product improvements that will be protected by patents of one form or another.

AN INVITATION TO COURT

On their own, IPRs are not enough. Except when they were obtained for purely defensive reasons—"If I have it, it means you can't"—**IPRs become valuable only when they are exploited and enforced.**

At the beginning of the 20th century, the great American patentee Thomas Edison described a patent as merely an invitation to a lawsuit. In the same vein, Lord Hoffmann, one of the great IP judges and a member of the Court of Final Appeal in Hong Kong, noted in a speech marking his retirement as a British judge in June 2009:

> "[During the Industrial Revolution in Britain, from the late 18th until the mid-19th century,] whether you could enforce a patent or not seemed to depend mainly upon how much money you had for the purpose of litigation and partly upon luck. And the same seems to be largely true today."

An IPR is not going to strike a competitor dead like a bolt of lightning. Where it requires registration (and many don't), applying for it and having it granted in a particular country is just the first step. Then comes the hard part—of building a sustainable long-term business using the IPR.

CHANGING A LIABILITY INTO AN ASSET

Many IPRs are liabilities not assets. To take only one example: the mere fact that you have managed to get a patent, and spent good money doing so, does not mean you have the right to use the invention covered by it. If there's an earlier patent belonging to somebody else, your later one may infringe upon it. It's then a game of attack—saying the earlier shouldn't have been granted or that you don't infringe it—or defence, in trying to get a licence to use the earlier patent, perhaps in return for letting its owner use yours.

A patent is a right to stop others from using the invention described in it. But like all rights it withers away unless *you* enforce it, because nobody else is going to do that for you.

Wanted: determination (and deep pockets)

Singapore-based Trek 2000 International has built up a valuable portfolio of IPRs to protect its portable storage and other digital devices. A 2007 case study of the company for an IP Starter Guide published by IPOS revealed that its trademarks Trek and ThumbDrive had both been registered in Singapore, China and India, and were pending elsewhere. Meanwhile, it also owned over 150 granted patents covering its technologies in a variety of countries.

The company's Chief Financial Officer Gurcharan Singh explained to IPOS: "We filed our patent for the ThumbDrive® USB Flash Drive solution in 2000. That year, we went to [computer show] Cebit to showcase [it], as the world's first and smallest ThumbDrive® USB Flash Drive. When we went back to Cebit the following year, we had some 50 competitors from Korea, China, Taiwan and more. Unfortunately, we

could not do anything about this as our patent was pending at the time. So when we received our Singapore patent in 2002, we took actions to protect our assets.

"IP litigation is very expensive—this case cost Trek close to S$5 million [approx US$3.6 million] and took up a huge amount of time and resources. On hindsight, we would have looked for an alternative solution, such as an out-of-court settlement, or arranging a licensing deal."

Not surprisingly, when in January 2010 Trek launched its latest product, the FluCard (designed to link devices wirelessly), its strategy was different. It teamed up with one of its shareholders, industry giant Toshiba, which will manage and oversee the IP protection of the device.

IT'S A CHANGING WORLD

If you haven't any IPRs or don't know what to do with them, be afraid. Be very afraid. They are the currency of, even the visa to enter, many areas of modern commerce. Their importance has increased hugely over the past 30 years.

A final word of warning at this stage: in many instances IPRs are *cumulative*. Just because the patent on a product has expired doesn't mean it's free for others to copy without fear of infringement. There may then be trademark or design rights.

On Valentine's Day 2006 the New Zealand Court of Appeal accepted that a previously patented vine tie was properly registered as a trademark. There is also copyright in the underlying drawings. And, if you're getting the inside information on how to make the product from one of your competitor's former employees, that may be an abuse of trade secrets.

Similarly, much commercialisation of IPRs involves multiple rights. Franchising a business will involve trade secrets (how to do it), copyrights (showing how to do it or plans of outlets), as well as trademarks such as Jollibee or McDonald's. All of these will be licensed as a package by the owner to the franchise outlets, usually for an upfront fee and then continuing royalties based on sales.

> "In many instances IPRs are cumulative. Just because the patent on a product has expired doesn't mean it's free for others to copy without fear of infringement. There may then be trademark or design rights."

Build and bill

Even the IPRs—real and alleged—in children's toy bricks have been fought over in many courts around the world. The Danish maker of the well-known children's toy Lego has sued many other manufacturers of toy bricks in Hong Kong, China and elsewhere who have copied the exact dimensions of Lego bricks so that theirs could be used interchangeably.

The interlocking brick system from which the Lego Group has made so much money was originally designed by an Englishman, Hilary Page. In the 1950s, Page obtained British patents for the interlocking mechanism and marketed the toy under the trademark Kiddicraft. As is so often the case, Page hadn't the time, money or perhaps the inclination to protect his invention outside his home market and had only patented it in Britain.

A Danish entrepreneur by the name of Ole Kirk Christiansen bought a Kiddicraft toy on a visit to England and realised its potential. Returning to Denmark, Christiansen copied exactly the dimensions of Page's bricks and their interlocking mechanism—what is now called "reverse engineering". With no patent in Denmark, there was nothing Page could do to stop this, even if he had wanted to.

Christiansen packaged his new bricks attractively in bright coloured boxes, put the Lego trademark on them and the rest is history. Before suing Tyco Toys in Hong Kong in the late 1980s, Lego bought from Page's executors any copyright still in force in the original designs.

In a 2006 case in Canada, Lego relied on the law of passing off (which can be used to protect the get-up of a product), but on earlier visits to the law courts around the world it had used patents (now long expired), copyright (in the drawings of its bricks, and even the re-drawings) and trademarks (the word "Lego" and in some countries the shape of the brick itself).

One Chinese competitor stopped from selling copy bricks was Tianjin Coko Toy Co, Ltd. In 2002, the Lego Group's IP holding company in Switzerland, Interlego AG, sued Tianjin Coko for copyright infringement. A Beijing trial court found 33 of the 50 Coko bricks to be infringing. Coko was ordered to cease manufacture of these bricks, publish a formal apology in the *Beijing Daily* newspaper, and pay RMB50,000 in damages to Interlego. On appeal, the Beijing High People's Court upheld the trial court's ruling.

On the other hand, the Hong Kong case between Lego and Tyco Toys is a good example of how it is dangerous to assume automatically that copying will infringe IPRs. That was something Christiansen knew only too well when he copied Page's toy.

In the 1990s Tyco Toys, Inc were the third largest toy manufacturer in the United States and much of that success arose from copying others. The most striking example of this strategy came when the company marketed Tyco Super Blocks, a building block set designed to be interchangeable with Lego bricks. Tyco's catalogue made clear: "Tyco works with Lego. Tyco Super Blocks connect to Lego. So your child can keep on building with either one." Referring to the Danish company, Tyco president Richard Grey told *Forbes* magazine in 1988: "We knew they had a reputation for being litigious." True enough, Lego did sue for copyright infringement, in Hong Kong where Tyco was having the bricks made. After an expensive three-year legal battle, which ended up in the Privy Council in London (because that was the final court of appeal for Hong Kong in pre-1997 days), Tyco won the case. The millions of dollars in legal fees proved to be well spent, as Tyco Super Blocks became a stable multi-million dollar product line before Tyco was taken over by toy giant Mattel in 1997.

EVOLUTION

What starts out as an IPR may evolve into something quite different. Say "Glaxo" today and you think of a pharmaceutical giant, but in 1907 Glaxo was the trademark registered by the Nathan family for a new dried milk product made in their Bunnythorpe factory near Wellington in New Zealand. After the huge and, for the Nathans, lucrative demand for dried milk from soldiers in the First World War, the Glaxo company moved into pharmaceutical research and production in 1936. Its headquarters eventually moved to London. Having merged with pharma rival SmithKline Beecham, it's now a set of initials—GSK.

Today, the fragmented and sometimes incoherent law of intellectual property is used both to help and to hinder the growth of businesses.

The word "hinder" is just as relevant as "help" in any meaningful explanation of how Invisible Gold works in the real world.

This is well known to Zong Qinghou who, with a RMB140,000 loan, founded the Hangzhou Wahaha Nutrition Food Factory in 1989. Its purpose was to sell the Wahaha nutrition drink developed by Professor Zhu Shoumin at Zhejiang Medical University. The product's trademark Wahaha (娃哈哈), which sounds like a laughing child and means "smiling child" in Mandarin, was chosen after a public competition and its logo of a smiling child established the product's carefree image even further. When Zong decided to enter the fragmented purified water market in 1996, he used the same trademark, by now well-known, and succeeded in selling RMB500 million worth of branded water the following year.

By that time, in March 1996, Zong's Wahaha had entered into a joint venture with French food giant Danone and agreed that the Wahaha trademarks would be transferred to the joint venture. Troubles began when the Chinese Trademarks Office refused to give its consent to the transfer, as is required by Chinese law. The two sides were then involved in a seemingly endless progression of court actions and arbitration proceedings, with claim and counterclaim: all about the brand and who could use it and for what. This was settled finally in November 2009. According to the *Financial Times*, a Swedish arbitration panel found that Zong had breached confidentiality and non-compete agreements with the French company. However, Danone agreed to sell its 51 per cent stake in the joint venture to its Chinese partner for US$450 million (€300 million).

> "Today, the fragmented and sometimes incoherent law of intellectual property is used both to help and to hinder the growth of businesses."

The neutral observer needs to realise that, for every successful business relying on a real or alleged IPR, there is at least one unsuccessful and restrained defendant. There may also be any number of others who, as a result of seeing writs flying around, are frightened into moving away from what may be perfectly legitimate business activities.

SEEING MAY NOT BE BELIEVING

In addition, there will be others who have changed their business behaviour due to actual or perceived IPR problems. In Malaysia a third of all patent applications have been rejected by the Malaysia IP Office since the country introduced local filing in 1986. The fact that a competitor has applied for a patent may mean little. Even if a patent has been granted it's not the end of the road. About a third (again) of all patents granted around the world are never used or exploited in any way, but they sit there on the patent register in a particular country and it is the brave (or stupid) business that ignores them.

Similarly, the fact that an IP right has been registered doesn't necessarily mean it is valid.

A WHITEWASH

This was a lesson that instant noodle maker Sichuan Baijia Food Co, Ltd ("Baijia" means, literally, "white family") learnt the hard way.

In July 2007 its dominance of the national market for starch noodles was challenged by a competitor from central and northern China, Henan Zhenglong Food Co, Ltd (using its registered trademark Baixiang—literally, "white elephant"). Baijia reached for its IP rights to try and force Zhenglong, whose own trademark Baixiang had been registered in January 2001, out of the market.

It looked to rely on its registered trademark Baijia, which it had used on its instant rice noodles packaging since 2000. This had even been recognised as a famous mark in Chengdu and in Sichuan province. But its registered trademark was for Baijia in a *horizontal* style and the packaging use was of Baijia in a *vertical* style.

In November 2007, Zhenglong sued in the Zhengzhou Intermediate People's Court, claiming that Baijia's unregistered, vertically printed trademark infringed upon its registered *vertical* Baixiang trademark, and asked the court to stop use of the mark. In its judgment at the end of January 2008, only 62 days later, the court ordered that Baijia immediately stop using the vertical Baijia trademark on its instant noodle packaging, as it infringed the vertical Baixiang registered mark. The Henan Higher People's Court rejected Baijia's appeal at the end of November 2008. Both marks are composed of two Chinese characters and printed vertically; both fonts are Xingkai; for both, the first character is Bai with identical pronunciation and meaning; Xiang and Jia, though of different pronunciation, look alike when written in the font of Xingkai. Thus, concluded the court, as a whole, Baixiang and Baijia look too similar.

Losing the trademark battle, Baijia looked to its design patents, arguing that Zhenglong's packaging was too similar. In late 2007 it lodged an administrative complaint alleging design infringement to the Henan and Zhengzhou intellectual property offices. Showing it knew how to play the IP game, Zhenglong immediately asked the State Intellectual Property Office (SIPO) to reexamine whether the design patent had been properly granted and to invalidate it. As a result the Zhengzhou office suspended Baijia's case and waited for the decision of SIPO on Zhenglong's request.

Undeterred (or perhaps badly advised), Baijia tried again and in mid-November 2007 sued Zhenglong for design patent infringement at the Weifang Intermediate People's Court. It sought an injunction and maximum damages of RMB1 million. (Hu Yuanqiang, the public relations chief of Baijia, explained that the case was not filed in Henan due to worries about local protectionism, but refused to answer why not in Sichuan.)

But then Baijia withdrew the legal action before a judgment could be given. At the same time, in June and July of 2008, SIPO decided to cancel four of Baijia's design patents for failure to meet statutory requirements. According to Zhenglong, these Baijia patents were those which had been claimed to be infringed.

The moral of the story is that before you spend money suing people you should check whether your Invisible Gold is real or just fool's gold. Conversely, if someone is trying to stop what you are doing by saying they have Invisible Gold, make sure it's real.

Too frequently this is forgotten by the IPR zealots, who accept no dissent in their headlong quest for broader, cheaper and more IPRs. But wait until they are on the receiving end of an action for infringement of one of these broad rights and see their attitude change. Already many Chinese owners of design patents in that country are following in the footsteps of those about whom a senior English judge warned 90 years ago:

> "It is not open to a manufacturer to take one or more leading features of different goods already on the market, and, by registering a Design showing merely a combination of these features, and without any real mental activity being required for its production, acquire a registered Design."

That may be true on the strict wording of the law. However, when the local Chinese companies do obtain a Chinese design patent (by copying products already on the market outside China or perhaps even those described in patent applications elsewhere), the question to be answered by the innocent foreign recipient of a warning letter from the owner of the undoubtedly invalid design patent is, which is less expensive—to buy them off through some sort of payment or to defend an expensive legal action before an inexperienced, and often chauvinistic, judge?

> "Before you spend money suing people you should check whether your Invisible Gold is real or just fool's gold."

Whether in England in 1919 or China in 2009, where a system is designed to make it easy to get IPRs, there will be those who abuse that system for commercial gain.

04 It all depends on your perspective

How IPRs are viewed will frequently depend on the perspective of the person looking at them. This is a fact often forgotten in the strident and unhearing exchange of claims and counterclaims that characterises much of the debate about IPRs.

Let's consider the different perspectives.

THE IPR OWNER

This person has spent time and money—usually both—obtaining the IPR and wants to ensure it was worth it. If the owner is a business (and today most IPRs are owned by businesses of one form or another), the IPR is an asset it needs to protect. If it's an individual it may be the result of his or her life's work. In the same way as you don't allow people off the street to eat in your canteen or wander in to use your computers without payment, why should they use your hard-earned IPRs without paying you for the privilege?

Aspiring software entrepreneurs are scrapping plans to start their businesses due to "lack of appreciation" of IPRs in the country, said Joey Gurango, the CEO of Filipino company Gurango Software in October 2008. He claimed that developers often abandon plans to start a business after learning how hard it is to recover the initial investment and get a decent price for their products. In a complaint echoed by many entrepreneurs around Asia, he noted that Filipino software firms have to sell products at prices 30 per cent cheaper than those from outside the country. As a result the Philippines is among the lowest contributors to software firms' revenues. He said:

> "Business is hard enough as it is without having to deal with piracy.... It's like having a store that has a back door open where people can just enter and steal your products. ... Let's not forget that behind those products, especially if they are locally made, are people that deserve to be compensated for their investments."

The IPR owner will also want an inexpensive and efficient way of stopping people from misusing the IPR it owns and will be dismayed that to do so usually costs a lot of money, and takes a lot of time and effort. Is it worth it? It can be—especially if you have deep pockets, but that's true not only in the world of IPRs.

THE CREATOR OR INNOVATOR

The person who creates or innovates may be the poor author or mad inventor who has laboured for years to write his or her masterpiece, or against all odds and conventional wisdom has come up with the greatest invention since the wheel or gunpowder. In those cases, and that of the small business as well, what is needed is an inexpensive and easy way to stop others from taking advantage of those labours without paying.

More likely today is that the creator or inventor is an employee of a larger business, receiving a wage or salary. Whatever they create or invent belongs as a matter of law to their employer, automatically. Computer programmers or research scientists are good examples. When Indian brains are used to design new software products in Bangalore, the IPRs will belong to the employers. In turn, those employers will have a contract with overseas companies such as GE, IBM or Microsoft that requires them to transfer the IPRs to them. In return, in some countries such as China and Japan but not in others such as India and Singapore, the employee is given a right under the law to share in the benefit his or her employer gets from such an invention; in China this is called a **service invention.**

With many works protected by copyright, the creator is a talented musician or writer. Piracy or counterfeiting takes money out of their pockets unless they are fortunate enough to be backed by a large company, such as J.K. Rowling is by Warner Brothers. More normal in Asia is the attitude of Chinese film director Li Chuan, who wryly admitted that if he were asked by a fan to autograph a pirated DVD of one of his award-winning films he would do so. Noting with a sigh that "a creator is not a businessman", he is always happy to have fans like his work.

THE EMPLOYEE

If the employee is an inventor he may benefit directly from a share in the benefit his employer makes from his invention and indirectly too, in the form of increased salary or bonuses, if his employer's business does well as a result of success with products or services he has helped create.

Even if not a creator or an innovator, all employees of a business based on IPR—such as a biotech company that patents its new anti-viral drug and protects it under a trademark like Tamiflu—share in the benefits brought by the added value protected by the IPRs.

If you are an employee of a business built on "me-too" or look-alike products—in the pharmaceutical and food industries such products are common—you may dislike the IP system because it's a threat to your employer's survival if sued for infringement. Real or perceived, it still costs a lot to defend a legal action.

In the worst case, you may be employed by a business that knowingly infringes other's IPRs, copying without payment. But, in the end, it's still a job … and perhaps the only job in town.

So, if you can't beat them, what about co-opting them?

After years of trying to stem the ever-increasing tide of fake software, Microsoft's anti-piracy strategy in China has recognised this ugly fact of life in many parts of Asia. The US corporation moved to work constructively with local authorities to encourage them to build legitimate businesses rather than turn a blind eye to, or even actively participate in, the illegitimate. In a very different sector, Japan's Honda entered into a cooperation agreement with one of the local Chinese companies that had illegally copied Honda products and manufactured them at significantly lower cost. This combination of Honda's technology and know-how and the Chinese company's low-cost production capability created a powerful new business.

Making a living

An article in the *Bangkok Post* of 25 May 2009 reported: "Ploy, an underground music and movie DVD vendor, is fully aware that it's wrong to sell pirated products. But she believes the lucrative business is worth the risk, as the fakes fetch more than double the profit she earns from selling genuine music and movie discs. More importantly, the entry costs and her risk of arrest are quite low, as Ploy usually sells only to long-time customers, mostly corporate employees.

"'I know it's wrong, but this gives us a living,' she said. 'We're just a small vendor; if you (police and authorities) want to arrest us, you had better take the producers who are the source of the process.'

"An unnamed customer said that even though he knew it was not right to buy pirated goods, the prices were irresistible. 'In the past, I bought genuine tape cassettes. But once CDs came along, I started buying counterfeit ones, as it's not worth it to buy the whole album when you only like a few songs,' he said."

THE PROSPECTIVE DEFENDANT(S) IN A LEGAL ACTION FOR IP INFRINGEMENT

It costs money to defend a legal action, even if you are successful. Many threats of infringement of IPRs are just that—threats—and go nowhere after the initial letter. But when the threat is followed up with a lawsuit, the defendant needs to think very carefully. Is the legal action worth fighting? Is it less expensive to just stop selling the allegedly infringing product? Is the IP right really infringed? Indeed, is the IP right what its "owner" says it is?

All too frequently infringement is in the eye of the beholder and how expansive a view of infringement the beholder has is often correlated directly to the depth of his pockets.

All legal action is a game of bluff and counterbluff, and IP infringement actions are no exception. If threatened with IP infringement or sued for it, a defendant must develop a clear strategy. Sometimes it's the correct strategy to fight. Sometimes it's not.

Made in China

The Chinese company BYD Auto provides a good example of how it can be the correct commercial decision to fight claims of IP infringement, to establish firmly that this company was not going to give in to its competitors when they alleged IP infringement.

BYD (the name has been claimed to be an acronym for Build Your Dreams) was founded in Shenzhen in 1995 by Wang Chuan-Fu to manufacture rechargeable batteries to compete with the expensive products from Sony and Sanyo. Both tried unsuccessfully to sue for patent infringement, as did Taiwan's Hon Hai (or Foxconn, the trade name of its Hong Kong subsidiary by which it is better known). BYD is now the second-largest maker of lithium-ion batteries in the world.

In 2003 BYD purchased an ailing state-owned car company. By mid-2005, BYD Auto had launched its first car, a small sedan called the F3, which at the end of 2008 was the bestselling sedan in China. Industry observers claimed the F3 was a copy of the Toyota Corolla but Wang insisted he was always careful not to infringe other's intellectual property. "By synthesizing good ideas in China from Toyota and others, BYD created its own cars quickly," he said, believing there was no better way to learn the ropes of the auto industry than benchmarking against the industry's leaders. A Toyota spokesman told the *Wall Street Journal* that the Japanese company did not intend to take BYD to court over the F3. "In general, we're always prepared to take legal action if we can determine there is a clear case of infringement," said company spokesman Hitoshi

Yokoyama in Beijing. Obviously BYD Auto had succeeded in staying on the right side of the line—in China. Mimicking or, kindly, "paying homage to" a competitor's product is not always to infringe its IP rights. (Certainly the BYD copying is not limited to Toyota, as BMW, Mercedes and Porsche have all seen their cars paid homage to by BYD.)

In September 2008 MidAmerican Energy Holdings Co, majority-owned by billionaire investor Warren Buffett's Berkshire Hathaway Inc, bought a 9.9 per cent stake in BYD for HK$1.8 billion (US$230 million), having earlier had its offer to buy 25 per cent rejected by Wang, who was not prepared to sell more than 10 per cent of his company. Wang was No. 1 in *Forbes Asia*'s 2009 list of China's richest, with a net worth of US$5.8 billion as a result of the increase in his company's share price after the Buffett investment. Buffett's longtime partner Charlie Munger told *Fortune* magazine earlier in the year: "This guy [Wang] is a combination of Thomas Edison and Jack Welch—something like Edison in solving technical problems, and something like Welch in getting done what he needs to do. I have never seen anything like it."

Wang's fellow founder Xia Zuoguan stepped down to be a non-executive director in 2008 in the midst of another acrimonious legal fight, this time with Taiwan's Foxconn Industries about alleged theft of trade secrets. However, this prevented neither his appearance too in the *Forbes Asia* China's Richest list in 2009, with a net worth of US$1.3 billion, nor his company's electric car being the talk of the Detroit Motor Show in January 2009.

THE TEACHER

This person wants to be able to use whatever materials are most appropriate to aid in the difficult task of explaining the subject, whether geography, urban economics or law, but is subject to ever-tightening budgetary restrictions which limit the books he or she can buy or, increasingly, the databases he or she can access. Surely for your teaching you should be able to take 20 copies of a chapter in a textbook to give to your students without worrying about IPR infringement? In most countries you can't.

On the other hand, what about the poor teachers who have spent many years writing their excellent student textbooks: shouldn't they at least receive some royalties from their publishers too? Why should their efforts, at home at night and over the weekend, go unrewarded except in terms of recognition?

THE GOVERNMENT

On the debit side of the balance sheet, the government has to consider:

- its tax revenues from the domestic and international sales of brand-owning, creative and innovative businesses;
- the employment, and tax revenues, provided by these three categories.

On the credit side:

- the sums spent on educating tomorrow's creators and innovators;
- the funds provided to customs and police to enable them to chase the pirates and the counterfeiters;
- the cost of providing an effective court system to resolve IP disputes quickly and fairly;

- the sums paid by the state for expensive IPR-protected drugs (in Vietnam, for example, the authorities have deliberately adopted a restrictive view of what pharmaceuticals can be protected by patents, because patents are perceived as one of the reasons why local drug prices are so high).

Then there are the lost opportunities and hidden costs that don't appear on the country's balance sheet but are just as real as those that do:

- the losses in tax revenue caused by counterfeiting and piracy (although, in some countries like China, this may be counterbalanced by the employment it offers in the poorest districts and provinces);
- the cost of treating citizens harmed by counterfeit drugs or safety-critical products like car-brake parts;
- the bullying of small- and medium-sized businesses by deep-pocketed corporations who know how to play the anti-competitive edges of the IP game where "might is right";
- the loss of vibrancy and creativity in the cultural life of the country if piracy makes the musicians, filmmakers, authors and playwrights think it's not worth the effort;
- loss of the incentive to innovate, with all the consequences that brings for a country's future economic prosperity.

THE TAX-PAYER

The tax-payer is happy that IP-creating companies and individuals like J.K. Rowling or Jackie Chan pay taxes.

But perhaps the same tax-payer is not so happy that the police and other public officials, like customs officers, spend a lot of time chasing infringements of these privately owned rights when they could be chasing drug traffickers and organised crime gangs. Would the tax-payer change his mind if he knew that drug traffickers and organised crime are heavily involved in counterfeiting and piracy?

THE MAN AND WOMAN IN THE STREET

They don't really care, one way or the other, about IP. It's all too complicated until:

- the flow of new and improved drugs dries up because research is no longer worth investing in, without the reward given by patent protection;
- replica shirts of their children's favourite football club become too expensive as brand owners wring the last cent out of fans;
- their children are sued for illegal downloading of music;
- the cheaper replica shirt they bought outside the football stadium turns out to be a fake and loses its colour the first time it's washed;
- food prices start to rise because farmers can't afford to buy patented seeds;
- food prices start to rise because diseases attack the crops grown by the farmers who didn't buy disease-resistant patented seeds;
- she buys a look-alike product in the supermarket without realising because it looks so similar to the branded product she always buys and when she gets home it just isn't the same.

And so on.

THE INTERNATIONAL POLICY MAKER

He or she must try to strike the right balance between the level of protection necessary to encourage people and businesses to create and innovate, and the need to keep to a minimum restraints on free and fair competition. The right balance will depend on the starting point of the policy.

For example, the rights and wrongs of the ongoing battles between drug patent owners and health authorities depend on your perspective. There is no one right or wrong answer.

For the AIDS sufferer at death's door, the health authority with a limited budget, the US government during the anthrax scare post-9/11, the private right in a patent should be overridden where the public interest demands. Or so the Thai health authority argued in January 2007 when against the objections of the US it granted compulsory licences of Abbott Labs' patented HIV drug Kaletra and Bristol Myers Squibb's patented blood thinner Plavix.

For the shareholder in Ranbaxy, Dr Reddy's, GSK, Novartis or Pfizer who has risked his or her pension monies investing in a business searching for an AIDS cure, a new anti-malarial vaccine or a better drug for heart disease, patents provide fair protection if that risky investment makes good.

What policymakers must bear in mind always was well-summarised by Stanford University economist John McMillan:

> "Whatever course of action is chosen, it has some shortcomings. 'Weakening intellectual property means less innovation,' say those who favour stronger protections. They are right. 'Strengthening intellectual property, by excluding some users, shrinks the total value of ideas,' say those who favour weaker protections. They are right, too. Unconditional assertions about intellectual property are rarely valid. The trick is to find the right balance."

05 What's the fuss about?

Having described the rights that can make up Invisible Gold, got the myths out of the way and considered the different perspectives, let's now look at why IPRs are so important to businesses everywhere and why they have become such important weapons on the battlefield that is world trade.

Creativity and innovation are the lifeblood of a sustainable and growing economy in the 21st century, especially after the dismantling of tariff and other barriers that in the past sheltered so many economies from the winds of competition.

Creativity and innovation provide not only improved living standards but also the added value from which particularly US and European companies have benefitted for so long—an added value that IPRs help to protect. The World Trade Organisation (WTO) rules that require almost all countries to have an effective system for the protection of IPRs mean that for both countries and businesses there is no longer any choice: you either play the IPR game or you leave the field.

But, IPRs alone are not enough and not all IPRs are equal. Businesses everywhere now need to understand what for decades has been second nature to American, European and Japanese technology companies and brand champions:

- first, how to acquire and nurture their Invisible Gold reserves; and
- secondly, what to do with them once they have them.

If they don't make the effort to understand, they will be left behind in the inevitable death spiral of endlessly trying to shave the last cent from production costs. There will always be somebody who can do it for less.

WORLD-CLASS COMPETITION

In 2004 it was argued by a leading world figure that in the 21st century, world competition will revolve around competition for intellectual property rights. Who said it? No, not Bill Gates but Chinese premier Wen Jiabao during a visit to Shandong Province. He has repeated it many times since, as the Chinese government has focused on reducing the revenues flowing out of the country to foreign IPR owners by encouraging local innovation and creativity.

Another practical effect of Wen Jiabao's world view was seen in March 2009, with the startling rejection by China's competition authorities of Coca-Cola's generous US$2.4 billion bid for the country's leading juice maker Huiyuan, after Coca-Cola refused to give up the brand to get approval. Ownership of one of the most valuable Chinese brands, even for a 200 per cent premium over the market price on the Hong Kong stock exchange, was a step too far for the Beijing policy makers.

Since Wen Jiabao's visit to Shandong in 2004 the importance of IPRs in China and elsewhere in Asia has increased in leaps and bounds. Even in a recession-torn international trade arena the need to encourage and protect innovation and creativity, to move up the added-value curve, remains at or near the top of the agenda for most governments in Asia. In June 2009 Premier Wen exhorted Chinese businesses to take advantage of the downturn in economic activity to look carefully at their product lines and improve technology.

This has acquired an even greater urgency in Asian countries, which have recognised that it is dangerous to be over-reliant on export markets in Europe and North America that may take years to recover from the global financial crisis. For example, in August 2009 the Deputy Chairman of Singapore's sovereign wealth fund, the Government of Singapore Investment Corporation (GIC), Dr Tony Tan, suggested that the island-state should move from its cost-effective production model to become "an economy of ideas" and the products and services the country exports should "have a high technological content and higher value-added", both of which would mean a greater role for IP rights—Invisible Gold.

GLOBAL IMBALANCE

Whether it's China with its all-embracing 2007 National IP Strategy, the island-state of Singapore with its long-term investments in life sciences, or India where Tata has applied for as many as 36 patents covering parts of its revolutionary Nano car, countries throughout Asia are determined to redress the global imbalance of trade in IPR-protected products and services.

Rightly or wrongly, that imbalance is not going to change soon. As the governments of the Big Five IP countries—Britain, France, Japan, Sweden and the USA—know very well, they are the only countries to have a positive balance of payments in IPRs. Their economies make more money from their own IPRs than they pay for those belonging to foreigners. Compare this with South Korea, for example. In 2008 around US$5 billion in royalties was paid to foreign patent owners but only US$1.9 billion was received by Korean companies for use of their patents. One way in which the Chinese government has been trying to redress its country's balance of IPR payments is in developing its own proprietary protocols and standards for areas such as 3G telecoms (the Chinese standard is called TD-SCDMA), wireless LAN (WAPI), DVD (EVD) and operating systems (Red Dragon), so that IPR payments do not flow out of the country to the likes of Qualcomm, Sony and Microsoft.

Understandably, the Big Five are determined to keep their comparative IPR advantage as the actual making of the products moves inexorably to the lowest-cost location. It's all about capturing added value—the difference between the cost of making the product or providing the service and the price charged for it. IPRs allow you to do that.

Knowing how to play the Invisible Gold game, how to play within the rules while sometimes bending them, has become crucial for businesses large and small, whether trading at home or abroad.

It's true that many of those rules were written in the late 20th century largely to protect the interests of US, European and Japanese corporations (as described vividly by Cambridge economist Ha-Joon Chang in his 2002 book *Kicking Away the Ladder*), but they are not going to change soon. Complaining about them does not help build businesses today. Instead, countries and businesses must get engaged in creating and using their own Invisible Gold. In some areas Asia has already made great strides: in 1994, Japan, South Korea and China accounted for 7.6 per cent of international patent applications; by 2008, they accounted for 26.1 per cent.

THE TRIPS AGREEMENT

What has brought IPRs to centre stage in international business, trade and diplomacy is a little-known side agreement to those regulating global trade through the WTO: the 1994 **Trade-Related Aspects of Intellectual Property Rights**, or **TRIPs, Agreement.**

The TRIPs Agreement has made IPRs and their enforcement a major world trade issue, rather than primarily a question of private rights belonging to individuals and businesses, which they had been for the previous 200 years of their existence.

TRIPs means that all countries must play the IPR game because without an IPR system they will not be allowed in the Club of Nations that is the WTO. No longer can a country build its economy rent-free on the intellectual endeavours of foreigners; that option is not available any more. To put it another way, the international trade rules of the 21st century do not allow countries like China, India or Indonesia to do what the United States did in the late 18th and 19th centuries, and Japan did in the mid-20th century: ignore IPRs belonging to other countries.

“No longer can a country build its economy rent-free on the intellectual endeavours of foreigners; that option is not available any more.”

Today's rules don't allow a developing economy to transition at a time of its choosing from an economy copying from others without charge to one creating its own intellectual capital base—that is, to move from being IP pirates to IP proprietors. TRIPs requires that IPRs must be respected, enforced and paid for, or else the threat of trade sanctions and complaints to TRIPs dispute resolution panels will quickly arrive. For those countries without their own IPRs, that means a future of continuing dependence on foreign intellectual capital, which they have to pay for.

IPR IMPERIALISM?

Don't think it's only in multilateral trade talks like those of the WTO that IPRs are discussed and fought over. The same occurs in bilateral trade talks, which often result in free trade agreements (FTAs) like that between Singapore and the USA signed in 2004, and between China and the ASEAN group of countries two years earlier (which came into effect on 1 January 2010).

Unfortunately, as Sir John Sulston, who shared the Nobel Prize for Medicine in 2002 and is the British scientist behind the Human Genome Project, lamented in his November 2006 BP lecture at the British Museum:

> "When the EU or US fails to get its way in trade negotiations they bypass the multilateral solution in favour of so-called free trade areas. This is imperialism by another name. All the bilateral agreements of the US, for example, have included intellectual property clauses that favour its industries. The consequence is a race to the ethical bottom in trading standards."

OR UNJUSTIFIED CRITICISM?

All this activity has meant that IPRs are hugely important but little understood outside the IP departments of major companies and in the rarefied reaches of trade ministries. This has led to widespread but frequently ill-informed criticism of many aspects of IPRs and even challenges to the very notion of privately-owned intellectual property. There is a need to step back and consider dispassionately the manifold benefits of a system whose purpose is to encourage and protect creativity and innovation for the benefit of all.

For example, it's too glib for Joseph Stiglitz, another Nobel Laureate, to claim, "The global intellectual property regime denies poor people access to life-saving drugs." No, it does not; it is politicians who do that. After all, who would invest the hundreds of millions of dollars it takes to develop a new drug if it were not for the protection of the patent system and its potential rewards?

As the Undercover Economist, Tim Harford, commented in his *Financial Times* column on 9 May 2009 dealing with the economic value of government promises:

> "Governments occasionally override patents, or threaten to do so, in times of emergency. The makers of anti-anthrax drug Cipro [German company Bayer] and flu-fighter Tamiflu [Swiss business Roche] have both had their arms twisted in recent years. Pharmaceutical companies contemplating investing billions of dollars in an HIV vaccine must be given pause for thought by this; does anyone seriously think that the inventor of such a vaccine would be allowed to charge what the market would bear, free of political interference? And so a vaccine seems less likely."

Like many others, the world of IPRs is not black and white but has large tracts of grey. There are rarely right or wrong answers. It all depends, on where you are and who you are. It's a world of checks and balances. In some aspects, the checks have been forgotten or are too weak; in others, the balance has been lost, the protection doesn't go far enough or, more likely, provides theoretical protection that is rarely worthwhile enforcing.

INTELLECTUAL PIRATES?

Critics argue that the TRIPs-mandated IPR rules are unfair and legitimise theft of IPRs from Asia.

In 2009 Asaffa Endeshaw, well known in academic circles for his trenchant attacks on the TRIPs Agreement and its impact on developing nations, noted "three main tendencies in current Asian IP law:

- an attempt by nations to keep abreast of any additional demands of the industrial powers and to introduce all manner of new laws or revision of old ones considered to be important for foreign investors;
- a continuation of Asian reluctance to confront foreign nations (chiefly the US and EU) as regards the forms and contents as well as enforcement of such laws;
- a desire to keep costs of the IP system down and help local businesses benefit from better access to such a system … "

He warned that "foreign, particularly US, criticism and attendant heavy-handed moves to compel Asian nations to implement IP laws are being viewed, more and more, through Asian eyes, as crossing the boundaries of propriety and might easily backfire."

On similar lines, the Indian anti-globalisation activist Vandana Shiva contends that for many Indian farmers IPRs mean "intellectual piracy rights", giving the examples of the wound-healing properties of turmeric and the neem tree which have been cultivated by Indian peasant farmers for centuries and used as a pesticide and medicine.

Despite the law saying that patents should only be granted for novel inventions, in the mid-1990s an American university managed to obtain a US patent covering a method of wound healing using turmeric powder. American and Japanese corporations have also managed to obtain patents covering the pesticidal and medicinal properties of the neem tree, with no royalties going to Indian farmers.

In the turmeric case, after the University of Mississippi Medical Center was granted its US patent in March 1995, it was challenged by the Council of Scientific and Industrial Research (CSIR) of India, which today is the leading Indian patent applicant. After spending a lot of money, CSIR succeeded in having the patent revoked in 1997.

Around the same time, a European patent on a pesticide based on chemical compounds from the neem tree was challenged by the Research Foundation for Science, Technology and Ecology from India and the International Federation of Organic Agriculture Movements. The patent had been granted in 1995 by the European Patent Office (EPO) to the US Department of Agriculture and W.R. Grace, a Florida-headquartered chemical corporation. Again, the Indian challenge was successful and the patent was revoked by the EPO in 2000. Despite an appeal, the revocation was upheld by the EPO in 2005.

Is all this fair? Should the patents have been granted in the first place, leading to the spending of a lot of money to challenge them, which could have been used for better purposes? The answer to both questions is, "Definitely not." But business (and international trade) is rarely fair and every system involving subjective decisions—such as whether an invention is really "novel"—is imperfect to a greater or lesser degree.

TO ATTACK IS THE BEST DEFENCE

In addition to the ultimately successful challenge to the patent grant by CSIR, the Indian government responded constructively to the

1995 patenting of the wound-healing properties of turmeric at the US Patent Office, even though these supposedly novel uses had been known for millennia.

One of the many problems faced by patent offices around the world is that they are often unaware of **prior art** (patents must be novel and what is already published—the prior art—may, or should, not be patented) and grant patents for so-called inventions that are, in fact, common knowledge. This is a particular problem in the area of traditional medicine, for example in China and India. Substances derived from plants may have been used for thousands of years. Yet patents are still granted, especially in Western countries ignorant of these ancient medical traditions, which are often recorded only in languages such as Sanskrit, Mandarin, Hindi, Arabic, Urdu and Tamil, in which not too many patent examiners are fluent!

To try and alleviate this problem, and to stop its traditional knowledge base being exploited in this way, India has created the Traditional Knowledge Digital Library (TKDL) database. Starting in 2000 with a task force of experts, this was unveiled on 2 February 2009 and is now available online, via an access agreement, to the patent examiners at the EPO to help in checking for prior art in the case of patent applications based on Indian systems of medicine.

The Indian way is to try and make it harder for others to obtain IPRs wrongfully. The alternative is to be proactive and get the rights before anyone else does. In February 2007 the Indonesian government cited "intellectual property concerns" when refusing to send avian flu virus samples to Britain after the outbreak at a Bernard Matthews chicken farm in Norfolk. Only after they had done an exclusive deal with US healthcare multinational Baxter on a potential vaccine did the Indonesians release the samples to British labs.

What both the Indian and Indonesian governments appreciated

when dealing with the turmeric and avian flu issues, respectively, is that the only constructive and meaningful response to the IPR system's present imbalance must lie in encouraging self-innovation and creativity in Asia. This can then be coupled with a more effective use of the IP system by businesses throughout the region, both in their home market and on the global scene.

As Peter Chou, CEO of the leading Taiwanese smartphone company HTC, told the *Financial Times* in June 2009:

> "There is tremendous knowledge and experience required to become a global consumer company ... accumulating the experience and being able to go out to do great innovation and make sure the product is really people-centric and the marketing too—all this is still quite challenging for Asian companies."

To put it in Invisible Gold terminology, innovation, product design and branding are the fundamentals needed to succeed both in Asia and elsewhere.

NOT SEEING *IS* BELIEVING

These IPRs are exclusive private rights arising from the laws of patents, designs, copyright, trademarks, trade secrets, semiconductor chip rights and plant varieties (and, depending on the country you are in, a few others). To put it more pompously, they are legal rights protecting products of the intellect—assets that are intangible, invisible; you can't put your hands around them.

It doesn't matter whether you love them or hate them, IPRs are not going away in the foreseeable future. Their importance, commercial and political, is increasing rather than diminishing. They are the Invisible Gold reserves of every country and its businesses. In the 21st century they must be given the focus and attention that bricks and mortar were given in past centuries.

"IPRs are legal rights protecting products of the intellect—assets that are intangible, invisible; you can't put your hands around them."

As Chinese researchers Jun Hong and Hao Wu commented in their analysis of the sugar industry in Guangxi province (which comprises 94 enterprises responsible for 60 per cent of the country's sugar production): "[The] Guangxi sugar industry should pay more attention on patent strategy so as to achieve industrial upgrading and sustainable development."

ALL-PERVASIVE

What the IPRs are depends on where you are. The position in every country is different despite a complicated network of international conventions that aims to harmonise national laws.

To a greater or lesser extent, there are now IPRs in all countries.

As part of the price paid to enter the WTO—which it did in December 2001, only 10 years after Deng Xiaoping's famous South China Speeches promoting further reform—China has introduced an advanced IPR system at breakneck speed over the past 25 years or so, in parallel with the explosive growth of its economy. During a speech at the 4th Strategic Economic Dialogue in New York in June 2008, Chinese Vice-Premier Wang Qishan noted: "The Chinese people only learned about the term 'intellectual property' in the past 10 years." (Notwithstanding this, in the initial stages of its development Qingdao Haier Group issued an internal patent strategy document as early as 1987. Today it is one of the world leaders in the manufacture of white goods such as refrigerators and an expert user of the patent system in China and abroad.)

The other Asian economic miracle of recent years, India, at the same time as releasing many of the bureaucratic shackles of the Licence Permit Raj put in place first by Nehru and then his daughter Indira Gandhi, has watered-down its highly-protectionist IPR policies in areas such as pharmaceutical patents (although they remain highly controversial). Meanwhile, Indian companies have gone on the prowl for IPR-rich foreign acquisitions. When Tata Steel paid US$12 billion for the Anglo-Dutch steelmaker Corus in 2007, it acquired over 80 US patents and more than 1,000 research staff, whereas previously it had not a single patent in the USA.

Knowledge of the importance of IPRs and how they can be used as commercial weapons is spreading across Asia. Businesses are realising the need to innovate and create, to generate and find Invisible Gold, in order to avoid being vulnerable to the next fashionable and cheaper manufacturing location.

Either because they want to or are forced to do so by their international competitors, many Asian businesses are joining in and building up their reserves of Invisible Gold. Once built up, they are being used against competitors. An article by Ng Tze-wei in the *South China Morning Post* on 7 July 2008 described how Chinese businesses "are becoming savvier about their [IP] rights. And more foreign businesses, ranging from Hong Kong clothing brand G2000 to IT giant Intel, are finding themselves on the defensive."

Great leap forward

An interesting example of a Chinese business using IP rights as a core asset is Shenzhen-based Netac Technology.

The company was founded in May 1999 by Deng Guoshun and Cheng Xiaohua, a software and hardware engineer, respectively, who had both previously worked for Dutch electronics giant Philips in Singapore. With that experience of an IP-based multinational behind the two founders, the new company filed for patent protection of the core technology for its USB flash drive shortly after its formation.

A couple of years later, while the patent application was still being examined by SIPO, Beijing Huaqi Information Technology Co, Ltd launched a new USB flash storage drive, similar to Netac's product OnlyDisc but made in Taiwan. Deng claims that Netac had approached Huaqi to offer a licensing or manufacturing deal; Huaqi rejected this.

When the Chinese patent was granted in 2002 Netac sued Huaqi and its Taiwanese suppliers in the Shenzhen Intermediate People's Court. The Taiwanese settled quickly but Huaqi fought on until the court decided in favour of Netac in June 2004. (Huaqi appealed but the case settled finally in July 2006.) A commentator quoted on the company's website makes the point: "[I]n a country that counterfeits everything from toothpaste to cars, being officially declared real—with a patent case—can be great for business."

Having been vindicated in the legal action against Huaqi, Netac then took on the might of Japanese giant Sony, again suing for infringement of its Chinese patent covering flash memory data storage.

Asked to comment on Netac's legal action, Sony China Chairman Kei Kodera claimed that before Netac got the patent there had already been over a million flash cards sold. He went on to say he found it unusual that Netac had sued for patent infringement, alluding to the fact that, under the law in China, patents for inventions should only be granted if they are "novel". In response, Zhang Zhoukuan of Netac pointed out that it takes about three years to apply for and finally obtain a patent for an invention in China. Once the patent is granted, it is effective from the date the application was filed. Zhang accused Kodera of covering up Sony's alleged infringement and playing dumb about patent procedure in China.

Whether that was true or not, the legal proceedings were brought to an end in November 2006 when Sony agreed to purchase flash products from Netac. Vice President Vincent Zhong of Netac commented in an interview with *Managing Intellectual Property*: "Before that maybe some people thought that Netac just wanted to go for litigation and only litigation. But that is not the case—we are in the business world and business is the most important interest for us."

With that success under its belt, Netac took the highly unusual step of suing US corporation PNY Technologies in its own backyard. Early in 2006 the Chinese company brought legal proceedings for infringement of its US patent (granted at the end of 2004) in the Eastern District of Texas, a place not known for favouring foreign IPR owners. But again the legal action was settled, in March 2008, when PNY entered into a licence agreement with Netac.

FOLLOW UP IS NECESSARY

There is a need for follow-up. All too frequently in Asia (as indeed elsewhere), official policies on IPRs concentrate unduly on how important it is to apply for the rights but remain quiet or even silent on what the IPR owners should do after that. In a refreshing exception to this, in a 2005 report to the ASEAN Secretariat, "Maximizing the Contribution of IP Rights (IPRs) to SME Growth and Competitiveness", authors Stuart Macdonald, Tim Turpin and Amelia Ancog cautioned that:

> "... many of our recommendations are concerned with ensuring that SME managers have information about what IPR to use and when. Appreciating when not to resort to IPR is particularly important. So, too, is another of our recommendation themes: the use of IPR must be part of a SME's overall business plan. IPR can never be a magic bullet to replace strategy.
>
> "Very few managers of SMEs in the ASEAN region have any familiarity at all with IPR. They have much to learn and there is a clear responsibility here for policy makers to arrange help and advice, but always in the context of SME business planning. What policy makers must not do is sell IPR to SME managers as if they were a homogeneous sector. In some cases, encouraging SMEs to resort to IPR may distort their business plans and actually reduce overall competitiveness. While SMEs are disadvantaged in most elements of competitiveness, they do have the advantage of flexibility. They can be quick to market, exploiting niches with new products and processes. If the IPR system is to be of value to SMEs, it is in the context of flexibility and conduciveness to business strategy. The

> singular advantage of flexibility for SMEs is threatened by a cumbersome IPR system.
>
> "This is not to say that ASEAN SMEs should ignore IPR. The TRIPS regime is a reality. ASEAN SMEs must adapt to this reality. Policy makers have a role to play in helping turn abuse of IPR into constructive technology transfer. Above all, ASEAN policy makers should always bear in mind that IPR is a tool of large firms and the developed world. To make this tool useful for SMEs in the developing world will require all the skills its policy makers can command."

In other words, all businesses are different and need to use IPRs differently—some more, some less. What they can't do is ignore them.

A NUMBERS GAME

Everywhere, the numbers of IP rights are exploding:

- It took around 120 years after its establishment in 1790 for the US patent system to grant the first million patents, but in the past 15 years two million were granted, leading some commentators to predict gridlock. In his provocative 2008 book *The Gridlock Economy*, Columbia Law School professor Michael Heller warns: "Private ownership usually creates wealth. But too much ownership has the opposite effect—it creates gridlock. Gridlock is a free market paradox. When too many people own pieces of one thing, cooperation breaks down, wealth disappears, and everybody loses.

  "There has been an unnoticed revolution in how we create wealth. In the old economy—10 or 20 years ago—you invented a product and got a patent; you wrote a song and got a copyright

> ... Today the leading edge of wealth creation requires assembly. From drugs to telecom, software to semiconductors, anything high-tech demands the assembly of innumerable patents. And it's not just high tech that's changed. Cutting-edge art and music are about mashing up and remixing many separately owned bits of culture."

- As far as Europe is concerned, Ciarán McGinley of the European Patent Office has noted that in the 10 years up to 2005 "both the number of claims and the number of pages per application have shot up". The reasons included "an unnecessary export of US-style drafting to Europe; a fee regime that is too lax; and the usual hide-and-seek behaviour of patent attorneys".

- From a standing start in 1985, when its first modern patent law came into force, China had granted 1.7 million patents by the end of 2006. The five-millionth patent application was made in March 2009. Although the vast majority of these was for design patents and utility model patents (which protect minor inventions), even in the more complex area of invention patents Chinese applicants were granted more than 50 per cent of the 36,000 granted in the first half of 2009. China's earlier attempts to introduce a functioning patent system had failed. Harvard Professor William Alford in his study of IPRs in Chinese civilisation, *To Steal a Book is an Elegant Offense*, noted that a 1912 law resulted in between 360 and 692 patents in its first 30 years. An earlier Qing dynasty law in 1889 was no more successful. In post-1949 Communist China, patents were replaced by inventor's certificates. Only four were issued between the mid-1950s and 1963 when it was declared that all inventions were the property of the State, with payments made to the inventors of between 10,000 yuan for a first-class invention and 500 yuan for a fifth-class one. Shortly after, the start of the Cultural Revolution ensured that intellectuals ("the stinking old ninth category") had more important matters on their minds.

DON'T THROW THE BABY OUT WITH THE BATH WATER

Notwithstanding the problems arising from this massive growth in patenting activity over recent years, it is important that the many advantages of the patent system are not forgotten in the chorus of criticism. As Professor Joseph Straus of the Max Planck Institute in Munich cautions:

> "As with all fuels, [the patent system] will surely contain some debris, which has to be filtered out in order to optimize the combustion performance of the engine. The latter is definitely in need of fine lubricants. As the main administrators of the patent system, the most prominent task of the patent offices is properly filtering the fuel and taking care of the lifetime lubrication of the engine. The backlogs of pending applications ... revealed by WIPO [2007] statistics, that is more than 950,000 in the United States, more than 800,000 in Japan, about 400,000 in the Republic of Korea, some 250,000 in the European Patent Office and some 200,000 in China and Canada, indicate that the system as it stands is facing extremely serious problems and could be compromised altogether. However, the solution cannot be an attempt to contain and suppress the flow of the fuel, which the global economy and especially its emerging players need so badly."

06 Why now in Asia?

Reflecting its growing importance, the economies of Asia accounted for nearly 22 per cent of global GDP (in inflation-adjusted 2005 US dollar terms) by the end of 2009. Roughly 29 per cent was held by the 27-member European Union. The USA's share lay between the two at about 27 per cent (down from 50 per cent at the end of the Second World War).

Also, in China and India, Asia is home to two of the countries in the group known by the acronym, BRIC (Brazil, Russia, India and China), invented by Goldman Sachs economist Jim O'Neill in 2002. (O'Neill told the *Financial Times*' Gillian Tett that the only reason he didn't call the group of emerging economic powers the CRIB was that he thought the child connotation of that acronym could be thought patronising). In O'Neill's later invention, the N-11 or Next Eleven countries to emerge, Bangladesh, Indonesia, Korea, Pakistan, the Philippines and Vietnam are included from Asia—along with Egypt, Iran, Mexico, Nigeria and Turkey.

In addition to these and the many other reasons already described as to why IPRs are of increasing importance in Asia, there is also the fact that many Asian economies are moving to the next stage of their development.

INTRA-ASIAN TRADE

In an era of increasing regional and global trade under the watchful eye of the WTO, no longer do governments in Asia, or can they, build up their local industries shielded from the winds of external competition by high tariff barriers and overt local preference. Instead, cross-border competition within Asia is increasing.

In 2005 over half of all Asian exports of goods went to other Asian countries (if you include Australia and New Zealand in Asia). Asian economies have become more tightly integrated. The rest of Asia is the largest export market for Japan, followed by the US market and the 27 countries making up the European Union. Also, for the first time since the mid-19th century, Japan now exports more to China, Hong Kong and Taiwan than to the United States, and China has replaced the United States as Korea's top export market.

This increase in intra-Asian trade carries with it a need for businesses throughout the region to develop new methods of protecting their markets. As Peter Williamson, Professor of International Management and Asian Business at the Judge Institute in Cambridge, warns in his 2004 book *Winning in Asia*:

> "The cost advantages that allowed Asian companies to take market share from high-cost suppliers in the United States and Europe will be of little help in winning the battle for Asian markets. The primary competitors, whether they be other Asian firms or multinationals operating in Asia, will all enjoy the same Asian cost advantages. Low costs will be an entry ticket into the game. New sources of advantage will be necessary to win in the next round of competition for Asian markets."

In many cases, those sources of advantage will include Invisible Gold, especially in view of Williamson's contention that "Asia today has a striking innovation deficit compared with its global competitors. But … this does not reflect an inherent lack of creativity or potential for innovation. The reality is that, over recent decades, it simply didn't pay most Asian companies to allocate a significant slice of their investment resources to innovation."

THE REGIONAL GIANTS

Today, not only does it pay to make such an allocation but it is only those businesses which do that will survive and prosper. This can be seen from the Asian companies featured in the FT Global 500 List, which operate in sectors with significant IP exposure.[1] The Asian presence has become much more broadly spread geographically between 2000 (*see Appendix 1, Table 1*)—when the 72 entries were dominated by Japanese corporations, which comprised over three-quarters of the Asian companies listed—and 9 August 2007 (*see Appendix 1, Table 2*), by which time Chinese and Indian companies were featured in the 63 Asian entries and the Japanese share had fallen to close to half.

As the following diagrams illustrate, Japanese companies no longer dominate the list in the way they did just 10 years ago at the turn of the century. They comprised just over half of the Asian companies in 2009, compared to more than three-quarters only nine years earlier. On the other hand, in the same period China including Hong Kong SAR increased its share from around seven per cent to

[1] Excluding financial and insurance, energy, real estate (including transport infrastructure) companies.

19 per cent (mainland China appearing in the 2009 list with 11 per cent, having not had even the one per cent required to appear in 2000) and India from four per cent to 10 per cent. South Korea and Taiwan maintained and increased slightly their shares at six per cent and five per cent, respectively.

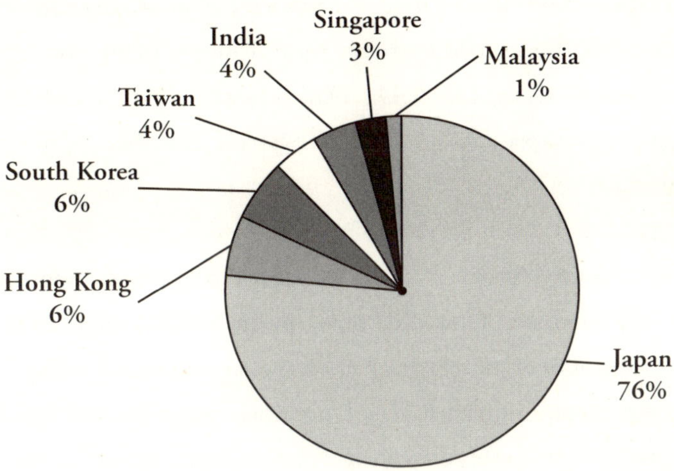

Figure 6.1 National breakdown in 2000

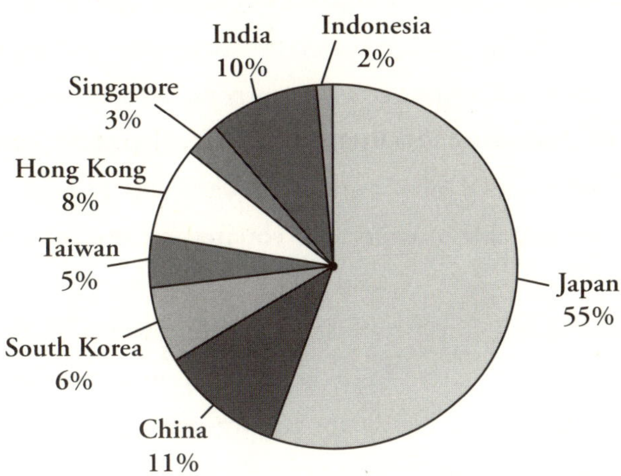

Figure 6.2 National breakdown in 2009

IGNORANCE ISN'T BLISS

Even though IP rights have become hot topics of debate in domestic and international trade circles all around Asia, there still remains frightening ignorance about how they can and should play a critical role in the development of Asian economies in coming years.

In an April 2004 article in *The Financial Express*, after reviewing figures on what he considered the poor foreign patenting activity of Indian enterprises, Dr A.D. Damodaran, former Director at the Thiruvananthapuram Regional Research Laboratory of India's CSIR, warned:

> "Even after a five decades-long post-independent development followed now by a decade-long additional promotional efforts [sic] since the signing of the WTO/TRIPS Agreement, Indian R&D of 'possible industrial use' has 'Miles to Go' to emerge even as a reasonable player in the field, with the TRIPS-compliant patent regime straightaway only reinforcing the hold of the foreign agencies in extending their IP monopolies to this country as well ...
>
> "[A]ny further delay in eradicating the 'massive patent illiteracy' could very well corrode our national technological-industrial edifice itself. The task is huge, and yet the Faustian Alternative must be faced squarely by all who yearn for an honourable place for our country in the comity of nations."

If you think it doesn't affect you, think again. From counterfeit drugs that replace active ingredients with chalk, to the genetically-modified food you eat, IPRs are an ever-present part of everyday life in Asia, and increasing in significance all the time.

HEADY INFLUENCE

As just one indicator of that significance, the respected specialist magazine *Managing Intellectual Property* publishes an annual list of the 50 most influential people in the intellectual property world. Nine of those in the 2009 list are from Asia; three others can claim an Asian connection.

Table 6.1 Asians among the 50 most influential people in the IP world

Name	Country	Who they are	Highlights
Toichi Takenaka	Japan	Chairman, Japan Intellectual Property Association	Helped shape Japan's IP policy as head of the Japan Intellectual Property Association (JIPA), one of the country's most active IP organisations. Also chairman of Astellas Pharma.
Lee Jeong Hwan	South Korea	Executive vice-president, Intellectual Property Centre, LG Electronics	Helped found the Korea Intellectual Property Association in June 2008.
Kong Xiangjun	China	Deputy chief judge of the IP tribunal of the Supreme People's Court	Streamlining China's courts.
Tian Lipu	China	Commissioner, SIPO	Implementing the National IP Strategy in China.
Wu Handong	China	President, Zhongnan University of Economics & Law	Chairman of the Intellectual Property Rights Law Association of the China Law Society.

(continued overleaf)

Name	Country	Who they are	Highlights
Song Liuping	China	Chief legal officer, Huawei	Leading China's No. 1 patent applicant.
Alongkorn Ponlaboot	Thailand	Deputy Commerce Minister, Thailand	Chairman of the National Committee on Prevention and Suppression of IP Rights Violations.
P.H. Kurian	India	Controller General of Patents, Designs & Trademarks, India	Reforming India's bureaucratic IP system.
Lu Guoqiang	China	Deputy Director-General, Shanghai IP Administration	Helped found the IP chamber of Shanghai's Higher People's Court. Set up the Shanghai Intellectual Property Arbitration Institution, first of its kind in China, in October 2008.

Another Asian in the 50 Most Influential List was **Margaret Chan, Director-General, World Health Organisation (WHO).** Under her leadership, the WHO is becoming increasingly active on IP issues, particularly in the area of access to medicines protected by patents. The organisation's Global Strategy and Plan of Action of Public Health, Innovation and Intellectual Property was approved in 2009. It set out a plan of how the WHO will increase access to medicine and fund R&D for neglected diseases while at the same time respecting IP rights. The plan of action aims to be completed by 2015.

Other influential personalities certainly important in Asia were the essentially global phenomena **the illegal downloader** and **the IP blogger,** which would include highly-informative blogs such as *ipdragon* (on China) and *spicyipindia.*

A WORLDWIDE EPIDEMIC

Don't think that innovation and creativity are the preserve of North American and European companies: Taiwanese and South Korean businesses dominate certain technology areas, owning swathes of patents.

Think of an iconic American product, the iPhone. The key to its simple interface is a screen that can respond to multi-point touches. This makes rapid text entry possible and allows keyboard-like and mouse-type navigation of Web pages and the phone's own applications. The screen is built by a German company, Balda AG, which originally produced high-quality cameras but switched to precision plastic components for the mobile phone industry in 1998. By 2006 Balda was bleeding red ink and laid off 1,500 of its workforce in Germany. That same year, however, via its Singapore-based investment holding company, it bought a 50 per cent stake in TPK Holding. This is a company set up in 2003 by Taiwanese entrepreneur Michael Chiang to specialise in touch screens from two to eight inches in size and which, through its wholly-owned TPK Optical Production, runs a production facility in Xiamen. So, the touch-screen technology itself is neither American nor European but Chinese, originally developed by TPK in its design facility in Taiwan to help the rapid input of the Chinese language's character-based alphabet.

On the other side of the coin, the iPhone, assembled in China for Apple by Taiwan's Hon Hai, is a good example of how the country needs to improve its own rate of innovation and creativity because less than five per cent of the US$280 manufacturing cost actually stays in China.

In Taiwan, companies used to be able to focus on low-end products and survive by making them cheaper, but "now it's all about intellectual property", a local businessman comments, in a country where R&D expenditure has soared to over US$8 billion from less than US$2 billion in 1990.

In India many companies have made the same transition. Pune-based Bajaj Auto, the world's fourth-largest motorbike maker, has turned to the patent system to help in its battles with Chinese copycats. In May 2009 the Indian company announced that the Indian Patent Office had granted it a patent covering multi-spring vehicle shock absorbers. Bajaj first introduced the shock absorber on the Bajaj Boxer CT 100 commuter motorbike in July 2005 and had sold over five million bikes using it by March 2009—a success that brought in its wake copies, such as the NeXus motorbike marketed in Nigeria and the Nebula brand in Kenya and Uganda, made by Chinese manufacturers. A Chinese company, Taian Chiran Machinery Company, even made an almost exact copy of Bajaj's hugely successful Pulsar motorcycle to sell in Latin America and had the cheek to call it the Gulsar. In late 2005 Bajaj succeeded in stopping Taian from selling these copy Pulsars to Sri Lanka where they were being marketed under the brand Ranomoto.

This is all a far cry from the mid-1990s when business writer Gita Piramal commented of Bajaj in her book *Business Maharajas* that "its product would need substantial technological upgrading to make it internationally acceptable". Indeed, as head of the Bombay Club of industrialists, which opposed liberalisation, company chairman Rahul Bajaj was one of the most vocal opponents of the steps taken in the early 1990s by Narasimha Rao and Manmohan Singh to dismantle the Licence Permit Raj, charging that Indian "national interests and national pride" must be protected "until there's a level playing field".

UP, UP AND AWAY

In October 2006, WIPO's Director General Dr Francis Gurry referred to the meteoric rise in the number of patent applications in the 10 years up to 2004. In that period, the number of patents filed by residents in South Korea increased by 268 per cent, while the number of patent applications from residents in China increased by 488 per cent. The average increase in the number of patent applications around the world was 42 per cent, according to Gurry.

Some think in that very increase lie the seeds of the system's downfall. With the deluge of new applications, patents are granted with less and less concern for whether they actually contain anything truly inventive. In April 2008 Ciarán McGinley of the European Patent Office commented disparagingly of the filing upsurge in the United States:

> "US-based CEOs are playing an increasingly macho game of having the largest patent portfolio such that patent application volumes are more important than substance."

SPROUTING TECHNOLOGY

From India to China, Asian companies are starting to transition from reliance on foreigners' technology to developing their own. In 1982 when the founder of Reliance Industries, Dhirubhai Ambani, obtained a prized licence to build a polyester yarn plant at Patalganga in Maharashtra, he turned to American giant Du Pont for the technology. Today Reliance, the largest private-sector conglomerate in India and headed by Dhirubhai's son Mukesh, files for its own patents on polyester technology developed at its own Technology Centre in Raigarh as it dominates world trade in yarn.

Chinese companies and universities are starting to play the IP game too, although it remains true that around 60 per cent of invention patents in China are granted to foreign companies or joint ventures.

R&D DOLLARS AND SENSE

In the same vein, Kishore Mahbubani, a former diplomat for Singapore, described the rapidly-changed outlook in his 2008 book *New Asian Hemisphere*:

> "It is stunning to see the degree to which Asians have come to dominate research in science and technology. The Asian mind, which once appeared to be handicapped in this area [as described in Mahbubani's earlier book *Can Asians Think?*], has overwhelmingly taken to science and technology research. An October 2006 *Time* magazine cover story, 'Asia's Great Science Experiment', cited some impressive statistics … [including]
>
> "Asian nations have dramatically increased their government spending on science: between 1995 and 2005 China more than doubled the percentage of its GDP invested in research and development, from 0.6 per cent to 1.3 per cent, while South Korea's funding has risen from US$9.8 billion in 1994 to US$19.4 billion in 2004. Such cash infusions have lured many seasoned Asian researchers from the west, where science budgets are stagnating or, in some countries, even dwindling …
>
> "The science push has already yielded results for Asia's developing economies: their share of high-tech exports rose from seven per cent in 1980 to 25 per cent in 2001, while the US share declined from 31 per cent to 18 per cent, according

> to the US National Science Foundation. At the same time, the Asian share of all published scientific papers climbed from 16 per cent in 1990 to 25 per cent in 2004."

REALISM REQUIRED

Impressive though the figures cited by Mahbubani are, Asian businesses and policymakers should not get carried away. The reality is that the West together with Japan still dominates many areas of science and technology. Whilst it is true that R&D spending in Asia has been increasing, more than 80 per cent of the 700 largest R&D spenders still come from only five countries: the United States dominates, followed by Japan, Germany, the United Kingdom and France.

Paradoxically, much of the "Asian dominance" to which Mahbubani, now dean of the Lee Kuan Yew School of Public Policy at the National University of Singapore, refers has resulted in IPRs *owned by Western and Japanese companies* because of the trend to outsource R&D to Asia. When Philips, Intel, Microsoft or Sony set up R&D centres in China or India, for example, the inventions that come out of them will be owned by Philips, Sony, etc, and not by Asians. It is also worth mentioning here that of the 50 major companies in the bodies that develop standards for the information and communication technology (ICT) sector, 25 are from the United States, 12 from the EU and eight from Japan. In the top 10 are IBM, Microsoft, Fujitsu, Intel, Hewlett-Packard, Hitachi, Sun Microsystems, Nokia, Ericsson and Texas Instruments. Only five companies from emerging countries (all from Asia) feature as minor players. In order of importance these are Samsung (Korea), Huawei (China), LG (Korea), Lenovo (China) and ZTE (China).

Later in his book Mahbubani refers to the considerable success of India's CSIR and its Director General Dr R.A. Mashelkar, noting that it earned US$1.26 billion "from doing contract research for the likes of GE". This is certainly an impressive achievement.

However, it should not be forgotten that most contracts for R&D outsourcing would require that all the intellectual property generated in the course of carrying out the research would belong to the company paying for the research, and not to the institution carrying out the research, although it may be given limited rights to use for research purposes only. Rather than creating IPRs it owns, the long-run benefit of such activity to the host nation lies in the enhanced expertise of its researchers. It is the job of that host nation to provide the infrastructure for those researchers to use that enhanced expertise in building their own businesses with their own IPRs.

To take one example of how this can work for the benefit of Asian countries: chip design. Instead of the global centres of excellence established between the 1970s and 1990s (such as Silicon Valley), there are a number of new clusters developing in Asia in places like Hsinchu, Taipei and Tainan (in Taiwan); Shanghai, Suzhou, Hangzhou, Beijing, Shenzhen and Xián (in China); Seoul, Incheon and Daedok Innopolis (in Korea); Bangalore, Noida, Chennai, Hyderabad, Mumbai, Pune and Ahmedabad (in India); Penang and Kuala Lumpur (in Malaysia); and Singapore. Although much of the work carried out in these centres will result in IPRs owned by the global leaders in the ICT sector, it will also result inevitably in the creation of expertise that can be nurtured for the benefit of businesses established in the host nation.

Another measure often used to show who is more innovative—who owns more technology—is the number of patents and patent applications. Indeed, the highly respected Gurry told a Singapore audience in July 2009 that, looking at today's patent numbers, Japan, China and the Republic of Korea now own more than a quarter of the world's technology.

The underlying premise, that Asia is becoming more innovative and is increasing its use of the patent system, is of course correct. It is also important to encourage more Asian inventors to file for patents in what Gurry has described as a "knowledge arms race".

"... most contracts for R&D outsourcing would require that all the intellectual property generated in the course of carrying out the research would belong to the company paying for the research, and not to the institution carrying out the research."

But the "quarter" claim is a step too far and is based on a number of false assumptions. These include:

- Not all patents are equal. Many are for minor, incremental improvements, with one or perhaps two claims, of little value to anyone. Others are for truly groundbreaking inventions (like the MP3 player navigation technology patent owned by Singapore's Creative Technology, which in August 2006 Apple paid US$100 million to use) with many separate claims, all of which can be relied on in court to stop a competitor. Under pressure to be more effective, to bridge the gap between academia and business, many educational institutions around Asia have demanded that their researchers file for patents. The more patents filed the more kudos the researcher gets. So, patent applications are made for every development, however small, however unimportant. If the application is actually granted and makes it onto the patents register, it is often dropped quietly when renewal fees become due and more commercially-minded colleagues realise it is of no marketplace value at all. But by that time it has entered the statistics and the academic has had his or her promotion or bonus, so he or she is very happy.

- Many Chinese patent applications are for designs not inventions (in the USA and China, although not in most other Asian countries, *patents* are awarded for designs as well as inventions). This is not to suggest that design is unimportant. In fact, in many industries it as important as technology, but apples should not be compared with oranges: many of the "patents" used to support the Asian technology growth argument have nothing to do with technology.

- Also, many Chinese patent applications are for **utility models,** a lesser form of patent to protect minor inventions for up to 10 years, which some Asian countries have but most do not (and nor does the USA). Huge numbers of utility models, which are granted without any examination as to utility, are applied for by domestic Chinese businesses, although (perhaps to its cost) the system is used infrequently by non-Chinese.

Bus journeys

A striking example of how utility models can be used successfully by a determined non-Chinese business came in March 2009 when the Beijing No. 1 Intermediate People's Court ordered the Jiangsu province-based Zhongwei Passenger Bus Co Ltd, its parent company Zonda Industrial Group and its Beijing dealer to pay RMB21.16 million (US$3.1 million) in damages and legal costs to Neoplan Bus GmbH, a MAN AG subsidiary. The German company had obtained a design patent for its Starliner bus in China in

September 2004. After coming across the A9 copies of its Starliners manufactured by Zhongwei in the spring of 2006, Neoplan soon sued Zhongwei to stop producing and selling the A9 bus at only a third of the Starliner's price. Since its launch in 2006, the A9 had been successfully exported to Southeast Asian countries and Eastern Europe due to its low price. In an attempt to put its German competitor on the defensive, in January 2007 Zhongwei sued for libel as a result of its claim at a Beijing press conference that the Chinese company was "copying", but the German company eventually prevailed in its design patent legal action.

- The vast majority of patents is never commercialised and few are kept in force for their full term but instead are abandoned or lapse when a renewal fee is not paid. In Europe, where the full patent term is 20 years, it has been estimated that the average length of time patents are kept in force is only seven years.

- Technology does not equal patents. Much technology and many inventions are never patented. Instead the technology owner relies on speed to market, branding, trade secrets, continual improvement and complementary services to get and keep ahead of the competition.

THE BALANCE REDRESSED?

Although it is undoubtedly correct to say that Asian contributions to innovation will increase as the likes of Singapore, China and India compete to attract R&D centres run by foreign businesses but staffed with local talent, the question that can only be answered in the long term is whether this will lead to Asian countries owning a greater proportion of the world's IPRs. It is those IPRs that permit what economists describe as "rent extraction", either through premium pricing or royalty streams for the right to use them.

To take but one example: although Microsoft employs hundreds of engineers in its Beijing R&D facility specialising in computer graphics and language simulation, the IPRs generated there will be owned not by those engineers but by the US software giant. On the other hand, the intangible and long-term benefit obtained by China lies in the value to its engineers of working for one of the world's most innovative and well-run businesses.

There is little excuse if Asian businesses don't also have the foreign rights to their creative and innovative products. Almost every country in the world now has a legal system for the protection of IPRs, both those of its own citizens and those of foreigners. Gone are the old days such as those in Japan following the introduction of its patent system in 1885 when foreigners were not allowed even to file for a patent. Today, where countries may differ is in the respect they give to IPRs and the effectiveness of the methods available to enforce them, but they all have IP systems.

THE TYRANNY OF THE KPI

As the world has globalised, the language and procedures of the management guru and the business school have permeated many institutions and businesses around Asia. Much of this can only be good, as processes and planning replace chaos and making things up as you go along.

On the other hand, one of the favourite tools of the management consultant is the KPI or Key Performance Indicator. Achieving a

KPI has become the badge of success, no matter how the business is actually doing in the marketplace where competitors and customers don't care about the latest trend in business school thinking. The problem with IP-related KPIs stems from the KPI-setters not understanding what IP rights are for—and how, when numbers are the performance measure, quantity often replaces quality.

There are Asian businesses (and indeed academic institutions) where a person's KPI—and thus their status in the organisation—is the number of patent applications they can file in the relevant measurement period, despite the fact that a patent application means nothing except an application number. Even if the KPI is the number of patents granted in the measurement period (which is a lottery in itself because of the huge backlog of applications at many patent offices), again it is valuing what you can measure rather than measuring what you value. This is usually a waste of time and money in the cause of measurement. It doesn't matter whether the patent application or even the patent if it is granted (and many don't get that far) is for anything of commercial value. That's somebody else's problem, somebody else's KPI. For example, seven of the top 10 invention patent owners in the biotechnology field in China identified by Chen Qiongdi in her 2010 study are universities (Fudan, Zhejiang, Shanghai Jiaotong, Qinghua, Nanjing Agricultural, Wuhan and Nanjing Agricultural) but she characterises the rates of exploitation of those patents as "very low".

Delhi-based lawyer Kruttika Vijay made the same point, on the *spicyip* blogspot, about the headline-grabbing figures for the patenting activity of India's publicly-funded CSIR:

> "Scratching the surface a little deeper reveals this glory to be a tainted one. A massive investment has been put into

the filing and maintaining of all these patents, by the CSIR. The important question to be asked at this point is, how many of these patents have actually been marketed, or commercially utilised in any way? How many of these patents serve a purpose? Several academic works point out that 60 to 70 per cent of the technologies and research processes developed by the CSIR remained unutilised or could not be commercialised. Is the aim purely to have a large number of patents (CSIR as of October 2008, is said to have 3016 patents in force) just so that we can boast about our statistics? Most of us are aware that the kind of investment such activity requires is colossal—and while on the one hand all this investment is being pumped in—there seem to be very feeble signs of any returns. In fact, as per statistics obtained from Mint, in 2004 to 2005, the latest period for which data is available, CSIR filed 50 patents and generated Rs4 crore in royalties and licensing. However, it also spent Rs10 crore in filing for the new patents and in maintaining existing ones. It appears to be a rather futile exercise then, to relentlessly file patents at the cost of taxpayer's money, which are just a financial drain and are incapable of generating any financial returns. Thus, while it was crucial to promote IP awareness amongst the scientific community, the no-holds-barred way this was approached emerges as unsatisfactory in the extreme—as what has resulted is a large number of patents requiring a correspondingly huge investment but with no returns."

Don't make the mistake of thinking something is valuable merely because you can measure it. It is far better to work out what you value and then see if you can measure it.

PART TWO

The Asian IP Landscape

Part Two first examines the IP landscape in the different countries making up the Asian region, looking both at the general state of development of the country in the intellectual property field and at examples of how local businesses have developed and exploited IPRs in their domestic markets and elsewhere. After that, it looks at examples of how Asian businesses have been commercialising IPRs: through buying and selling, and taking and giving licences to use. Finally, there is a relatively brief treatment of the counterfeiting and piracy problem in Asia, a subject that dominates whenever IPRs are mentioned in the media and elsewhere.

It is possible to provide here only a snapshot (and one from a relatively high level) of the importance of Invisible Gold in a particular country; there is no attempt to provide a comprehensive description. The examples cited are just that and not meant to be representative. Nevertheless, it is hoped that they give a flavour of the unheralded Invisible Gold reserves to be found all around Asia and provide a form of road map to the areas in which Asian companies will compete with their international counterparts in the years to come.

07 It takes all sorts

Countries around Asia feature in every different category of IPR development: from the advanced relying on its own innovation and creativity (Japan), to those moving—at varying speeds—from imitator to innovator (China, India, Taiwan and South Korea); those aiming to use in the development of their own Invisible Gold the technology and know-how introduced by foreign investors (Singapore, Indonesia, Malaysia and Thailand); to the newly industrialising countries—the NICs—still highly dependant on foreign technology and assistance (Vietnam, Cambodia and Laos). *Appendix 3* contains a timeline of significant events in the development of the intellectual property infrastructure in Asia.

What is consistent in all Asian countries is a wish to improve their IPR position. As the different economies evolve, the importance of IPRs of all kinds increases, whether they belong to foreigners or are locally generated. And there are more and more of the latter.

Take brands first: businesses throughout the region are acutely aware of the critical importance of brands and the need to constantly nurture them. In Brand Finance's 2010 list of the Global 500 Brands, which puts monetary values on companies' brand equity, nearly 20 per cent are Asian companies (*Appendix 2*). The top three are Toyota (with a brand value of US$27.319 billion), China Mobile

(US$18.673 billion) and Mitsubishi (US$17.805 billion), with Tata being the highest Indian company (US$11.216 billion). (The possibility of considerable volatility in such valuations can be seen in the firestorm of criticism that surrounded Toyota at the beginning of 2010, with its inevitable and speedy impact on brand value).

LEADING EDGE

Three of the top four most popular patent offices are in Asia. In 2006, the US Patent & Trademark Office (USPTO) received the largest number of patent filings (425,966), followed by the Japanese Patent Office (JPO; 408,674), the Chinese SIPO (210,501) and the Korean KIPO (166,189). Between 2000 and 2006, filings at SIPO and KIPO increased by 26.3 per cent and 8.5 per cent a year (average annual growth rate), respectively. By contrast, patent filings at the JPO decreased by 0.4 per cent a year.

> “As the different economies [in Asia] evolve, the importance of IPRs of all kinds increases, whether they belong to foreigners or are locally generated.”

In the same year, the total number of patents in force across the world was estimated to be around 6.1 million. Applicants from Japan (approximately 1.6 million) and the United States of America (approximately 1.2 million) owned the majority.

Further illustrating the IPR leadership of these two countries: all of the top 20 university applicants using the international patent filing system, the Patent Cooperation Treaty (PCT), are from the United States of America (15) and Japan (five). The University of California is by far the largest PCT applicant from the university sector, with the highest ranking non-US universities being Kyoto and Tokyo universities in Japan.

ELECTRIC EXPANSION

Electrical engineering, a technical field in which Asian countries such as Japan, Korea and Taiwan excel and which includes computer technology, telecommunications, electrical machinery, apparatus, energy and audio-visual technology, was the most active technical sector according to the number of patent applications. A high number of applications were also filed in the fields of optics and medical technology. Now that China is moving rapidly up the technology curve, there seems little doubt that its influence is going to increase in these fields. As Kishore Mahbubani notes admiringly:

> "In China, there is a deep and profound hunger for education. Parents invest a huge amount of their savings to send their children to regular schools and to provide private tuition. The education they aspire to for their children is a modern Western secular education with a heavy bias towards science and technology. Almost every Chinese parent wants to produce an Einstein or a Bill Gates—both are equally revered in China."

CHINDIA

The two recent Asian arrivals on the world economic scene, China and India, have built their economies at breakneck speed over the past 20 years in vastly different ways, each playing to its particular strengths. China's economy is roughly three-and-a-half times bigger than that of India: GDP in 2008 for the two countries stood at US$4.2 trillion and US$1.2 trillion, respectively.

China has become the world's factory, taking advantage of its huge but poorly paid population as it sucks in technology and more than US$60 billion in foreign direct investment (FDI) a year. In its 2009 Person of the Year (Chairman of the US Federal Reserve Ben Bernanke) feature, *Time* magazine paid tribute in No. 3 position to The Chinese Worker, noting that "[b]y their millions, they leave their families to work in faraway factories and stoke the world's fastest growing economy".

What is sometimes forgotten in the increasingly strident calls for the introduction of protectionist measures to stem the flow of imports from China, is that the massive FDI has resulted in more than 70 per cent of the country's exports coming from businesses owned not by local Chinese or the government but by American, European, Japanese, Taiwanese and Hong Kong companies. These have provided the much-needed management expertise, technology and access to foreign markets. At the same time, the Chinese market itself has grown massively. The rest of the world waits anxiously to see if Chinese consumers will help the global economy emerge relatively unscathed from the recession that followed the 2008 to 2009 financial crisis. A noteworthy consequence of the recession affecting some countries, like the USA and Britain, more than it has others is that 2008 saw more cars sold in China than in the USA.

(At the beginning of 2010 General Motors took the radical step of appointing engineer Hans Demant, the head of Opel's German operations, to the new position of Global IP Head. A statement from GM said, "In the fast-moving global automotive industry ... the value and treatment of intellectual property is critical.")

In areas like business process outsourcing (BPO), India has used its intellectual capital and freed itself from the stultifying effects of the dead hand of bureaucracy and red tape during the Licence Permit Raj. This way of regulating business—which, in the words of Indian software entrepreneur Nandan Nilekani, "turned economic competition into a game with a crooked wheel, as bureaucrats who managed licences became the gatekeepers to industry"—lasted from Independence through the rule of Nehru, his daughter Indira and grandson Rajiv until 1991. It was in that year that Prime Minister Narasimha Rao and his Finance Minister Manmohan Singh responded to the country's latest financial crisis by starting to dismantle the controls in critical areas, including drastically reducing import tariffs.

Today, in places such as Bangalore the likes of TCS and Nilekani's Infosys provide back-office services for businesses all over Europe and North America, while GE, Texas Instruments and other Western IT giants have flocked there to tap lower-cost Indian brainpower in developing the next generation of IT products. However, the level of FDI is only six to seven per cent of that which has flowed to China. As a result India has been forced to become more capital efficient in a range of industries. A *Business Week* analysis of the largest listed companies in both countries showed that the average Indian company had a 16.7 per cent return on capital in 2004, compared to only 12.8 per cent in China.

ASEAN

Before looking at intellectual property at the country level in Asia, the role of ASEAN should be mentioned. The Association of Southeast Asian Nations (ASEAN) members are Brunei Darussalam, Cambodia, Indonesia, Laos, Malaysia, Myanmar, the Philippines, Singapore, Thailand and Vietnam.

Speaking to the Foreign Correspondents' Dinner in 2004, Singapore's Minister Mentor Lee Kuan Yew recognised, in his usual no-nonsense fashion, that it would take many years for Asia to develop an economic community because it is very diverse and not as homogenous as the West. However, he felt that "[w]hat will pull [ASEAN] together is the need to be sufficiently competitive against two huge countries now in the World Trade Organisation and wanting to industrialise and join the export markets: India and China".

As MM Lee predicted, the ASEAN grouping has indeed made significant trade liberalisation steps since and, although attracting criticism, has established itself as a leading regional grouping in Asia.

In the field of intellectual property rights, 2009 saw the coming into effect of the ASEAN Patent Examination Cooperation (ASPEC) Programme, which aims to reduce the time taken to deal with patent applications from applicants who have filed in at least two of the ASPEC member states.

Of far greater significance in the long term, in 2002 a China-ASEAN FTA was signed at the Eighth Summit in Phnom Penh, Cambodia, providing duty-free access to the Chinese market for over 600 agricultural products from the original six ASEAN countries of Brunei, Indonesia, Malaysia, the Philippines, Singapore and Thailand (with the other less developed member countries following later).

FREE TRADE

This FTA came into force on 1 January 2010 and the China-ASEAN Free Trade Area (Cafta) was born, despite some last-minute concerns that Indonesia would attempt to renegotiate certain aspects. Many in that country and elsewhere in ASEAN remain unconvinced about whether the FTA is in their interest. For example, on the day the FTA came into force, Indonesian business magazine *GlobeAsia* carried an article entitled "Free Trade With China: A Dangerous Commitment" by an academic at Paramadina University, Wijayanto, who complained:

> "The election is over, but our leaders spend too much time on domestic politics, neglecting the survival of our nation in the global economic arena.
>
> "In the past, China's dynasties spent centuries to build the 6,000 km Great Wall of China. It is estimated that over two million people died during the construction process. They spent tremendous energy and time to protect their interests from the nomadic people in the north.
>
> "We have our Great Wall in the form of trade rules, taxes and tariffs to protect our industry from the 'invasion' from the north. Unfortunately, instead of maintaining it, we demolish it by signing [the FTA]. Consequently, we will compete with a much stronger nation without the proper weapons, protection or strategy. The chance to win is very limited.
>
> "I am confused how I should celebrate this New Year, since it will usher in the new free trade agreement. We will face new opportunity, new challenges. The trouble is that the challenges are double or triple the opportunity."

While also bearing in mind that the Great Wall did little to protect anyone, it is worth recalling here the more pragmatic view of FTAs expressed by Mahbubani: "In theory, an FTA is a trade agreement. In practice, it represents a strategic calculation that the two parties have long-term interests in forging a closer partnership or that one party has an interest in strengthening the other."

However interpreted, the entry into force of this FTA is merely one indication of the expanding level of trade relations with and within Asia. This expansion is bringing with it an inevitable increase in the importance of IPRs as a commercial asset and competitive advantage.

08 Japan

Let's look briefly at the position of Japan, which is in an IPR league of its own in Asia. It is the advanced Asian economy that most resembles the developed economies of Western Europe and North America. Over recent years, it has also allied itself with those economies as the rules of the IP game have been settled by world bodies such as the WTO. Japanese multinationals in various industrial sectors have featured in lists of the world's largest companies since the 1970s and these companies have learnt how to play the IP game as effectively as any. The Japanese government too has long recognised the importance of IPRs to the country's medium- and long-term future, although it is only in the past decade that IP has come to the fore of the government's economic planning. Japan's manufacturing base has already experienced the hollowing-out being felt today by other Asian countries, as industry goes in search of the latest, least expensive manufacturing location. Increasingly, what is left at home is the clever part of today's business models: the added value protected by IPRs.

Japan's experience with IPRs falls into five distinct phases:

1. its re-engagement with the rest of the world from the Meiji Restoration in the mid-19th century until the last years of the century;

2. the period between the turn of the century and the end of the Second World War when Japanese industry dominated a number of industrial sectors;
3. the period from 1945 to the early 1970s when Japan rebuilt itself after the destruction wrought by the war years;
4. from the early 1970s to the early 1990s when Japanese companies again started to dominate many areas of world trade; and
5. the period since the early 1990s in which a deflationary Japan has struggled to reinvent itself to meet the twin challenges of China and India.

RE-ENGAGING

In the period between the Meiji Restoration, in 1868, and the introduction of the country's first effective patent law, the Patent Ordinance (Law No. 7) in 1885, thousands of young Japanese were sent abroad to learn about American railways, British textiles and metallurgy, French and German law—in fact, everything "foreign".

Even Kintaro Hattori, founder of Seikosha, became the largest watchmaker in Japan by the mid-1890s through imitating American *bon bon* clocks. Later, when the First World War started in 1914 Seikosha benefitted greatly from the earlier dominance of German alarm clocks on the British and French markets: British and French orders switched to Japan. Hattori's Tokyo factory worked with double shifts to fulfill the surge in orders. By the end of the decade Hattori's company had both established itself in overseas markets and held 70 per cent of the domestic watch market.

In the more prosaic field of condiments, there was also consolidation and progress.

Kikkoman—then known as Noda Shoyu Co—was founded by merger in 1917, in an attempt to bring some order to a fragmented Japanese market in which there were over 1,000 soy sauce makers. The families that merged their businesses into Noda Shoyu (the company adopted the name of its most famous brand, Kikkoman, only in 1964) can trace their roots back to 1661, when the Takenashi family started brewing Japanese-style soy sauce or *shoyu* in the town of Noda; today this is called the Chiba prefecture. In a 2004 article on the history of Kikkoman, William Shurtleff and Akiko Auyagi of the SoyInfo Center of Lafayette, California, noted: "Kikkoman labels now state that the company was founded in 1630, but there is no proof of or even reason to suggest such an early date."

The Mogi family (current chairman Yuzaburo Mogi is a member) started brewing *shoyu* in the same town from the mid-18th century. Shortly after, in 1782, they started using the Kikkoman brand name, which is composed of three characters: *ki*, the character for "a tortoise, which represents longevity and good luck"; *ko* meaning "top quality"; and *man* meaning "10,000". The brand name should be translated as "good luck and fine quality for 10,000 years". The trademark was first registered in Japan in 1885, in Germany in 1886 and in the USA in 1906, although by 1917 it was only one of the 200 brands belonging to the new company formed of the Takenashi and Mogi family businesses. Within six years these had been rationalised down to only 16, the most important of which was Kikkoman.

MITI AND INDUSTRIAL POLICY

When rebuilding its economy after the Second World War, Japan chose to limit the role of foreign direct investment. Instead, through its powerful Ministry of International Trade & Industry

(MITI, created in 1951), the country encouraged its targeted industries to take licences of foreign technology they could then develop further. The policy was summarised by *Time* magazine's Asia business correspondent Michael Schuman in his 2009 book *The Miracle: The Epic Story of Asia's Quest for Wealth*:

> "The purpose of Japan's industrial policy [at this time] was not only to produce rapid growth, but also to alter the entire structure of the Japanese economy toward advanced industries and create companies that could compete in the global marketplace in new, high-value sectors. In orchestrating this shift, Japan's bureaucrats set in place a pattern of development followed by most of the other [successful] Asian countries ... Economies first generated rapid growth by producing low-cost, low-tech products with their low-wage labour, then steadily transitioning into more expensive, more technologically complex goods as development progressed."

During the post-war Occupation, which came to an end only in April 1952, the military authorities headed by the Supreme Commander of the Allied Powers (SCAP), General Douglas Macarthur, dismantled many of the financial coalitions known as the *zaibatsu* (headed by Mitsui, Mitsubishi, Yasuda and Sumitomo), which had previously dominated Japanese industry. However, along with a later change of heart by the Americans, these economic reforms were hampered by wealthy and influential Japanese who obviously stood to lose a great deal. There were also those who consistently resisted any attempts at reform, claiming that the *zaibatsu* were required for Japan to compete internationally in the post-war world, and looser industrial groupings known as *keiretsu* evolved.

MATSUSHITA IN THE FIRING LINE

In March 1946 the SCAP designated the Matsushita group as being subject to the dissolution decree affecting the *zaibatsu*. Company founder Konosuke Matsushita later recalled his reaction; in his autobiography, he wrote:

> "At the time we received notice of our designation as a *zaibatsu*, I realised that the authorities did not have their facts straight. For one thing, Matsushita Electric was not among those enterprises that had been in business for generations; for another, it had not had a hand in controlling Japanese industry as had the big combines. I had started from nothing and built up the company little by little; it was a mere 20-odd years since it had been founded in the Obiraki-cho tenement house. We were little more than a small electric shop grown rather large, and yet we were being treated like the great Mitsui, Mitsubishi, and Sumitomo concerns. In a way, I suppose, it was an honour to be put in such illustrious company, but I was sure it was all an absurd mistake."

Lobbying hard whilst trying to keep his business functioning as inflation ravaged the country, Matsushita succeeded in having the *zaibatsu* designation lifted at the end of 1950. Once this shadow had lifted, the company founder looked overseas for help in rebuilding his struggling company, but not at any cost.

Matsushita identified Dutch concern Philips, with whom his company had already worked prior to the war, as his preferred partner for a technology link-up. However, he was unwilling to pay the six per cent technology licence fee demanded by the Dutch. He was prepared to accept the US$550,000 upfront payment and give Philips

30 per cent of the shares in the joint venture, but the licence fee was a step too far. Rather than rejecting the fee outright, Matsushita appealed to the Dutch sense of fair play, reasoning that he would pay a fee for the technology if the Dutch would pay a management fee. After all, the success of the joint venture would depend as much on its management, provided by Matsushita, as its technology, provided by Philips. There was also an important element of pride at play in the negotiations. Matsushita noted: "In the early fifties, Japan was still a poor, weak nation, and Europeans were inclined to think they could throw their weight around."

After much to-ing and fro-ing, and threats to call off negotiations, a deal was signed in October 1952. It recognised the sensitivities on both sides: a technology licence fee of 4.5 per cent would be paid to Philips by Matsushita and a three per cent management fee by Philips to Matsushita. The contractual joint-venture lasted for its initial 15-year term, during which the fees were reduced to three per cent and two per cent, respectively, and was then extended for a further 10 years, with 2.5 per cent flowing in each direction, until 1977.

SAVVY MANAGEMENT

Matsushita recognised all too clearly that it was important for the two parties to appreciate and value properly each other's contributions; that was critical to the long-term success of the joint venture. Still, he bemoaned the fact that "most businessmen do not seem to recognise that management know-how has as much value as technical know-how".

This was brought home to Matsushita again the following year when he was asked by the Industrial Bank of Japan to take over the management of the Victor Company of Japan (JVC), the failing former subsidiary of RCA that had already been through the hands of Nissan and Toshiba. What sparked Matsushita's interest was his recollection of JVC's well-known trademark of the dog Nipper listening to "His Master's Voice". When he started to analyse JVC he realised that although it owned some outstanding technology, it lacked good management. Matsushita therefore installed one of his best, albeit controversial, managers, the former admiral Kichisaburo Nomura (who had been Japan's Ambassador to the US at the time of Pearl Harbour). Under his management the company gradually returned to its former glory and remained majority-owned by Matsushita until 2007, illustrating again the need to marry good technology with effective management.

Man's best friend

JVC provides a good example of the territorial nature of IP rights. Within Japan JVC is best known for the Victor trademark, coupled with the logo of the Nipper dog listening to "His Master's Voice". However, JVC does not own these trademarks outside Japan, and instead has used the Nivico name (a contraction of Nippon Victor Company). For the same reason, the HMV chain of stores is present in Japan but is not allowed to use the Nipper logo or the His Master's Voice trademark; it uses a stylised image of a gramophone player.

EXPORT OR DIE

By the end of the 1950s Japan's economy had been rebuilt sufficiently to start exporting manufactured goods again. Indeed, Sony's Akio Morita recollected later that at this time, the general view of

Japanese industrialists was export or die. Even the traditional soy sauce made by Kikkoman was establishing itself and its distinctive bottle in foreign kitchens. By setting up a US subsidiary in 1957 the company set itself firmly on the path of international expansion, which today has resulted in global sales of over US$4 billion a year, with 55 per cent of its profits generated outside Japan.

Recognition that many Japanese companies were succeeding in export markets came in 1962 when *Time* magazine featured Matsushita Electric and its founder (described as "the Henry Ford of Japan's appliance industry") in a cover story about the revival of Japanese industry. Japan's return to the club of the world's advanced economies was sealed with Tokyo's hosting of the 1964 Olympics.

The late 1960s saw a return to a high rate of economic growth in Japan after the recession that followed the Tokyo Olympics. Companies like Canon increased the exports of cameras to the USA and Europe and, at the same time, diversified into areas such as photocopiers. Investing heavily in R&D, Canon was licensing its plain paper copier technology to US corporations by 1972 and started to earn more from licensing out its technology for others to use than it paid to buy in technology.

PICTURE PERFECT

This was a far cry from the early 1950s when the founder of Canon, Takeshi Mitarai, approached the president of Bell & Howell, the established Chicago photographic firm, to ask if he would represent Canon in the American market. He was told in no uncertain terms that this would be considered only if the Bell & Howell brand was put on the products, because Japanese brands had a poor reputation. Realising the importance of establishing his own brand rather than relying on someone else's, Mitarai decided to set up his own selling organisation rather than rely on a US company.

The same happened to Sony's Morita in 1955 when he rejected a similar requirement, which accompanied an order from the US company Bulova to buy 100,000 of Sony's new transistor radio. Morita underestimated his own company's potential, however, when he told the Bulova executive: "Fifty years from now, I promise you that our name will be just as famous as your company name is today."

Kikkoman took the route of expanding its business by developing new products based on its existing technological expertise in the fermentation field. It established Seishin Pharmaceutical Co, Ltd in 1961. Two key products developed by Seishin have been Molsin, a proteolytic enzyme, and Stalase, an amylolytic enzyme, both widely used pharmaceutically as digestive enzymes, often along with antibiotics.

DOMINATION AND SLOWDOWN

In the 1970s and 1980s the Japanese industrial model had huge successes and became the envy of the industrialised world. There are many books lauding the corporate titans that came to dominate whole industry sectors, such as cars and electronics, through their drive for continuous improvement and efficient manufacturing.

In its niche market Kikkoman continued to expand and in the 1980s established a state-of-the-art research facility. This laboratory focused on applying biotechnology and enzymology to create new seasonings and foods. Its significant achievements included the improvement of a proprietary microorganism employed in the production of soy sauce. Also, scientists were able to create an enzyme that produced gallic acid, used in the semiconductor and pharmaceutical industries. Initially created for industrial production, this enzyme developed into one of the company's most lucrative commercial products. Company researchers were also the first to isolate luciferase and produce it for industrial use. Luciferase, which is an enzyme that makes fireflies glow, is used in food production facilities to test for microorganisms. Luciferase also found commercial applications in hospitals and the semiconductor industry.

Another research success involved the development of the *Oretachi* orange, a fruit that is resistant to cold temperatures. Based on cell-fusion techniques, this knowledge was licensed by Kikkoman to help orange growers around the world. After Kikkoman purchased Del Monte's Asia-Pacific business in 1990, the company began research into new tomato varieties and its researchers developed a new method of inoculating tomato plants against a common virus, and developed hardier and juicier tomatoes.

Kikkoman also continued to develop and market enzymes for industrial use. By 1997 the company had a portfolio of 12 enzymes it sold to other food manufacturers, laboratories and cosmetic manufacturers. Using its core know-how, Kikkoman also developed soy-based pharmaceuticals, such as the estrogen product Isoflavon.

In 1995, as Japan reeled under the pressures of a deflating economy, Kikkoman appointed a new president and CEO, Yuzaburo Mogi. Mogi, who was educated in the late-1950s at Columbia Business School in New York, is an outspoken businessman who was also chairman of the Committee on Infrastructure for New Industries. At the World Economic Forum in Davos, Switzerland, in 1997, he spoke openly on topics rarely raised in public by Japanese corporate leaders: taking risks, innovating broadly, deregulating the Japanese economy. He also criticised the frequently stultifying management style and structure of Japanese companies.

These criticisms were echoed in *Can Japan Compete?*—a book written in 2000 by business strategy guru Professor Michael Porter of Harvard Business School and two Japanese colleagues, Hirotaka Takeuchi and Mariko Sakakibara. The authors stated baldly:

> "Almost none of the conventional wisdom [for Japan's success in the 1980s] is true. Japan's much-celebrated bureaucratic capitalism is *not* the cause of Japan's success; in fact, it is most closely associated with the nation's failures. ... The core of the problem is that the government mistrusts competition and therefore is prone to intervene in the economy in ways that harm the nation's productivity and prosperity."

REPOSITIONING

The problems identified by Mogi and Porter remain as entrenched more than a decade later. In his analysis of where the three Asian giants, China, Japan and India, are today, Bill Emmott, former editor of *The Economist*, contends that:

> "[Japanese companies'] poor productivity performance in the 1990s means they have a chance to catch up with foreign rivals by copying techniques pioneered elsewhere; their high level of spending on research and development, totalling 3.2 per cent of GDP, one of the highest in the OECD area, gives them a lot of scope for innovation; their lack of M&A in the past means there is a lot of potential in new combinations and strategies in the future. The question is whether Japanese managements will want to take these chances."

In a wide-ranging speech to the Diet in March 2002 aimed at transforming his country from being one of "follow-on" or "catch-up" innovation to be instead a hotbed of "breakthrough" innovations, then-Prime Minister Junichiro Koizumi announced the creation of an IP Strategy Headquarters within the Cabinet. Just over a year later, the Strategy HQ published its *Strategic Programme for the Creation, Protection and Exploitation of Intellectual Property*.

One of the results of the Strategic Programme is the practice adopted by Japanese companies of publishing a detailed annual report on their IPRs. An excellent example is that issued by Kikkoman Corporation: it illustrates how much more extensive the company's IP assets are than might be suggested by its core soy sauce product.

In a November 2009 briefing on Japan's technology champions, *The Economist* focused on the unsung success of many of the country's medium-sized electronics companies: the Ministry of Economy, Trade and Industry (METI) estimates that Japanese companies have more than 70 per cent of the global market in at least 30 technology sectors. Each of these companies is worth more than US$1 billion. Noting that little-known Japanese companies dominate critical technology niches in electronics, engineering and materials science, the briefing explained:

> "Around 75 per cent of motors for hard-disk drives in computers come from a firm called Nidec; 90 per cent of the micro-motors used to adjust the rear-view mirror in every car are made by Mabuchi. Often the products are components, materials or equipment used to make other equipment: TEL makes 80 per cent of the etchers used in making an LCD panel; Covalent produces 60 per cent of the containers that hold silicon wafers as they are turned into computer chips.

> "In some instances the companies' only real rivals are also Japanese, making the country indispensable even if there is more than one supplier. Shin-Etsu has 50 per cent of the market for the photomask substrate, used to place patterns on semiconductors, but the other producers—Covalent, NSG, AGC and Tosoh, all hail from Japan too."

However, the briefing also quoted the concern expressed by the CEO of Covalent, Susuma Kohyama—who led the management buyout of the company from Toshiba in 2006—that Japanese companies need "to think a lot more openly". This echoed one of the criticisms expressed by Yuzaburo Mogi in Davos more than 12 years before and suggests there has been little progress in the interim.

09 The Little Dragons (or Asian Tigers)

Whether as Little Dragons or Asian Tigers, Taiwan, Hong Kong, the Republic of Korea (ROK) and Singapore certainly make their presence felt. Known in Asia under the former name, which recognises their integration with China, and in the West under the latter, the group had an annual per capita growth rate of six per cent or more between 1960 and 1990. This led to a doubling of per capita income every 12 years.

Over the 20 years since, two of the Little Dragon economies, Taiwan and Hong Kong, have become inextricably intertwined with that of mainland China. China's computer, consumer appliance and semiconductor industries have been built largely by combining low labour costs with Taiwanese technology, investment and management. By as early as 2002, over 40 per cent of Taiwan's electronics industry had migrated to the mainland. Critically, ownership of most of the IPRs and around 70 per cent of China's electronics exports remain in Taiwanese hands. At the same time, the Hong Kong SAR has become integrated into the Greater Pearl River Delta region, where Hong Kong businesses have been responsible for much of the light manufacturing and dominate the export trade in everything from furniture to clothes. The other two, the ROK and Singapore, have also each moved rapidly up the added-value curve to establish themselves as leading developed economies, although in different ways and sectors.

TAIWAN

At the time of its takeover by the Kuomintang under Chiang Kai Shek at the end of the 1940s, around 80 per cent of Taiwan's industrial capacity was owned by the state. After 1953, the country was forced by American pressure to open its economy and compete internationally. As part of that process, driven by Premier Chen Cheng, FDI was encouraged, the currency devalued and import tariffs lifted. By the early 1960s trade was increasing at 22 per cent a year as the share of public sector enterprises in the economy fell to less than 50 per cent, and less than 20 per cent a decade later. By the time Chiang Kai Shek died in 1975, Taiwan boasted one of Asia's most prosperous economies. Francis Pike notes in his short history of modern Asia since the Second World War, *Empires at War*, that "[w]ith some 706,500 companies in 1983, Taiwan achieved the distinction of having more companies per capita than any other country in the world. Taiwan also gained the lesser distinction of becoming the counterfeit capital of Asia".

One of the most successful private enterprises dating back to that period is Formosa Plastics, founded by Wang Yung-ching, which became the country's leading conglomerate by the 1980s.

The Industrial Technology Research Institute (ITRI) was founded in 1973, a non-profit R&D organisation specialising in applied research in industrial technology, technical services and business development. The institute, a collection of engineers who focused on creating new technological products that could be commercialised and exported, began licensing in technology from American firms and circulating it to Taiwan's private sector. Today, over 150 leading IT Taiwanese companies are spin-offs from ITRI—Acer and UMD among them. The institute itself has over 3,000 patents to its name, and apparently applies for five patents per day.

A noteworthy service developed by the institute is the Taiwan International Patent Auction (ITRI-TIPA), under which Taiwanese companies can obtain patents from sellers worldwide. ITRI plays a matchmaking role by assessing a particular patent's marketability in Taiwan and matching the international patent seller to a local buyer, offering full support to both parties during the auction process. The institute also provides local firms with patent portfolio development assistance. Its Technology Transfer and Service Center (TTSC) manages tech transfer between ITRI and Taiwan industry, with more than 1,400 patents being sold or exclusively licensed to domestic firms via its Chinese auction platforms.

The Hsinchu Science-based Industrial Park was another initiative to contribute to Taiwan's economic miracle. Established in 1980, it was designed to attract many local and overseas Chinese technology businesses to set up and invest in Taiwan. The government hoped to create an incubator effect, where the managers and engineers would learn from one another and technology would breed technology. In 2002, 335 high-tech firms had set up operations in the industrial park, most of them engaged in the six major industries of biotechnology, telecommunications, optoelectronics, computers and peripherals, precision instruments and integrated circuits. Combined sales for the firms totalled over NT$705.5 billion, providing jobs for approximately 100,000 employees. The National Science Council was so encouraged by the success of the Hsinchu park that, in a bid to balance industrial development in north and south Taiwan, a Tainan Science-based Industrial Park was established in 1996 and divided into semiconductor, precision machinery and agriculture and biotech industry zones, promoting further research into new technologies. By the end of 2002, 93 firms had applied for a place in the Park, with investments totalling NT$1.3 trillion. Total sales of firms located there amounted to NT$103.1 billion.

Taiwan transformed itself from a low-cost manufacturing hub into a world-class centre for electronics in a relatively short period of time. The Made in Taiwan concept has taken on new meaning, having once signified only that Taiwan was a conveyor-belt that produced virtually all of the world's consumer products. It may remain a manufacturing arena, but one that is highly specialised in electronics and a global centre for IT production. In 2005, Taiwan produced 70 per cent of all notebook PCs and 80 per cent of all PDAs.

There is space to mention only a few examples of Taiwanese success stories in the electronics/IT arena in which Invisible Gold—in the form of patents, designs, brands and trade secrets—is so important.

Acer

Stan Shih's company Acer may not have been born had Qualitron Industrial Corp not succumbed to the market and gone bankrupt. Taiwan, and indeed the world, would have missed out on what has become the world's second-largest PC manufacturer behind Hewlett-Packard. Starting out distributing electronic parts (like its Chinese competitor Lenovo), the company turned into a PC manufacturer. Shih himself pioneered a manufacturing method that has become a PC industry-standard way of making computers—the "fast-food model", in which each of Acer's overseas regional business units assembled computers from components flown from Taiwan. Local customers would then be sold computers "hot and fresh" off the assembly line. Shih has also focused on innovation, building up a large patent portfolio and cross-licence agreements. In 1996, Acer owned 400 patents worldwide but 10 years later it owned approximately 1,000 on PC-related inventions alone. The company also has a profit-sharing plan where some of the income generated from patent licences is split with the engineers who applied for patents.

In the last decade, Acer has begun to focus on its brand. When the company spun-off its manufacturing operations into Wistron Corporation, it reduced its labour force and concentrated on marketing and brand-building strategies using its existing distribution channels. Revenues have steadily been increased, rising from US$4.9 billion in 2003 to US$16.65 billion in 2008. Yet its workforce remains small, with just under 7,000 employees globally. Acer has also brought established PC brands under the Acer umbrella, buying American rival Gateway for US$710 million and acquiring a 75 per cent controlling interest in Packard Bell.

In its 2008 annual report, Acer's trademarks accounted for 66 per cent of the value of the company's IP assets, whilst the company's patents only accounted for 5.7 per cent. Acer's brand value is estimated at US$1,265 million (NT$39,835 million) and came in third in the 2008 *Taiwan Top Global Brands Survey.*

Despite impressive revenues and IPRs to its name, Acer admits it has a constant struggle in becoming a real recognised brand. In his book, *Me-Too Is Not My Style*, Shih spoke about the problems of being associated with the Made in Taiwan brand: "[Reasons for the negative image of Made in Taiwan] are twofold. First, many poor-quality products are sold under Taiwan brands while many of the fine-quality products are manufactured for foreign brands (OEM). Second, although there are good Taiwan-made products, there is not enough promotion or marketing of them."

Marketing and promotion remains a recurring issue. As the world eagerly awaited the launch of Apple's new tablet computer in January 2010, people had long forgotten—or didn't know in the first place—that Acer had produced its own tablet computer eight years earlier in collaboration with Microsoft. The PC, with impressive technology for its time such as hand-recognition software, fared dismally in the marketplace. Within 11 months of launch, Acer had sold only 100,000 units, a mere five per cent of its overall notebook sales. At the time, Acer and Microsoft were arguing about the level of licence fees to use the Windows XP operating system and Acer chairman, J.T. Wang, felt that Microsoft did not put in the resources required to make the product a success.

The example goes to show you can have all the innovation and technological quirks in the world but a product will often fail without the push provided by a respected brand.

ASUSTeK

ASUSTeK (Asus) has become one of the world's leading electronics and computer hardware companies, and it all started with the motherboard. By November 2009, a mere 20 years after its formation, Asus was the world's largest motherboard maker with a 29.2 per cent share of the global market. It has also been in *BusinessWeek's* InfoTech 100 and Asia's Top 10 IT Companies ranking for 11 years straight, since 1998. However, the company is so much more than just mo-bos.

In the 1980s Taiwan was struggling to make its mark in the then-rapidly-expanding computer industry, limited to producing components for PC-makers. At the time those PC and component makers had to wait up to six months to receive engineering prototype samples for motherboards. So, four engineers working at Acer at the time—T.H. Tung, Wayne Hsieh, M.T. Liao and Ted Hsu—sought advice from their mentor Johnny Shih about creating a new company that could take the industry forward in Taiwan. The four named their company Asus—the last four letters of the Greek mythological winged-horse Pegasus, who represents the inspiration of art and learning. They took the last four letters of the name—"asus"—to be at the top in alphabetic listings.

Formed as a company offering consultancy services to motherboard manufacturers, Asus wanted to work with local industry manufacturers to create state-of-the-art designs to put Taiwan on the electronics map. Unfortunately, as the IT industry in Taiwan was still based on manufacturing generic parts for sale under someone else's brand name, it was hard to get established alongside the big PC players. It was not until Intel's announcement of its 486 processor at the beginning of 1989 that Asus changed from imitator to true innovator.

Using the founders' extensive motherboard design experience, along with the technical information published by Intel, Asus produced its own 486 motherboard design without access to a 486 processor. Asus then approached Intel for a licence to make the 486 processor. Intel was said to be slow to greet its visitors when the Asus team came to its headquarters; design flaws in their own 486 motherboard had the Intel team rushing around trying to find solutions. The legend then goes that the Asus workforce managed to fix Intel's motherboard problem within minutes, to the amazement of the Intel team. Consequently, Intel agreed to try the Asus 486 motherboard on its processor and it worked perfectly.

This put Asus on the road to being the world's No. 1 motherboard manufacturer, becoming a key partner of Intel by supplying motherboards directly to the American company. In what Asus president, Jerry Shen, called the company's "second wave", between

1993 and 1998, annual profits jumped from US$10 million to over US$300 million. One in three motherboards now sold in the world are made by Asus. Not bad for a company that started out in a tiny apartment in Taipei. The value of the Asus brand was estimated at over US$1.3 billion in 2009.

As already mentioned, Asus offers more than motherboards. Shen believes the company is in its third phase: creating its own branded products. The Eee PC netbook was launched in October 2007 (the "Eee" name originating from its ad slogan, "Easy to learn, Easy to work, Easy to play") and has been hugely successful all around the world, being named the 2008 Product of the Year by *Forbes* and the UK's *Stuff Magazine.* Asus' good reviews from tech and gadget blogs alike prompted one technology trend blogger, Mike Elgan, to write in his 2008 article entitled, "The Most Hated Company in the PC Industry": "Who in the hell are Asustek and why does Microsoft hate them more than any other company in the industry? Why does [sic] Apple, Dell and Palm Computing hate them? And why does Intel love them?"

Asus apparently grabbed mini-netbook market share before Apple, Dell and other competitors had a chance to respond, then proceeded to pile the pressure on by setting a very low price point for its netbooks. In addition, according to Elgan, "the Asus Eee PC is demonstrating to the world that its success depends on aggressively 'avoiding' any Microsoft product", whilst retaining an ever-closer relationship with Intel through the use of its processors.

Despite the envy felt by big-player competitors, things have not been all glorious for the Taiwanese company. In a June 2009 *New York Times* interview, Asus Vice-Chairman Jonathan Tsang admitted that whilst the company was doing well in Europe and Asia, it has failed to become a well-known brand in the US.

Perhaps to deal with this problem, in the same way as its down-the-road competitor, Asus decided to brand-split, splintering its operations into three separate companies. Its name-brand product business still remains as Asustek, and its original equipment manufacturing (OEM) operations (now called Pegatron Technology Corp) were also split from its original design manufacturing (ODM) operations (now Unihan Technology Corp).

With scores of patents to its name and heavy expenditure on R&D, like many technology companies Asus has scores of patent litigation cases to deal with. It outlined in its 2008 Annual Report 11 separate cases of alleged patent infringement, general IPR infringement and violation of trade secrets filed against it by Japanese, Australian and US companies.

Hon Hai

Founded in 1974 by Terry Gou with the mundane aim of making plastic parts for television sets, Hon Hai Precision Industry Co Ltd is the No. 1 electronics contract manufacturer in the world and owns more patents than any other Taiwanese company except Taiwan Semiconductor Manufacturing Company (TSMC). Gou has since gone on to become the richest man in Taiwan.

HTC

Set up in 1997 by Cher Wang, Taiwan's richest woman and daughter of Formosa Plastics tycoon Wang Yung-ching, High Tech Computer or HTC is a leading smartphone and PDA designer and manufacturer. In addition to making for the likes of Vodafone and Deutsche Telekom, HTC has had its own brand of handsets running on Windows Mobile since 2006. It was also the first manufacturer to use Google's Android operating system in its mobile phones.

With her husband Chen Wenchi, Cher Wang had already made a success of chipset maker Via Technologies in the 10 years before HTC was formed. This had a massive 40 per cent of the global market by 2001. But it met the irresistible force of industry leader Intel and its cohorts of lawyers, which sued Via for patent infringement in many countries. By the time the legal fights were settled in 2003, Via was a shadow of its former self and had to rethink its strategy. Today, Via is one of the world leaders in energy-efficient processors but has changed its geographical focus to one much closer to home, mainland China. In the China market it adopts a collaborative model, supporting and working for the long term with growing IT manufacturers.

Since the death of her father in October 2008, Cher Wang has also been elected to the board of the family group's flagship company, Formosa Plastics, which she told the *Financial Times* in August 2009 "is still in a time of transition" after her father's death.

It is not only Formosa Plastics that is in a time of transition: so is the Taiwanese economy. Commentators argue today that Taiwan's economy is in slow structural decline and, to prevent it hollowing out further, it needs to attract FDI, perhaps from the mainland as economic ties grow between the two countries.

HONG KONG

Since the early 1980s Hong Kong's manufacturing industry has moved almost completely across the border into mainland China to take advantage of the lower labour rates and other costs. What has been left in the Hong Kong Special Administrative Region (SAR) are the higher added-value elements of design and marketing, showcased annually in its highly successful Business of Design Week, which now includes well-attended sessions on the intellectual property law aspects.

Fenix Group is a Hong Kong company that illustrates the change in the business model. Founded in 1972 by Anthony Keung and his Japanese partner Ozumi Ogino, Fenix was set up as a supplier of Japanese yarn. It evolved into a knitwear trading and manufacturing company that then diversified by starting a fashion retailing business in the 1980s. It has become one of the major Hong Kong fashion retailers, operating 12 high-fashion brands and more than 100 shops worldwide, including its own brand Anteprima. In 2003 Keung noted that Hong Kong clothing companies, which previously depended on manufacturing for about 70 per cent of their revenue, had by then reduced this to only 20 per cent. Design work increased from 20 per cent to 50 per cent, while brand development work increased from 10 per cent to 30 per cent of revenue.

As one of the leading financial centres in Asia, Hong Kong also attracts companies from its Great Pearl River Delta hinterland and further afield to list on its stock market, and their Invisible Gold assets are often an important but relatively unremarked feature.

It's not only outsiders that generate Invisible Gold. To cite a few examples:

VTech

VTech followed the then-trend of producing cheap and cheerful electronic products when it was founded in 1976 in Hong Kong. It subsequently found its value-added niche in the world of electronic learning products (ELPs)—educational toys and games for children. Its first ELP (book-type version) came to market in 1980, and within six years V-Tech had become the largest manufacturer of ELPs sold in the United States.

Successful as it was in the ELP market, the company refused to rest on its laurels. At the beginning of the 1990s it launched the world's first fully digital cordless phone in the USA, using its experience in radio frequency technology.

Perhaps because of its simple yet catchy name, VTech has had to protect the Invisible Gold attached to its name. In 2005 it successfully brought a domain name dispute before the mainland's National Arbitration Forum against a company named V-Tech China Co, Ltd, which had registered the domain name vtechchina.com for a website featuring links to VTech's products, and other logos resembling those used by the Hong Kong company. The Forum ordered the domain name be transferred to VTech. A similar case was brought against the Forsyte Corporation, a Bahamian company, for registering vtech-jouet.com in Ottawa and Ontario. Again, the domain name was found to have been registered in bad faith and was transferred to VTech because *jouets* is the French word for toys, and the website contained links to products made by direct competitors of VTech.

Playmates Toys

Hong Kong-based Playmates Toys is one of the biggest toy manufacturers in the world, building success from producing licensed toys for almost half a century.

Playmates established its reputation as a "good product, good quality toys" company, but it was a business built on making generic toys for other companies. It was only when venturing into the promotional toy business through its US-based subsidiary that the company had real success with its own brands. Cricket, the talking electronic baby doll, was a great success for the company in the mid-1980s, more than doubling its revenues from US$32 million in

1985 to US$78 million in 1986. However, the fickle nature of the toy industry was seen a year later when Playmates launched a newer electronic version of one of its dolls named Jill—a doll that could blink, talk and swivel her neck, selling at a lofty US$200. Playmates recorded a loss of US$4.8 million in 1987 as management realised too late that American parents were not prepared to pay US$200 for a doll, however clever she was.

After that the company returned to its core business of paying to use successful brands developed by others. When two would-be comic book artists dreamt up the idea of crime-fighting martial-arts trained turtles with Renaissance-period names and a penchant for pizza, Playmates could hardly have known it would play a pivotal role in creating one of the most successful brands in the history of the toy industry. After being approached by a licensing agent, Playmates launched its Teenage Mutant Ninja Turtles (TMNT) toy line in 1988.

The TMNT gained an unenthusiastic response at first. However, Playmates' aggressive promotion of the turtles, even paying for the first five episodes of their cartoon series, led to US$23 million worth of the TMNT toy line being sold by the end of 1988. By 1990 the TMNT line had captured more than 60 per cent of the US market for action figures, and sales hit US$500 million by 1991. Illustrating the staying power of a good brand, in October 2009 Playmates signed a deal with Nickelodeon securing the global master rights to TMNT, which had been bought by the television company's licensing arm for US$60 million from the TMNT co-creator Peter Laird and the Mirage Group.

As animated characters have graced the silver screen over recent years, Playmates has continued to make the accompanying dolls and toys, securing more and more master toy licensing rights for model characters. Coneheads, Star Trek: The Next Generation and The Addams Family are examples of the characters featured on the company's toys.

Li Ka-Shing

No description of Hong Kong or its toy companies, however brief, can fail to mention "Superman"—not Clark Kent but Hong Kong's wealthiest man, Li Ka-Shing, who started on the path to his massive fortune making plastic heads for the GI Joe toy.

When Li took control of the venerable *hong*, Hutchison, on 1 January 1980, his plastics company Cheung Kong Ltd was already Asia's largest plastic flowers supplier. He also had a lucrative real estate portfolio, and was moving into the construction business. Today, Li's tentacles reach into many sectors of the Hong Kong economy and are highly visible on the Mainland too.

Reflecting his keen awareness of the value of Invisible Gold, in a 2007 *Forbes* magazine interview Li warned on the issue of IP rights in China:

> "Personally, I take IP very seriously ... IP offenders must be brought to justice, even if you have to pay $1.10 in legal fees to recover $1 of loss."

A couple of examples of Invisible Gold in the Li empire will need to suffice.

Cheung Kong subsidiary CK Life Sciences Holdings is an oncology-focused manufacturer of nutraceutical and pharmaceutical products. With a market capitalisation of HK$5.3 billion in January 2010, CK Life has grown rapidly in the past decade, acquiring nine companies in North America, Australia and elsewhere. Notable purchases included an 80 per cent stake in Vitaquest, the largest US customised maker of branded nutritional supplements, for HK$1.3 billion (US$309 million) and a 75 per cent stake in Canadian company WEX Pharmaceuticals, a leading company involved in the treatment of cancer pain, which was bought in 2009. With a large R&D expenditure (over HK$61 million in 2008), the company invests heavily in building up its Invisible Gold portfolio. It first seeks US patents for its inventions, then applies for further patents elsewhere. CK Life also has trademark registrations worldwide. At 30 June 2009, the company's patent and trademark portfolios were valued in the balance sheet at HK$5.25 million and HK$84.05 million, respectively.

Another company in the Li Ka-Shing stable is Hutchison China MediTech Ltd (Chi-Med), which specialises in the development of pharmaceuticals, health care and consumer care products based upon traditional Chinese medicine (TCM) and botanicals. Chi-Med conducts analysis through its R&D arm on traditional herbal remedies to determine their ingredients. For instance, in December 2009, Chi-Med started a three-year collaboration with pharmacologists from Cambridge University to investigate the anti-ageing properties in selected herbal remedies, including in Chi-Med's patented cardiovascular drug, the She Xiang Bao Xing pill, which is sold under the Shang Yao brand. Chi-Med's main drugs in development are in the oncology and anti-inflammatory area, some in the early stages of clinical trials before being placed on the US and Chinese markets. R&D revenues from its collaborations reached US$2.3 million in 2008, a 156 per cent increase over the 2007 figure of US$0.9 million.

In addition to its R&D focus, Chi-Med has invested a great deal of time in its TCM-based products under the brand name, Sen. In

2002 the Sen TCM therapy store was opened on South Molton Street in London's Mayfair, and eight others have been opened in other trendy areas of Central London, including Hampstead, Chelsea and Notting Hill. Sen also sells in France through French retailer Perfumeries Marionnaud, a subsidiary of Hutchison's retail arm, AS Watson, and in Hong Kong.

Chi-Med's China health care division markets the Baiyunshun ("white cloud mountain") brand through one of its joint ventures, Hutchison Whampoa Guangzhou Baiyunshan Chinese Medicine Company Limited (HBYS), a company set up by Shanghai-based Baiyunshan and Hutchison with a US$15.1 million cash investment in early 2005. HBYS is responsible for the popular prescription gallbladder drug Dan Ning, which had sales of nearly US$3 million in 2008, having been granted process and formula patents by the China State Patent Bureau in mid-2007. HBYS was also granted 17 patents in 2008 by the State Intellectual Property Office.

Embry Form

Some of Hong Kong's clothing companies have also realised the need to move away from competing merely on cost. "Superbrand" Embry Form is the leading lingerie brand in Hong Kong and was one of *Forbes Asia*'s Best Under a Billion list of companies in 2007. Hong Kong-based Embry has been producing high-quality lingerie under the brand names of others for over 30 years and continues to supply lingerie items to trading partners in Japan and the UK. But the company is now so focused on its own popular brands, Embry Form and Fandecie, that it only accepts orders from its OEM customers when spare production capacity is available. Although the Embry in-house design team collaborates with French lingerie specialists, it ensures that it retains all IPRs in creations, designs and other material created during those collaborations. The company has numerous patents and design registrations protecting its creations. The protected innovations include "lotus-shaped cups for ladies' undergarments", a "strapless bra with decorative ornaments", and "a panty corselet without buckle structures", the last having been invented by the company's CEO, Liza Cheng.

Showing its awareness of the need to build its IPR portfolio, at the time of its listing on the Hong Kong Stock Exchange in November 2006, Embry had 37 and 53 registered trademarks in China and Hong Kong, respectively (and other registrations in Australia, Singapore, Malaysia, Japan, Vietnam, Indonesia, Taiwan, the Philippines, Thailand, Korea and France), 37 patents, nine registered designs and a number of registered domain names.

REPUBLIC OF KOREA

Around 50 per cent of South Korea's manufacturing base was destroyed during the Korean War, which ended in 1953.

In his book *Bad Samaritans*, Cambridge University economist Chang Ha-Joon gave an enlightening summary of the extent of the transformation of his home country since his upbringing in Seoul during the two-decade-long rule of President Park Chung Hee from 1961 to 1979:

> "Today, Korea is one of the most 'inventive' nations in the world: it ranks among the top five nations in terms of the number of patents granted annually by the US Patent Office. But until the mid-1980s it lived on 'reverse engineering'. My friends would buy 'copy' computers that were made by small workshops, which would take apart IBM machines, copy the

> parts, and put them together. It was the same with trademarks. At the time, the country was one of the 'pirate capitals' of the world, churning out fake Nike shoes and Louis Vuitton bags in huge quantities. Those who had more delicate consciences would settle for near-counterfeits. There were shoes that looked like Nike but were called Nice, or shoes that had the Nike swoosh but with an extra prong. Counterfeit goods were rarely sold as the genuine article. Those who bought them were perfectly aware that they were buying fakes; the point was to make a fashion statement, rather than to mislead. Copyrighted items were treated in the same way. Today, Korea exports a large and increasing quantity of copyrighted materials (movies, TV soaps, popular songs), but at the time imported music (LP records) or films (videos) were so expensive that few people could afford the real thing. We grew up listening to pirate rock 'n' roll records, which we called '*tempura* shop records', because their sound quality was so bad it sounded as if someone was deep-frying in the background. As for foreign books, they were still beyond the means of most students. Coming from a well-off family that was willing to invest in education, I did have some imported books. But most of my books in English were pirated. I could never have entered and survived Cambridge without those illegal books."

President Park's ceaseless nurturing of the *chaebol*, the Korean equivalent of Japan's *keiretsu* family-run business groupings, was hugely successful and has resulted in the dominance of the Korean economy even today by the likes of domestically-focused Hanwha, Lotte, Doosan and Kumho, as well as multinationals such as Samsung, LG and Hyundai. The last-named showed the determination of Korean companies to compete with the world's best when it produced the home-grown Pony subcompact car in 1975, combining an engine and transmission licensed from Mitsubishi, some parts from the Ford Cortina it was already assembling in Korea, an Italian design, and management know-how from the former managing director of British Leyland, George Turnbull.

Within 25 years Korea was transformed into an industrial powerhouse, albeit one frequently racked by labour unrest and allegations of corporate corruption. Today it leads the rest of the world in the extent of Internet penetration amongst its population. However, at the same time there is much soul-searching within the country as to the position it will play in a world in which China and India are now so important. In an interview with the *Financial Times* in August 2009 Suh Nam-pyo, President of the Korean Advanced Institute of Science and Technology (Kaist), expressed his concern about whether an academic system that is based on rote learning can produce the free thinkers he believes are necessary to change the nation from one "improving and changing what others have designed to creating things nobody ever dreamed of".

On the world scene one Korean company stands out for its achievement in becoming a genuine global brand: Samsung.

Samsung

Samsung Group was originally an exporter of fish, vegetables and fruit when founded by Lee Byung-chull in 1938, seven years before Korea's independence from Japanese colonial rule. Until the 1970s its main lines of business were sugar refining and textiles.

Samsung Electronics was set up in 1969 with an initial investment of 330 million won. It is now just one of the 59 subsidiaries of Samsung Group. After the announcement in 1973 of President

Park's heavy industries programme (often called the Big Push, this was centred on shipbuilding, steel, metals, machinery, chemicals and electronics), it moved into the semiconductor industry by acquiring a 50 per cent stake in Korea Semiconductor.

Less than 10 years later, in 1983, it announced it was to start designing its own chips but few expected the company to grow to challenge, and even to overtake, the world's leaders in the field. In 1986 the company owned one US patent while Sony had 240. Until the early 1990s most of its products were made for others, such as Sears and Wal-mart, and its brand was invisible to consumers. Yet, 25 years later still, Samsung is one of the world's leading electronics companies and owner of patents the world over. It overtook Sony in numbers of US patents in 2004.

In November 2009 the *Financial Times* commented on a recent reverse to Samsung in a ruling of the US International Trade Commission (ITC) that it had infringed four LCD patents belonging to Japanese rival Sharp: "Of the 30 most recent cases on the ITC's website no fewer than five name Samsung as a respondent. Just to show that it can play this game as vigorously as any rival, in another couple of cases Samsung is on the other side, as complainant … [showing that] Samsung has potent technology of its own."

SINGAPORE

The explanation for Singapore's startling growth between its independence from Malaysia in 1965 and the late 1990s is simple, according to Stanford professor John McMillan: "The rapid growth in Singapore ... is sometimes described as a miracle, but it actually has a straightforward explanation. Singapore simply mobilised its resources. The primary source of growth was massive investment in physical capital. Singaporeans saved and invested as much as 40 per cent of their income. A further source of growth was investment in people. In 1966 more than half the workforce had no formal education; by 1990 two-thirds had completed secondary education. Singapore's growth, far from a miracle, was based on cumulative investment."

At ground level, this investment resulted in a 10-fold increase in real per capita income between 1965 and 2000: from US$500 (at constant value a sum equivalent to just under US$3,000 in 2000) at the time of independence to US$30,000 under then-Prime Minister Goh Chok Tong in 2000. This remarkable performance was reflected also in a GDP per capita annual growth rate of 5.1 per cent in the 25 years before 2000.

Singapore's geographical location, infrastructure, political stability and educated workforce all contributed to this. Up to the late 1980s the principal driver for the country's spectacular growth was foreign direct investment in manufacturing for companies based overseas, particularly in electronics, engineering, chemicals and pharmaceuticals. The government's success in attracting—and putting in place the infrastructure to attract—FDI led *Time* magazine's Asian business correspondent Michael Schuman to comment admiringly in his recent book *The Miracle*, "Singapore was probably the most carefully crafted and highly engineered of all of the newly industrialised states of Asia." As he notes, the country's founding Prime Minister and now Minister Mentor, Lee Kuan Yew, had put it bluntly in his autobiography: "We had one simple guiding principle for survival, that Singapore had to be … better organised, and more efficient than others in the region. If we were only as good as our neighbours, there was no reason for businesses to be based here."

By the late 1980s the country was already looking to the next stage of its development, and a modern copyright law was introduced. The then-Minister of Law and now Senior Minister, Professor S. Jayakumar, told Parliament that such a measure was necessary to provide the right climate for growth of creative industries such as publishing, computer software/IT and design.

In 2001 the Intellectual Property Office of Singapore (IPOS) was created as a statutory board within the Ministry of Law, with the mission of formulating and regulating IP law, promoting IP awareness and providing the infrastructure to bring about further development of IP in Singapore. It is now recognised generally around Asia that IPOS has achieved its mission to an impressive extent, as Singapore's position as the leading IP-protective nation in Asia attests. For instance, when Massachusetts-based IT company EMC Corporation chose Singapore for its regional disaster and data recovery centre, CEO Joseph Tucci told *Business Times*: "Singapore is ideally placed and has adequate laws to protect intellectual property which large companies can take advantage of."

The same year as IPOS was created, the Economic Review Committee was appointed to make recommendations on how to remake Singapore in view of the changes that made doubtful the long-term viability of the export-driven/FDI model that had brought the country such success. The Committee reported in 2003 and the Executive Summary to its report set out its vision of turning Singapore into a knowledge economy powered by innovation, creativity and entrepreneurship.

It has been constantly reiterated by the government since then that one of the key elements in achieving that vision is the protection, enforcement and commercialisation of IPRs. In 2005, for example, Singapore's then-Minister for Information, Communication and the

Arts, Dr Lee Boon Yang, exhorted other Asian Culture Ministers at a meeting in Hong Kong:

> "... without [a] robust IP protection framework, many creative industries will face difficulties in introducing their innovation to market and exploiting the full commercial values of such innovations ...
>
> "We should consider facilitating Asian countries coming together to share experience and raise awareness and capabilities in IP protection ... to help Asian creators protect their rights, encourage the creation of collective Asian content through collaborations and help them move beyond Asia with their creative work and penetrate other markets."

That focus continues: Philips, Seagate and Novartis have all set up multi-million-dollar research centres in the country to carry out high-value R&D. In 2007 Professor Ho Peng Kee, Senior Minister of Law, told one of the world's largest IPR gatherings:

> "Nowhere in the world is this evolution of IP's significance more apparent than in Asia. Regional countries are beginning to play increasingly major roles in the knowledge-fuelled global economy for which intellectual contribution and creativity are of paramount importance ...
>
> "This paradigm shift in Asia towards stronger IP protection and greater respect for IP will continue. The next decade looks likely to be a period of exceptional change to how IP is perceived in Asia. As these developments unfold, there will be many challenges to overcome and opportunities to capitalise on ...

> "Singapore is in the thick of these momentous regional developments. As a small country, Singapore has little choice but to capitalise on its human resources and intellectual assets …
>
> "With this realisation we embarked on our journey towards a robust IP regime a decade or so ago in support of our shift towards a knowledge-based and innovation-driven economy …
>
> "These initiatives have stood us in good stead and play a critical role in attracting R&D and high-value, IP-intensive investments into Singapore. This creates jobs and generates wealth for the nation. Hence by striking a good balance between the interests of stakeholders, we are reaping the economic rewards of IP …"

More important than words are infrastructure and support, which the Singapore government has put in place to make the country a regional hub for the development and commercialisation of IPRs. At the end of February 2010 Finance Minister Tharman Shanmugaratnam unveiled a package of financial support and tax measures aimed at making the country "one of the most compelling locations for private sector R&D in Asia". The infrastructure that already makes it compelling to many companies has built on the huge success of the Economic Development Board (EDB) in attracting FDI.

A*STAR

Singapore's Agency for Science, Technology and Research (A*STAR) is a government agency specialising in public-sector scientific research aimed at transforming Singapore into a knowledge-based economy. The agency oversees 14 scientific institutions and research entities. One of these is Temasek Life Science Laboratory (TLSL).

Since 2004 TLSL has collaborated with Singapore-listed ornamental fish company Qian Hu—which describes itself as "a knowledge company"—in a high-profile study of the reproductive behaviour of the arowana fish (commonly known as the dragonfish and the world's most expensive ornamental fish) in relation to its genome. A*STAR also collaborates with biotech companies seeking to develop highly specialised technology products, for example collaborating in 2007 with Australian-based firm BioChip Innovations, and with local firm SiMEMS in developing a silicon nanowire biochip used for DNA testing (described as the first of its kind).

A*STAR uses its commercial arm, Exploit Technologies Pte Ltd (ETPL), to market and exploit the IP created in A*STAR-funded research projects. For instance, Singular ID Pte Ltd was a company founded by Drs Adrian Burden and Peter Moran, former scientists at the Institute of Material Research and Engineering (IMRE). The spin-off nanotechnology company was set up to commercialise magnetic tagging technology used to combat counterfeiting in products. In setting up Singular ID, the founders entered into a licensing agreement with ETPL for the technology and developed Enxure, a high-technology brand security system that uses tags containing a unique magnetic feature providing a fingerprint that is very difficult to reproduce. The tags then can be incorporated into a product's label or embedded into it. The "unforgeable" barcode for the tags is supplied to manufacturers or brand owners to protect them against lost or stolen labels being used on fake products. Singular expanded its product range, set up subsidiaries in Italy and collaborated with Italian clothing companies tailoring technology to fabric labels, before being bought at the end of 2007 by Indian firm Bilcare Limited for S$19.58 million, apparently achieving for Exploit Technologies the highest return for one of its investments.

National Research Foundation

To give renewed impetus to the drive to transform the country into a knowledge-based economy, the Prime Minister's Office set up the National Research Foundation (NRF) in January 2006, to coordinate Singapore's different research agencies and to help implement a national R&D strategy.

The NRF allocates its managed fund of S$5 billion to support research and innovation programmes in the priority areas of biomedical sciences, environmental and water technologies (including clean energy), and interactive and digital media. In the latter fields the Media Development Authority (MDA) is also active. In May 2009 the NRF granted S$22 million to three local universities—Nanyang Technological University (NTU) S$6.5 million; National University of Singapore (NUS) S$9 million; and Singapore Management University (SMU) S$6.5 million—to encourage academic entrepreneurship and develop programmes to make innovation and entrepreneurship pervasive in the country. NUS has used its grant to aid faculty and researchers in commercialising their research.

SPRING Singapore

The Standards, Productivity and Innovation Board (SPRING Singapore) nurtures innovative SMEs and start-up firms, offering grants and other assistance to businesses who invest in their own R&D. Its mission includes helping in the country's economic growth from the bottom up by creating a competitive SME sector.

An example of the type of support SPRING offers is its innovation voucher scheme, under which SMEs with innovative ideas are provided with vouchers that can be redeemed at the participating Knowledge Institutions (KIs)—Nanyang, Ngee Ann and Singapore

Polytechnics, together with the Singapore Institute of Manufacturing Technology. The aim is to encourage collaboration between SMEs and KIs in the development of innovative ideas.

The chairman of SPRING, Philip Yeo, has been instrumental in much of Singapore's drive to become a knowledge economy, previously as chairman of the EDB from 1986 until 2001 and of A*STAR from 1999. In the latter position, which he left in 2007 to move to SPRING, he was labelled by *The Economist* in 2004 as "Singapore's man with a plan".

IE Singapore, Infocomm Development Authority

The alphabet soup of agencies involved in supporting and encouraging the development of Invisible Gold in Singapore and by Singaporean businesses continues with IE Singapore (previously known as International Enterprise Singapore), the outward-facing organisation whose mission is to help Singapore's companies when they expand outside the island state.

Meanwhile, the IDA (Infocomm Development Authority) helps nurture the country's infocomm companies both in and outside Singapore and leads the programme to achieve the goals of the "Intelligent Nation 2015" masterplan, which are (to quote):

- to be No. 1 in the world in harnessing infocomm to add value to the economy and society;
- to realise a two-fold increase in the value-add of the infocomm industry to S$26 billion;
- to realise a three-fold increase in infocomm export revenue to S$60 billion and to create 80,000 additional jobs;
- to achieve 90 per cent home broadband usage; and
- to achieve 100 per cent computer ownership in homes with school-going children.

Grenidea Technologies

A Singaporean company has succeeded even in converting waste into Invisible Gold. Grenidea Technologies was set up in 2000 by electrical engineer Dr Toh Peng Seng and chemist Dr Xu Yan to develop environmentally friendly products from agricultural and industrial waste. They called their natural-fibre biodegradable packaging AgroPack and obtained US patents. Today, the company's flagship product is branded AgroResin and its packaging is found all around the world, including in Sainsburys in the UK, COOP in Sweden and Coles in Australia.

Xu told *Business Times* in December 2004: "Our key value is growing around technology and know-how in materials engineering and process know-how … Singapore is so small; it's a place you grow your know-how, but it's not a place you commercialise your know-how. [Recognising its limitations, Grenidea has used a licensing strategy.] Our strength is in R&D, and we're going to help market and develop applications and build turnkey solutions. So we'll have two commercial clusters—one in manufacturing licences and the other in marketers/distributors."

As Xu recognises, Singapore is too small a country in which to build a large business, except obviously in areas such as telecoms or utilities. Singaporean companies have been active in building up their reserves of Invisible Gold outside the country also. In China alone, investment by Singaporean companies reached US$40 billion by the end of 2009.

The world's my oyster

In food (a subject of huge importance to most Singaporeans), for example, Tat Hui manufactures the Koka and Sanwa brands of instant noodles and exports over 100 million packets a year to more than 25 countries, while Singapore Food Industries has been active in acquiring foreign brands such as the UK's New Covent Garden Soup.

Food Empire's flagship brand of instant coffee, MacCoffee, which has had a number of trademark fights in Singapore with the fast-food giant McDonald's, is a market leader in Russia, Ukraine and Kazakhstan. Set up in 1994 and listed on the Singapore Stock Exchange mainboard in 2000, the company sells to more than 40 countries. In 2004 company founder and chairman Tan Wang Cheow noted that the MacCoffee logo was emblazoned on everything from a TV dating show in the Ukraine and pop concerts by Ukrainian band Alibi, to Euro Cup qualifier football matches. Other brands owned by the company include Klassno, Orienbites, Kracks and MacCandy.

Alongside the giants such as Singapore Airlines, SingTel and Keppel, the many other Singaporean companies active in building up their Invisible Gold portfolios outside the country include Haw Par with its global brand Tiger Balm, Creative Technology with its patented Zen MP3 player and Soundblaster sound cards, and OSIM with its patented massage machines. As long ago as March 2003 an international study put the value of the OSIM brand at S$203 million, and that will undoubtedly have increased significantly.

Less well-known TT International markets under its consumer products brand Akira just about everything electronic, from stereos to flat-screen TVs. With its marketing efforts focused outside Singapore, Akira products are popular in African countries such as Nigeria, Angola and South Africa, as well as in ASEAN countries, Eastern Europe and the former Soviet Union.

This small selection of examples highlights the fact that many Singaporean businesses have invested heavily in creating the sustainable competitive advantage that IPRs help provide. The country is on the way to achieving its aim of being the IP hub of Asia where the streets are paved not with gold but Invisible Gold.

External validation

Reflecting the success of the government's drive to create an infrastructure conducive to business and the creation of Invisible Gold, Singapore was ranked third of the 133 countries examined, after Switzerland and USA, in the World Economic Forum's *Global Competitiveness Report 2009–2010*. The Report commented:

> "Singapore moves up two ranks to 3rd place, remaining the highest-ranked country from Asia. The country's institutions continue to be ranked as the best in the world; at a time when confidence in governments in many countries has diminished, they are assessed even more strongly than in past years. Singapore places 1st for the efficiency of its goods and labour markets and 2nd for its financial market sophistication, ensuring the proper allocation of these factors to their best use. Singapore also has world-class infrastructure (ranked 4th), leading the world in the quality of its roads, ports, and air transport facilities. In addition, the country's competitiveness is propped up by a strong focus on education, providing highly skilled individuals for the workforce. In order to strengthen its competitiveness further, Singapore could encourage even stronger adoption of the latest technologies—especially broadband Internet—as well as the innovative capacity of its companies."

In the Report's assessment of innovation, the country was ranked 10th out of 133:

> "The final pillar of competitiveness is innovation. Although substantial gains can be obtained by improving institutions, building infrastructure, reducing macroeconomic instability, or improving human capital, all these factors eventually seem to run into diminishing returns. The same is true for the efficiency of the labour, financial, and goods markets. In the long run, standards of living can be expanded only with innovation.
>
> "Innovation is particularly important for economies as they approach the frontiers of knowledge and the possibility of integrating and adapting exogenous technologies tends to disappear. Although less-advanced countries can still improve their productivity by adopting existing technologies or making incremental improvements in other areas, for those that have reached the innovation-driven stage of development, this is no longer sufficient to increase productivity. Firms in these countries must design and develop cutting-edge products and processes to maintain a competitive edge. This requires an environment that is conducive to innovative activity, supported by both the public and the private sectors. In particular, this means sufficient investment in research and development especially by the private sector, the presence of high-quality scientific research institutions, extensive collaboration in research between universities and industry, and the protection of intellectual property. In this time of crisis, it will be important to resist pressures to cut back on the R&D spending both at the private and public levels that will be so critical for sustainable growth going into the future."

10 China

In 1978 Deng Xiaoping launched China on a frantic march to modernisation. The massive impact of his Four Modernisations programme (of agriculture, industry, science and technology, and the military) was summarised by Hu Jintao in 2005: "In a short span of 26 years from 1978 to 2004, China's GDP increased from US$147.3 billion to US$1.6494 trillion with an average growth rate of 9.4 per cent. Its foreign trade rose from US$20.6 billion to US$1.1548 trillion, averaging an annual growth rate of 16 per cent ... The overall national strength of China has increased remarkably and the quality of life of its people has improved steadily. While inheriting and carrying forward their proud past, the 1.3 billion Chinese people are writing a new chapter in history as they march of one mind on the road of building socialism with Chinese characteristics."

Over the same period China introduced a comprehensive set of IP laws for the 21st century and made remarkable progress in implementing both judicial and administrative procedures. Many of the rights resulting from those laws are efficiently enforced. But, as can be seen from the daily reports of piracy and counterfeiting, much remains to be done in what is a vast and diverse country whose economy and infrastructure are developing at a breakneck pace.

The level of enforcement differs greatly depending on the IPR in question and the impact of labyrinthine political infighting at central and local levels. As the American political scientist Andrew Mertha has remarked in his analysis of the politics of piracy in China:

> "All of the pressure that the USTR [US Trade Representative] has brought to bear on China from 1991 up through the present day [2005] has translated to an astonishingly low degree of copyright enforcement. One could argue that the copyright bureaucracy is so strong that it has been able to withstand the US demands and hold its ground. In fact, the case is exactly the opposite: the copyright bureaucracy is so weak that it has been singularly unable to enforce China's own copyright-related laws and regulations, regardless of whether its representatives want to do so. Its weakness and inertia, not its strength and resistance, explain these outcomes."

Let's take a snapshot to get an idea of where China is in terms of Invisible Gold (*see Table 10.1*).

Table 10.1 The top 10 Chinese regions in which patent applicants were based (2006)

Province/ Municipality	No. of Patent Applications	Province/ Municipality	No. of Patent Applications
Guangdong	72,220	Beijing	22,572
Zhejiang	43,221	Taiwan	20,599
Jiangsu	34,811	Liaoning	15,672
Shanghai	32,741	Tianjin	11,657
Shandong	28,835	Hubei	11,534

Source: *SIPO Annual Report 2006*

In the second stage of economic reform (1985–1991), the focus of reforms in the country shifted to the urban sector and a comprehensive reform programme was launched. The officially stated goal was to change China's economic system so that resource allocation would be done by markets and the government would exercise control only indirectly through the markets. This included a reduction in the scope of planning, the strengthening of enterprise autonomy and accountability, the liberalisation of product and factor prices, the creation of both product and factor markets, and the liberalisation of foreign economic relations.

Many consumer markets were opened up and a wide range of foreign products and brands were imported for the first time into the Chinese marketplace. In addition, the first joint ventures between Chinese and foreign enterprises were established. This led to the introduction of Western capital, technology and management skills into the Chinese economy. As a result, some Chinese businesses started to develop respect for the power of brands, although this was frequently illustrated by copying foreigners' brands. On a more positive note, many of today's most successful Chinese brand names were also launched during this period.

TOP CHINESE BRANDS IN 2005/2006

On lines similar to the international branding company Interbrand, "Beijing Famous Brand Evaluation" has evaluated Chinese brands in China each year since 1995 by giving each brand a monetary value. The national brand champion since 2002 is Haier 海尔 household appliances (US$7.34 billion in 2004), followed by Hongtashan 红塔山 cigarettes (US$5.67 billion), and Lenovo 联想 ("lianxiang") computers (US$3.71 billion).

Table 10.2 The top 10 Chinese brands by brand value in US$ billion in China (2004)

Brand Name	Company	Major Products	Brand Value (US$ Bn)
Haier 海尔	Haier Group	Household appliances	7.45
Hongtashan 红塔山	Hongta Tobacco Group	Cigarettes	5.67
Lenovo 联想	Lenovo Group	Computers	3.71
Wuliangye 五粮液	Yibin Wuliangye Group	Liquors	3.71
FAW 第一汽车	China FAW Group	Automobiles	3.71
TCL	TCL Corporation	TV sets, mobile phones	3.70
Changhong 长虹	Changhong Electronics Group	TV sets	3.27
Midea 美的	Midea Holding Company	Electrical fans, aircons, microwaves	2.43
KONKA 康佳	KONKA Group Company	TV sets, mobile phones	1.37
Tsingtao 青岛	Tsingtao Brewery	Beer	1.36

Source: "Beijing Famous Brand Evaluation", 2004

TVs and household appliances

In addition to Haier and Lenovo, most of the other top 10 Chinese brands are also consumer electronics and household appliances brands. These are TCL (TV sets, mobile phones), Changhong 长虹 (TV sets), Midea 美的 ("meidi": electrical fans, air conditioners, microwaves) and Konka 康佳 ("kangjia": TV sets, mobile phones). Although they all held a top ranking in 2004, they had developed in very different ways over the prior decade. Haier, for example, had increased its brand value rapidly by some 35 per cent a year, while Changhong has stagnated since as long ago as 1998 because of the highly competitive market for TV sets where there have been fierce and continual price wars. As a consequence of low price levels, combined with strong distribution networks, the top five leading brands for televisions in China are local, namely Konka, Changhong, TCL, Skyworth and Hisense.

Alcohol and cigarettes

A brand that has suffered in recent years but remains very powerful is Hongtashan 红塔山. Hongtashan is China's leading cigarette brand and was China's second most valuable brand in 2004 (although it ranked first until 2002). Considered a status symbol by Chinese smokers, Hongtashan benefits from loyal customers throughout the country and at all levels of society. At the higher end of the market it competes successfully with global brands such as Marlboro. Similarly successful are the Chinese alcohol brands Tsingtao 青岛 beer and Wuliangye 五粮液 liquor. Both enjoy strong domestic brand recognition and high levels of consumer loyalty.

Tsingtao's success factors have been its nationwide expansion strategy of acquiring smaller regional breweries (in 1994 it acquired the Yangzhou Brewery and Xi'an Hans Brewers and has acquired more than 40 others since, to ensure a comprehensive national coverage) and its strong overseas sales. After acquiring a local brewery, Tsingtao introduces its production technology and management systems while maintaining the local brands. Only once the new subsidiary has achieved the necessary quality standards is it permitted to use the Tsingtao trademark and logo.

Motor vehicles

China's leading brand in the automotive industry in 2004 was First Automotive Works (FAW) 第一汽车 ("diyi qiche"). FAW was China's first company to produce automobiles in 1953, and has become well known after its 1991 joint venture with Volkswagen (VW). Its main models are the VW Jetta, the VW Bora and the Audi A6. In recent years, however, FAW has been challenged by national rivals such as Geely and Shanghai Automotive Industry Company (SAIC), which acquired the MG Rover brand. SAIC has two large joint ventures with VW (making the VW Santana, the Santana 2000, the Passat and the Polo) and troubled US giant General Motors (making the Buick G, the GL8 and the Buick Sail Compact).

BRANDING A GOOD IDEA

In addition to the market leaders, there are also new aspiring Chinese consumer brands that belong usually to a private or privatised enterprise that started with a good idea, determination and one or two employees during the 1990s. These businesses are typically led by a charismatic manager who was often the founder. Examples include Li Ning 李宁 sportswear, Yue-Sai 羽西80 cosmetics, Mengniu 蒙牛 dairy (which in 2004 sponsored the first Chinese astronauts to go into space), Wahaha 娃哈哈 beverages, Gome 国美 ("guomei") consumer electronics, Blocko 宝高 ("baogao") toys (including toy brick systems which compete—legitimately—with Lego toys, although the company founder David Cheng started in the 1990s by copying the Danish company's products), Alibaba 阿里巴巴 online marketplaces and Huawei Technologies 华为技术 ("huawei jishu"). All these have strong market positions and brand strength among Chinese consumers. Li Ning, for instance, successfully competes against global brands such as Nike and adidas in the China market and, to the irritation of the International Olympic Committee, got huge exposure during the Beijing Olympics despite not being a sponsor.

Sportswear

Li Ning is China's most famous brand name for sports shoes, sportswear and sports accessories, and is also viewed as having been one of the most successful Chinese companies since the end of the 1990s. It has grown rapidly over recent years, resulting in revenues in 2009 of RMB4.052 billion, which represents around a 10 per cent share of the sportswear market (compared with Nike's 16.7 per cent and adidas' 15.6 per cent). In 2004 the company had 2,800 independent brand stores in China.

The brand's identity is inextricably linked to the personality and charisma of its founder Li Ning, who was a star gymnast at the 1984 Olympic Games in Los Angeles. Li Ning founded the company in the early 1990s and started by copying US sportswear giant Nike. Over the years, he has moved the brand away from being merely a look-alike, although its logo still bears a close resemblance to Nike's swoosh. The business has developed its own designs and brand images, hiring a former Procter & Gamble manager Wu Xianyong to run its marketing and branding. By 2006 the Li Ning brand, using its ad tagline, "Anything is possible" (which, although strongly reminiscent of the adidas "Impossible is nothing" campaign, was developed earlier), was managing to compete successfully against the leading global brands through aggressive pricing coupled with equivalent quality—pricing being in the RMB300 to RMB800 range, compared to brands like Nike that retail for RMB2,000. Li Ning's own popularity helped the brand to generate high levels of awareness, acceptance and loyalty from its target markets. Except for a low-priced sub-brand Z-DO, which is sold in hypermarkets, the company does not segment the market and 92 per cent of its sales in the first half of 2009 were under the Li Ning brand itself.

Importantly, Li Ning was able to establish a strong distribution network not only in the major Chinese cities but also in many of the smaller Chinese cities, which are often denied access to leading brands. In October 2009 the company told *China Economic Review*: "The mainstay of our strategy remains second- and third-tier cities, where we see the most potential. We are still adhering to our target of having 10,000 stores by 2013." It opened over 550 stores in the first half of 2009 when it achieved a 51 per cent year-on-year increase in operating profits. Through this strategy Li Ning has succeeded in establishing itself as *the* brand in smaller cities, although the likes of Dongxiang and China Sports are making inroads.

The Li Ning company has also sponsored several key sports events involving Chinese sports stars like the national Chinese Olympics team and has been the marketing partner of the Chinese National Basketball Association since January 2005. In its first move outside its home market, the company announced a S$1 million one-year sponsorship deal with the Singapore national badminton team in July 2009 and opened its first flagship store outside China at the high-end Ion Orchard shopping mall in Singapore.

As Li Ning has recognised, much of China's rural population does not have access to most leading brands as they are not accessible in a cost efficient way due to poor physical infrastructure, weak distribution systems and wide geographic dispersion. As a result, though there are a few national brand champions like Li Ning, TCL, Haier and Lenovo available across the entire country, each region is most likely to be dominated by its local manufacturers and local brands. For instance, there were more than 260 television manufacturers in China in 2004, including foreign enterprises. They made 73 million colour TVs, or 44 per cent of global sales. However, there were only 50 brands in the market, down from over 100 only five years earlier.

Household appliances

The Haier Group is China's largest manufacturer of household appliances. Although officially incorporated in 1984, Haier can trace its origins to 1955 when a group of people formed a handicraft-producers' cooperative. In 1979, it was named Qingdao Home Appliance Factory and by that time was manufacturing washing machines. Although the company switched to the more profitable refrigerator business in 1984 and was renamed Qingdao General Refrigerator Factory, the factory, employing about 800 people, was almost bankrupt by the end of that year.

Zhang Ruimin, a former bureaucrat in the municipal government, was appointed director by the Qingdao Municipal Governmental Household Appliance Division and proceeded to turn the losses around. He focused the business exclusively on refrigerators and decided to develop a national brand, addressing product and service quality as the top corporate aims. In 1985, at a time when demand for refrigerators was high and they sold at prices equivalent to twice the average wage of workers, he ordered the destruction of 76 defective refrigerators with a sledgehammer to bring home to his employees the need for quality and discipline. Around the same time, Zhang entered a seven-year joint venture contract with German appliance maker Liebherr, to get access to its advanced refrigerator technology. When the joint venture contract expired in 1991, the Qingdao-Liebherr Refrigerator was a product name known in many parts of China.

Following direction from Central Government in Beijing, Qingdao General Refrigerator Factory was merged with several local freezer and air-conditioner companies to form Qingdao Haier Group in 1991. The brand name Haier was chosen in 1991 and is a direct translation of the German *Liebherr*, which means "Dear Sir" in English. The first foreign trademark registration was in the United Arab Emirates, to which it was exporting refrigerators. The Chinese characters 海尔 have positive connotations in terms of Chinese traditional values: 海尔 means "like a sea", endless and living. The same pronunciation "haier", but written 孩儿, means "brothers" and "lots of sons".

Today's Haier Group was formed in 1993 and Zhang Ruimin became the president. Zhang aimed to establish international sources of innovation and R&D, overseas manufacturing facilities and to create a global brand. In his own words, describing the challenge: "If not developing a brand now, it could only become more difficult in future … in order to meet the challenge of the multinationals, Haier must become a multinational itself."

To fund the construction of the new Haier Industrial Park in Qingdao (which was completed by 1995), Haier went public on the Shanghai Stock Exchange in 1993. In the same year, Haier diversified into the washing machine sector by forming a joint venture with Italian company Merloni Elettrodomestici and acquiring the Qingdao Red Star Electric Appliance Company. Red Star, also a collective enterprise, is said to have been Haier's most important acquisition, since it had debts the size of Haier's total profits at the time, so was given to Haier free of charge by municipal government officials to save the business and keep 3,240 workers in employment.

With governmental encouragement, Zhang developed a 10-year plan focused on expansion through further diversification and cross-provincial acquisitions of troubled companies. The aim was to enter the *Fortune 500* before 2010. By 1997, Haier had acquired 18 factories and entered the air-conditioner, TV and computer markets.

In 1999 it obtained approval to produce mobile phones. To acquire the technology to do so, it entered into a joint venture with China Construction Telecommunication Company (CCT) in Hong Kong to build a production plant in Qingdao in 2000. In 2003 Haier

Mobile Phones went public in Hong Kong and was renamed Haier Electronics Group in 2005. To diversify risk and leverage fully the value of the established Haier brand in China, Haier also expanded into industries other than appliances, such as pharmaceuticals, real estate, financial and travel service. In 2002, Haier even invested in the retailing sector by forming joint ventures with OBI, Germany's largest DIY retailer, and with China's Suning Appliance Chains. In general, these diversifications outside the household appliances area (including, most strangely, a foray during the 1990s into noodle restaurants under the trading name Haier Dasaozi, which means "elder sister-in-law") have been unsuccessful.

As a result of going international (in August 2003 the Haier neon advertising sign in Tokyo's upmarket Ginza district was the first featured there by a Chinese company), there were increased competitive pressures and fast-changing market needs. Thus, Haier continuously raised its R&D spend. By 2005 this was six per cent of global revenues, resulting in 5,469 domestic patents, although most were utility rather than invention patents. The company has pointed out that being innovative has two competing consequences: it risks having its innovations copied in its domestic market by Chinese pirates, but it is more competitive against global players both at home and elsewhere. If Haier is not perceived as an innovator, its international competitors would fear that Haier would just copy them and, as a pirate, Haier would not be allowed to enter developed markets due to IP rights. Similarly, where Haier has its own patents, its global competitors have to be careful not to violate these rights.

However, it remains the case that Haier is weak in invention patents in developed countries. It depends on key components and technologies bought from foreign companies, including high-performance electro-motors, compressors, controllers, magnetrons and sensors. To try and remedy this weakness, the company has continuously forged alliances to obtain advanced technologies from global players. In the high-tech sectors, it has partnerships with Microsoft (computer software), CCT (mobile phones), LG and Philips (digital television), Toshiba, Lucent Technologies and Ericsson (Bluetooth and GSM technologies), Fujitsu and Hitachi (plasma television). In the words of a company spokesman: "First we observe and digest the new methods, then we imitate them. In the end, we understand them well enough to design them independently."

In addition to these partnerships, the company's CEO, Zhang, has concluded that Haier can only compete with the multinationals' superior technology by combining greater speed in product development with a faster innovation-to-market time and clever niche marketing. When entering the US market, Haier kept to niches like the student dorm micro-refrigerator market that established competitors missed and in which Haier had 50 per cent of the market by 2003. Local manufacturing was established in South Carolina in 2000, to go with the Los Angeles Design Centre. In 2001 the company bought the Meneghetti SpA factory to start manufacturing in Europe, where it also has design centres in Lyon and Amsterdam.

Dairy products

The Chinese dairy industry provides an excellent, but chilling, recent example of how brand value can disappear if quality issues arise.

In September 2008 it was discovered that melamine, an industrial chemical normally used in plastics, had been used as an ingredient in many domestic infant milk powders, giving rise to urinary tract problems and kidney stones. A huge media storm ensued when six children died of complications and more than 250,000 others were affected. Even the Hong Kong share price of Mengniu

(蒙牛), China's leading dairy company, dropped from HK$20 on 16 September, when it was suspended, to HK$7.95, when it returned a week later, even though its products were hardly implicated.

After testing samples from almost 500 batches of products sold by the 109 companies producing baby milk powder in China, the National Administration of Quality Supervision, Inspection and Quarantine found that more than 20 dairy companies had used melamine in their products. The company most implicated was Sanlu Group (三鹿集团), in which New Zealand's dairy cooperative Fonterra had a 43 per cent stake and which had nearly 20 per cent of the Chinese market for infant milk powder when the scandal broke in early September.

On 24 September, Fonterra announced that it had written down by more than two-thirds, NZ$139 million, the carrying value of its investment, reflecting the costs of product recall and the impairment of the Sanlu brand "as a direct consequence of the criminal contamination of milk in China". By the end of the year Sanlu had gone into bankruptcy and its assets were sold at auction in March 2009. Beijing Sanyuan Food Group (三元集团) managed to purchase for only RMB49 million a 95 per cent stake in the Sanlu Dairy Company, together with its facilities, patents and the Sanlu brand name, which on its own had been worth many times the purchase price less than a year before.

By contrast, the unusually-named American Dairy, which—although listed on the New York Stock Exchange—has been selling premium-priced milk powders in China since 1962 under the trusted brands Feihe and Firmus, expanded its share of the infant formula market from two per cent when the scandal broke to more than seven per cent a year later.

Health care

One area in which Chinese business has developed a significant number of IPRs, particularly patents, is human and animal health care (including Traditional Chinese Medicine, where most appear to be easy-to-obtain utility patents rather than the stronger—and more difficult to obtain—innovation patent). This can be seen from the consistently higher number of patents granted in the sector. These form a relatively low percentage of those applied for, suggesting that Chinese companies have started to adopt, perhaps for competitive reasons, the useful commercial trick of applying for but not proceeding with patent applications.

Table 10.3 Patents granted in medicine, veterinary science and health (1994–2005)

Year	No. of Patent Applications	No. of Patents Granted
1994	6,227	2,891
1995	6,177	2,517
1996	6,203	2,084
1997	7,589	2,250
1998	5,720	2,554
1999	8,757	4,865
2000	9,296	5,285
2001	12,509	4,781
2002	13,196	5,418
2003	16,583	6,838
2004	17,448	9,094
2005	24,875	10,179
TOTAL	134,580	58,756

Source: *China Statistics Yearbook 2005*

Ninety-seven per cent of domestic applications for patents in the medical field were for traditional Chinese medicines. Foreign applicants filed 92 per cent of the applications for non-traditional pharmaceuticals, an area where Chinese businesses are not very active. However, Chinese applicants filed nearly half (48 per cent) of the patent applications for so-called "modern medicines".

Telecoms

In 1998 two companies had between them nearly 45 per cent of the telecoms equipment capacity in China: Zhongxing Telecom Equipment (ZTE) and Huawei.

Established in 1985 in Shenzhen, three years earlier than Huawei, ZTE is a state-owned company. It was started by a number of state-owned companies affiliated with the Ministry of Aerospace Industry and in its domestic market has grown in tandem with its biggest customers, China Mobile and China Unicom.

ZTE has developed a number of its own innovative products. In 2000, it launched the world's first CDMA mobile phone with detachable SIM card. This was followed in 2004 by the launch of the world's first CDMA-based digital trunking technology—GoTa (Global open Trunking architecture system), which incorporates many technologies developed by ZTE and protected by its IPRs. Certain core technologies developed by ZTE for the GoTa system were the first to be licensed by a Chinese telecoms company to overseas vendors such as Nortel and Motorola—recognising perhaps the better commercialisation abilities of these Western rivals.

By the end of 2009, telecoms network equipment supplier Huawei, founded in 1988 by former PLA officer Ren Zhengfei, had become the third-largest player in the world, after Ericsson and Nokia Siemens Networks. When interviewed by the *Financial Times* in August 2009, the CEO of Ericsson described Huawei as his company's greatest threat. Before the end of the year, the Chinese company had beaten Ericsson in the Swedish company's home market when it was chosen by Tele2 and Telenor to build their fourth-generation mobile network.

The Guangdong-headquartered company has had its share of critics like Hong Lu, CEO of UTStarcom, one of Huawei's biggest competitors in China. He has argued that "they are followers, not innovators. In the past, they have always done things that others have already done. … Real innovation will come from foreign companies opening their own research facilities on the Mainland."

Notwithstanding this, Huawei was the first Chinese company to top the list of Patent Cooperation Treaty applicants in 2008. The Treaty, administered by the World Intellectual Property Organisation (WIPO) in Geneva, provides a mechanism to make multiple national patent applications and is often used as a measure of how innovative a company (and indeed, a country) is. In 2008 Huawei filed 1,737 PCT applications. Japan's Panasonic was the second-largest user with 1,729 international applications, followed by Philips Electronics (Netherlands, 1,551 PCT applications), Toyota (Japan, 1,364 PCT applications) and Robert Bosch (Germany, 1,273 PCT applications). However, Ren Zhengfei was quoted in 2006 as saying:

> "During the past 18 years, Huawei has been investing a minimum of 10 per cent of our annual revenue into R&D, especially during the last few years, we had more than 25,000 employees and investment of seven or eight billion yuan (about US$1 billion) dedicated to R&D activities. However, so far we have not had one single original product invention. What we achieved is advancing our capacity of improving and integrating the function and feature of the products invented by the Western companies."

In addition, although the huge advances made by Chinese companies such as Huawei in filing for patent protection outside China are impressive and not to be underestimated, it must be noted that *Managing Intellectual Property* magazine has estimated that the rate at which Chinese PCT applications are converted into actual patents (about 30 per cent) is around half that of applicants from Japan, the USA and Europe. If these figures are correct they suggest that Chinese businesses are starting to play the perfectly legitimate game of filing patent applications, which can never safely be ignored by competitors, rather than proceeding to the considerably more expensive phase of actually obtaining, maintaining and enforcing patents.

THE NEXT STAGE

At the beginning of 2006, to show the seriousness of its determination to improve the country's science and technology, the Chinese government announced a 15-year Medium- and Long-Term National Science and Technology Plan with the aim of achieving three goals:

- first, to use science and technology to support and lead future economic growth;
- secondly, to "leapfrog" to the forefront of research in specified critical scientific disciplines; and
- thirdly, to focus on "independent innovation" to redress China's weak record of innovation in commercial technologies.

This involves increasing expenditure on research and development to two per cent of GDP by the end of 2010 and 2.5 per cent by 2020. Clearly, over the course of the 15-year plan there will inevitably be increased patenting activity in the priority research areas.

The broad priority areas chosen for investment were:

- Advanced storage technologies
- Alternative and renewable energy technologies
- Biotechnology and genetics
- Electronic components
- Environmental technologies
- Integrated circuits (IC)/semiconductors
- Manned space exploration
- Materials technology
- Nanotechnology
- Network and communication technologies
- Optical and biological computing
- Software and related services.

Illustrating the Beijing government's awareness of the importance of IPRs in encouraging investment, this list was mirrored in paragraph 16 of the National IP Strategy published in 2007. Therefore, many patent applications can be expected in these areas over coming years.

FUTURE UNCERTAINTIES

In his provocative 2006 book *The Writing on the Wall*, on the relationship between China and the West in the 21st Century, Will Hutton dismisses the view that China has embraced the need for technological innovation:

> "In reality indigenous Chinese enterprise has competed largely on the basis of low wages, has copied technology and has disregarded environmental costs during the reform

> period. Moving to an alternative model without substantial institutional reform will be beyond it. Any other narrative is implausible, whatever the official goals declared for the future may be."

The recent successes of companies such as Huawei, Lenovo, Haier, BYD, Netac and many others, coupled with the entrepreneurial drive and will to succeed of hordes of younger and smaller Chinese businesses, suggest that at the very least Hutton may have been premature in his dismissal of the Chinese challenge to the technological superiority of the West.

What he got right, however, was his strong avowal of the need for there to be "understanding and engagement" with China by Europe and the United States, rather than "enmity and suspicion". That was the case in 2006 and after the economic crisis of 2008–2009, it is so even more as calls for protectionism become ever more strident.

Paradoxically, in some thought-provoking comments, Xiang Bing, Dean of the Cheung Kong Graduate School of Business in Beijing, perceived the entrepreneurial drive of many Chinese business people as a potential long-term problem to be addressed:

> "Entrepreneurialism is in our blood, and that makes us open to new ideas and new people. But it means we can also be impatient, and without focus. In Chinese companies, middle managers are always trying to figure out how they can ultimately take over the company, or start their own company. This may also be because Chinese companies aren't as good at taking care of their employees. Compare China to Japan in this respect. It's difficult to imagine a Chinese company creating the next Toyota, let alone the next Google."

Similarly, to the question whether the PRC government's efforts to encourage innovation will bear fruit, Dean Xiang gave a measured response—the last part of which Hutton would undoubtedly endorse:

> "If the Chinese government sees it as being important, that's good, because it means they'll pour money into it, and change policies to make it easier to innovate, and possibly encourage education that's more creative. But you need more than all this—it requires a mindset shift on the part of business people."

11 India

India is one of the two great economic success stories of the past 20 years. It has leveraged its advantages into global dominance in areas as diverse as drug making and IT. In 2006 and 2007 the economy's growth rate was more than nine per cent, with manufacturing output increasing by more than 12 per cent.

Despite considering that a "talented pool of workers, along with abundant capital and investment, presents us with immense opportunities for creativity and innovation, which can in turn lead to rapid gains in productivity growth and GDP", Nandan Nilekani, one of *Time* magazine's 100 most influential people in the world and founder of Indian success story Infosys Technologies, lamented in his 2009 bestseller about modern India, *Imagining India: The Idea of a Renewed Nation*:

> "Our biggest businesses are building international brands, yet red tape continues to throttle the new entrepreneur and frustrate the small business owner. ... My years as an entrepreneur have especially brought home to me how much India, despite its recent tremendous growth, is straining against the challenges that hold it back. Today we are a nation that has barely scratched its potential."

In a similar vein, IPR expert Professor Shamnad Basheer commented in December 2009 on the appointment of Sam Pitroda as Innovation Czar (or, more formally, Infrastructure, Innovation and Information Adviser to the Prime Minister):

> "This appointment couldn't have come at a better time. For, despite India's rapid economic progress and technological proficiency, it has failed to produce any real innovation on its soil. Consider our software industry, which continues to remain content with a cyber coolie 'services' model, and our pharmaceutical industry that thrives on a copycat generic model. What is most puzzling is the fact that the very same brains that fail to create on Indian soil do so the moment they land on foreign shores. What ails? Do we really lack an innovation culture? How is it that a country that boasts of a Sushruta and rudimentary cataract surgery as far back as 600 BC does not have a single blockbuster drug to its credit?"

BIG BELLIES

At a more populist level, *White Tiger*, the 2008 Man Booker Prize-winning novel by *Time* magazine's Asia correspondent Aravind Adiga, exposed the harsh underbelly of India's economic growth. Its protaganist, the chauffeur-cum-successful entrepreneur Balram, sums up the new India: "In the old days there were one thousand castes and destinies in India. These days there are two castes: Men with Big Bellies, and Men with Small Bellies." In his imaginary correspondence with the visiting Chinese Premier Hu Jintao, Balram predicts proudly: "In 20 years' time it will just be us brown and yellow men at the top of the pyramid, and we'll rule the world."

As to IPRs, the country has had an IP system since long before its Independence in 1947. But 60 years after that, Justice Madan Lokur of the Delhi High Court still complained, "The government is not organised and not able to get its message [about the importance of IP] across."

Even on what should be one of India's Invisible Gold successes, entertainment industry commentator Gerrie Lim asserts in his *Idol to Icon* book about celebrity brands: "The Bollywood film genre remains a cult taste ... [and] the ultimate truth is that the most famous Indian person in the film world today is of Hollywood and not Bollywood: the director M. Night Shyamalan ... the Alfred Hitchcock of our time."

Also, the much-heralded flow of engineering graduates out of the country's universities, on which so much hope for future innovations is placed, is not everything it seems. While graduates in technical subjects are plentiful, trusting the standard of university education sometimes leads to disappointment. Although the top-ranking universities such as IIT (Indian Institute of Technology) are renowned for the high level of research and teaching, there are widely varying standards among higher education institutions. Commentators acknowledge that the variance is much greater in India than in Europe and North America, where the education standard of top-level universities can be trusted.

PATENTLY CLEAR

As far as patenting activity in India is concerned, a massive 80 per cent of patents applied for are owned by foreigners and the aggregate numbers are roughly those applied for in China 10 years ago.

The top domestic patent filers are:

- the Council for Scientific and Industrial Research (CSIR, with roughly five times the applications of the second most prolific Indian filer; it is also the top patent filer in India, with numbers exceeding patents filed by foreigners such as Qualcomm, Bayer, Philips and Microsoft);
- Ranbaxy Laboratories (now majority-owned by Japanese pharma company Daiichi Sankyo);
- Dr Reddy's Laboratories;
- Indian Institute of Technology;
- Bharat Heavy Electricals;
- Orchid Chemicals & Pharmaceuticals;
- Cadila Healthcare;
- Cipla;
- Steel Authority of India (which, perhaps understandably, files nowhere other than in India); and
- Larsen & Toubro.

With the exception of Bharat, Steel Authority of India and Larsen & Toubro, these are also more or less the leading Indian filers of patents outside the country.

Noticeable by their absence are the country's IT powerhouses, TCS, Wipro, Infosys, Satyam (re-named Mahindra Satyam in June 2009 after being taken over by Tech Mahindra), HCL and Cognizant. Tata Consultancy Services (TCS) is the leading patent filer in this sector but with less than five per cent of the number filed at home and elsewhere by leading private sector filer, Ranbaxy.

Motor vehicles

Notwithstanding the dominance of foreign patent filers, companies like Tata Motors and Bajaj, in the car and motorcycle fields respectively, are increasingly using patents and designs as competitive weapons. Hardly a new car or motorcycle launch takes place in India without allegations from competitors of infringement of this or that alleged IP right. Even Mahindra & Mahindra's FES (Farm Equipment Segment) company has 12 patents covering tractor technology granted in India. In June 2008 it received its first US patent, entitled "Method for Producing Gears and/or Shaft Components with Superior Bending Fatigue Strength and Pitting Fatigue Life from Conventional Alloy Steels".

After a year in which his group had taken a controlling interest in troubled IT company Satyam and planned the launch of its sports utility vehicles (SUVs) in the USA—M&M's Scorpio model was India's first SUV—Anand Mahindra, MD and Deputy Chairman, told Singapore's *Business Times* in January 2010 that his aim is for Mahindra to become "the first and best-known Indian brand around the world". This is certainly a far cry from its origins in 1945 as Mahindra & Mohammed, assembling jeeps under licence from the off-road vehicle's US owner, Willys-Overland. The business became Mahindra & Mahindra on Partition when Ghulam Mohammed became the first Finance Minister of the newly independent Pakistan, before becoming Governor General in 1951.

Pharmaceuticals

The Indian pharmaceutical industry is one whose success was based largely on the lack of patent protection for pharmaceuticals in the country between 1970 and 2005. Particularly after 1978 when Italy came into line with all other countries in the European Community by introducing patent protection for pharmaceutical products, India became the country of choice for much of the world's production of "me-too" copies of products protected by patents elsewhere but unprotected in India. (These copies are sometimes called "generics", although that term also includes products that may not be protected by patents either any longer or ever.)

Today the industry is adjusting to the changed IP environment brought about by India's membership of the World Trade Organisation (and the TRIPs Agreement), which required the country to give protection to novel pharmaceutical products. There remains considerable controversy about what exactly a "novel" pharmaceutical product is. Switzerland's Novartis is just one of a number of foreign companies embroiled in extensive litigation—and lobbying—trying to have this resolved in favour of the research-based pharma industry that spends billions developing new drugs and relies on such patent protection.

In 2005, the first year of the new regime permitting pharmaceutical product patents, many of the nearly 18,000 registered local Indian pharmaceutical companies had increased considerably their spending on R&D in New Drug Development and Novel Drug Delivery Systems. The largest spenders were Ranbaxy and Dr Reddy's Labs (DRL), with expenditure the previous year of US$75 million and US$64 million, respectively. Others that realised the new imperatives and spent significant sums on R&D included Sun Pharmaceuticals, Wockhardt (which subsequently ran into financial difficulty after over-expanding and in 2009 was forced to sell its animal health business to US company Abbott Labs for US$130 million), Lupin (a successful participant in the CSIR public-private initiative described below), Cadila Healthcare, Torrent, along with biotech companies Biocon and Panacea Biotec.

Indian companies also went abroad to acquire the expertise they lacked. In 2005 and 2006 Glenmark bought Argentinian marketing company Servycal, Ranbaxy acquired South African firm Be-Tabs

Pharmaceuticals, and DRL bought for US$570 million the fourth-largest German generic drug maker, Betapharm Arzneimittel.

It was not one-way traffic only. For the pharmaceutical sector as a whole, 2009 was a year when Indian manufacturing capabilities took centre stage. For the first time, global pharmaceutical giants like Pfizer and GlaxoSmithKline (GSK) went shopping for Indian manufacturers.

GSK entered into a joint venture with Hyderabad-based DRL to develop and market generics and formulations. Analysts viewed this as a win-win deal for both. Whilst GSK gets high-class manufacturing at one-fifth of the amount it pays elsewhere, DRL enhances its geographical reach in markets like Africa and Latin America without having to spend a rupee on developing a distribution system.

Biotech

There have also been encouraging signs that Indian biotech companies, like Biocon, Avesthagen and Bharat Serums & Vaccines, are starting to mature into respected global players. For example, Avesthagen claims to have "a pipeline of over 160 patents", although by 2008 only two had been granted in India and seven elsewhere. It has collaborations with industry giants such as France's bioMerieux in the field of diagnostics and Switzerland's Nestlé Nutrition in the field of food nutrition, where nearly half of the company's patent applications have been filed.

The company was set up in 2000 in Bangalore by molecular biologist, Dr Villoo Morawala Patell. She had previously spent some time unsuccessfully trying to make the business succeed as a public-private partnership. Echoing a frequent complaint, she remembers that at that time the public side of the equation (the academic institutions) did not treat patents as a priority and the private side (the venture capitalists) were apprehensive about the public-private model.

By contrast, Villoo's description of her company's internal processes today shows it to be a sophisticated user of the IP system:

> "By means of competitive IP intelligence [ie, using databases to examine others' patent applications and granted patents], we assess the technology and patent landscape associated with the current and future products/technologies [to see what competitors are up to and to avoid going into areas where there are already too many patents] ... The essence of Avesthagen's R&D philosophy lies in building and strengthening the patent portfolio."

Medical devices

Similar sentiments are expressed by fellow Bangalore company Opto Circuits, run by Vinod Ramnani. In addition to growing through an aggressive programme of acquisitions, Opto has invested heavily in R&D in the medical devices field, spending 12 per cent of its income in 2009. As a result the company has developed its own products protected by patents, such as the bare metal stent Magic and its Dior drug-eluting coronary balloon (the latter developed by EuroCor, a business Opto acquired at the end of 2005 for only €11 million).

Of course, in a country in which the bureaucracy plays such a pivotal role, there is no shortage of initiatives aimed at generating innovation and encouraging creativity.

The Indian government's 2005 Biotechnology Policy set out a clear plan to develop biotechnology R&D in the country. The major initiatives proposed included encouraging R&D in academia, entering into partnerships with industry and direct support to industry, granting tax breaks and other incentives to biotechnology companies, as well as setting up biotechnology parks and special economic zones. To assist industry in bringing products to market quickly, the regulatory framework was to be streamlined through a new set of simplified guidelines for the approval of all recombinant DNA products. Also, a new biotechnology regulatory authority was created. A series of bio-clusters are being developed around existing biotechnology centres and identified institutes. The National Jai Vigyan Science and Technology Mission also provides support in developing new products and processes. Finally, the Small Business Innovation Research Initiative (SBIRI) is aimed at providing early-stage funding to scientists in private industry trying to develop high-risk, innovative or commercialisable products.

PUBLIC-PRIVATE INITIATIVE

The New Millennium Indian Technology Leadership Initiative (NMITLI) is a public-private partnership started by CSIR in 2000 to try to make India a global leader in the field of science and technology. The strategy of the NMITLI is to boost innovation and enable Indian companies to attain a global leadership position in selected niche areas.

Although there remain sceptics like Villoo who doubt the extent to which one can effectively mix academia with commerce, the Initiative aims to encourage cooperation between publicly funded R&D institutions, academia and industry. It supports two types of projects: those initiated as part of the programme, and those initiated by industry. In both cases, the most appropriate public institutions and industry players are identified and a joint project developed. More than 40 projects in various fields (eg, biotechnology, bioinformatics, agriculture and plant biotechnology, drugs and pharmaceuticals), involving over 400 groups in R&D labs, academia and industry had been supported by the beginning of 2009.

Areas receiving support included:

- new targets, drug-delivery systems, bio-enhancers and therapeutics for latent mycobacterium tuberculosis;
- novel herbal therapeutics for degenerative disorders;
- osteo-arthritis and rheumatoid arthritis;
- diabetes mellitus type II (NIDDM);
- hepatic disorders and hepato-protective agents;
- development of an oral, herbal formulation for the treatment of psoriasis;
- a new process for manufacturing Tamiflu® (the well-known Roche drug for avian and swine influenza);
- oral delivery of insulin; and
- development of lysostaphin (a novel therapeutic molecule).

One major achievement of the Initiative was the development of the first anti-tuberculosis (TB) drug in the past 40 years. This is the new antimycobacterial molecule Sudoterb developed by Lupin Laboratories in collaboration with other R&D partners. Tests on laboratory animals showed that, when given in combination with conventional drugs like rifampicin and pyrazinamide, Sudoterb was able to reduce the duration of tuberculosis treatment, from eight to six months initially, then to three months. In 2009 the new molecule started its Phase I clinical trials.

Another significant new drug developed through the NMITLI programme is Desoside-P, a single plant-based herbal drug for psoriasis that started Phase II clinical trials in 2009. Trials have shown that this Ayurvedic (traditional) drug is able to reduce psoriasis symptoms by about 70 per cent in 16 weeks. It is noteworthy that in these days of massive drug development spending, it cost only 700 million rupees for this drug to be developed by Lupin, who collaborated on the project with both an R&D laboratory (Central Drug Research Institute, Lucknow) and an academic institute (National Institute of Pharmaceutical Education and Research, Chandigarh).

START-STOP SYNDROME

Despite these initiatives, there remains a deep-seated reluctance in India to invest in start-ups or unproven businesses. Although the likes of Narayan Murthy and Nadathur S. Raghavan, both of whom made their money from the success of Infosys, are investing some of that money in start-ups, there remains a serious lack of venture capital funds to support small, growing businesses. As a result, many Indian entrepreneurs look outside the country for funding and, like biotech company Cellworks Group which started in Bangalore but now has its head office in California, even relocate to environments more amenable to supporting and financing innovation. In the longer run this can only be bad for India's chances of keeping up with its neighbour to the east in the battle to develop its own Invisible Gold reserves. However lucrative it may be in the short term to create and innovate for foreign companies that then own any IPRs, it is critical that Indian policy-makers appreciate the need to encourage in parallel the development of Indian businesses with their own IPRs.

12 Malaysia, Indonesia, the Philippines and Thailand

In Thailand, Indonesia and the Philippines, around half of each country's corporate assets is owned by 10 families, leading to the disparaging description of the countries' economies as examples of crony capitalism. Although not as concentrated on family lines, Malaysia's economy too has suffered from the external perception that the "crony" in its capitalism was the government—as indeed it was during Soeharto's 32-year rule in Indonesia, which ended with his resignation in 1998 after the economy contracted by more than 15 per cent in 12 months.

MALAYSIA

The first patent granted in Malaysia was in 1986 for Insect-Repellent Soap, following the country's 1983 Patents Act, positioning Malaysia as a relative latecomer on the patent scene. Within eight months, 1,000 patents had been granted by the national IP office and within seven years, 10,000 patents. Since 2000 there has been a steady increase in the number of patent applications by locals, with local patent applications increasing from three per cent in 2000 to 10 per cent and 12 per cent in 2004 and 2006, respectively.

The major producers of home-grown technologies were the

universities and government research institutes, with the total number of applications for patents from the universities in 2006 reaching 104, or 20 per cent of total domestic applications. Six of the top 15 patent applicants for the year were universities, along with three government research institutes. IP awareness in the country is slowly on the increase. The Malaysia Intellectual Property Office (MYIPO) received 8,000 trademark applications in 2009, two per cent more than in 2008. In the same year, a total of 3,468 patents were granted, but with only 270 of those to Malaysians. Local ownership of trademarks also lags behind foreign ownership, with only 29 per cent registered by Malaysians. The total local pool stands at almost 53,000.

To encourage further IP creation to fuel the growth of the economy, the government launched the National Intellectual Property Policy (NIPP) in April 2007. The expressed purpose of this policy is to harness IP as a new engine of growth for the enhancement of economic and social prosperity. The policy adopted multi-prong strategies for developing Malaysia as an IP centre, including improvement of the legal framework, capacity building, development of the infrastructure for IP transactions, encouraging the creation of IP-generated activities, public awareness, promotion of national IP interest, and foreign investment and technology transfer.

Other government initiatives include the Malaysian Institute of Microelectronic Systems (MIMOS), set up in 1987 under the Ministry of Science, Technology and Innovation (MOSTI) as a research agency to help stimulate investment in the information and communication technologies (ICT) and microelectronics sectors. For a while, however, it seemed that MIMOS itself needed some stimulation of its own as failed commercial ventures plagued the agency. Within three years of a new CEO, Datuk Abdul Wahab

Abdullah, being appointed in 2006, MIMOS had filed 191 patent applications, a stratospheric rise from the two filed prior to 2006. MIMOS' internal IP Reward Scheme, introduced by Abdul Wahab, has contributed to the agency's success. Employees are encouraged to have at least one patent disclosure accepted every year. For those patents that are commercialised, the employee inventor can receive up to RM500,000 (approx US$150,000).

The main beneficiaries of MIMOS' activities are local Malaysian companies who get the opportunity to take a licence to use the technology spoils. For instance, MIMOS' Semantic Search Engine has been an ongoing project. The technology interprets human language in a reasoned way, based on the logic of human thought. Head of the knowledge technology cluster at MIMOS, Dr Dickson Luckose, gives the example of an Internet search for an "inexpensive and teetotal Thai halal restaurant near the Jurong Point Shopping Centre in Singapore". The Semantic Search Engine would return restaurants that exactly match the requirements, rather than treating the word "halal" as a keyword and returning the results of restaurants advertising themselves as non-halal. It would also understand the words "teetotal", "inexpensive" and "near" to give an exact match. This technology was provided to Telekom Malaysia as part of a three-year R&D collaboration agreement under which Telekom Malaysia would invest between RM100 million and RM150 million.

Malaysia Biotechnology Corporation (Biotech Corp) is another agency under MOSTI, concentrating on the biotechnology field. It offers commercialisation grants for the start-up of Malaysian biotech companies and also sub-licences technology that it has acquired from foreign companies. In 2009 Biotech Corp signed a licensing agreement, worth AU$1.5 million, with the University of Sydney spin-off firm, Medsaic Pty Ltd, for its DotScan™ technology, a diagnostic test kit for leukaemia and lymphoma. Biotech Corp would then sub-licence the technology to a local company, in a way similar to when it obtained a licence from Nanobiotix in France in 2007 for the manufacture of nanoparticles. University Sains Malaysia was granted the primary sub-licence rights working with Nanobiotix in developing non-oncology applications.

Sri Kulai

The Sri Kulai brand is something the southern peninsular state of Johor can be proud of. All the praise goes to Liow Ren Jan, the creator of the Sri Kulai brand of microwaveable frozen ready-meals that are halal. The line includes a *dim sum* combo, *nasi lemak* and prawn *sambal*—three products that contribute 60 per cent of total sales. From his experiences in the cosmetics industry, Liow realised there was an untapped demand for ready meals in Malaysia. He markets his halal-certified meals as authentic Malaysian food, the answer to the Malaysian city-dweller's hectic life.

To start his venture, Liow bought existing local company Homito Sdn Bhd, both for its existing food business and to get access to its technology to make frozen microwaveable meals. He then set up AYS Sdn Bhd, the manufacturer and marketer of the Sri Kulai range of products and also a product-licensing arm, AYS Signatures Sdn Bhd. Liow invested RM3 million on the factory, equipment, know-how, working capital and brand-building. AYS now has its eyes on the Asian skies, already supplying eight meals to the low-cost Malaysian airline, Air Asia.

Pensonic

The success of the Malaysian electricals manufacturer Pensonic has been despite the fact that its name sounds very similar to the iconic

Japanese brand set up by Konosuke Matsushita.

Dato' Seri Chew Weng Khak's Penang-based business distributing Japanese-made small electrical appliances originally traded under the name Keat Radio Co. In 1982 Chew created the Pensonic brand—apparently meaning the "sound of Penang"—becoming a low-cost competitor to its Japanese almost-namesake Panasonic. Pensonic quickly became Malaysia's largest manufacturer and distributor of home electricals, with its products now sold in over 800 Malaysian outlets.

Unsurprisingly, Panasonic has not been happy about the Malaysian company's success, claiming it has enjoyed a free ride on the Panasonic global brand and is nothing more than a cheap knock-off version of the Japanese original. Panasonic was registered by the Japanese corporation as a trademark in Malaysia in 1971. Despite this, Pensonic claims not to have seen or known anything about the Japanese brand when the Pensonic brand was created in 1982 and it was subsequently registered in Malaysia in 1984. The two trademarks now coexist in 11 countries around Asia, including in China, Japan, Australia and Hong Kong.

In 2008 in Singapore, Panasonic successfully prevented the Malaysian company from registering its Pensonic mark (with a "P" device to represent Penang) because a substantial number of Singaporeans would confuse it with the well-known Panasonic brand. This can be contrasted with a Sri Lanka court case in 2009 where Panasonic lost its application opposing Pensonic registering its mark in that country, because the Japanese corporation had not objected when Pensonic was first registered in 1984 in Malaysia and even in Panasonic's home country of Japan.

When not fighting trademark battles, Pensonic has been active in bringing more brands into its portfolio, rather than simply resting on its laurels. In 2006 it bought the Cornell trademark rights for Singapore and Malaysia for RM870,000 from Amtek Holdings. It also continues to develop its own brands including a high-end steel appliance brand Lebensstil Kollektion—German for "lifestyle collection"—selling at almost five times the price of its Pensonic range. A lower-end brand Epicson (which again sounds rather similar to a well-known, this time Swedish, brand) that sells for around half the price of the Lebensstil range.

Selangor Pewter

On a more refined level, an Australian sales assistant's chat with the late Sultan Salahuddin Abdul Aziz Shah in 1979 was to change Selangor Pewter into brand royalty.

When asked where he was from, the Sultan answered he was from Selangor, to which the sales assistant replied, "Ah, Selangor Pewter." The legend goes that the Sultan was so impressed that Australians had heard of the brand, he conferred royal status on Selangor Pewter, which changed its name in 1992 to reflect the royal warrant. However, it is a century-long history of making quality pewter objects that has made Royal Selangor a Malaysian brand icon and one deserving of its royal title.

A young Yong Koon's arrival in Malaysia from China in 1885 with nothing but a pewter-smith apprenticeship soon became a small business producing ceremonial pewter objects for Chinese homes and temples. Under British colonial rule, Selangor Pewter broadened its business into making functional household pewter items such as cigarette tins, tankards, ashtrays and other commemorative items complete with the Selangor Pewter stamp.

Royal Selangor's products are now considered luxury goods, sold in famous stores including Harrods in England and the Wako and

Mitsukoshi stores in Japan. With a large presence worldwide, the company exports to more than 20 countries. Products also extend beyond pewter into gold, silver and precious jewellery. Indeed, Royal Selangor may be the world's largest pewter producer because of its purchase of long-established pewter brands, including the 300-year-old London maker of Crown & Rose pewter, Englefields, and Canadian company Seagull Pewter, the latter bought in 2002. Beyond pewter, in 1993 the company also acquired a pre-eminent UK silversmith brand established in the UK in 1645, Comyns, and inherited its treasure trove of over 35,000 drawings.

Royal Selangor's designs are the key to its successes—designs that have been internationally recognised. For instance, Royal Selangor's *Wine Celebration Funnel*—a "soft launch" spout with five stream openings—won three international design awards in 2002: the Red Dot Award from the Design Zentrum, Germany; the G-Mark Good Design Award from the Japan Industrial Design Promotion Organisation; and an IDEA2002 bronze medal from the Industrial Designers Society of America.

Top Glove

More prosaically, as one of the world's top three rubber producers, Malaysia dominates the rubber glove industry, supplying more than 60 per cent of the world's rubber latex gloves. One company—aptly named Top Glove—is the world's largest rubber glove manufacturer by production capacity, producing up to 31.5 billion gloves every year and holding 24 per cent of the world rubber glove market. As the H1N1 flu virus flew around the world in 2009, shares in Malaysia's rubber glove makers skyrocketed. Top Glove's share price, in particular, rose 181 per cent in 12 months.

Top Glove was founded in 1991 by Tan Sri Dr Lim Wee Chai

and his wife in Klang, Selangor, the Malaysian Silicon Valley for glove manufacturing. Dr Lim responded to the growing demand in the early 1990s for rubber gloves worldwide for protection of health care workers against AIDS and other infectious diseases. Top Glove expanded rapidly, with 19 glove factories in Malaysia, Thailand and China. With a corporate philosophy of continual expansion, the company spends between RM5 million and RM10 million annually on R&D.

Even the rubber glove industry is affected by IPRs: Top Glove successfully defeated a complaint filed against it and 30 other companies by American rubber glove firm Tillotson Corporation, at the US International Trade Commission (ITC) for infringement of its patent for its 616 nitrile rubber gloves (a glove made with a crude oil by-product rather than natural rubber). Success of Tillotson's complaint would have seen Top Glove and the other alleged infringers forced to make royalty payments of up to US$2 per 1,000 gloves imported into the United States. In August 2008 the ITC rejected Tillotson's claim.

Sime Darby

Once British-owned, Malaysian corporate giant Sime Darby began life as a management company for some 500 acres of Radell Rubber estates in Malacca. Today, as a result of its 2007 merger with Golden Hope Plantations and Kumpulan Guthrie, Sime has over 100,000 employees and is one of the world's largest plantation and palm-oil businesses with a land bank of over 633,000 hectares. It is a multinational company with 60 per cent of the group's revenues originating from abroad.

Sime Darby Technology Centre (SDTC) focuses on plant biotechnology and plant products as part of the group's research into the plantation business. In collaboration with bio-informatics company Synamatix, and having invested RM40 million in research, SDTC successfully deciphered the genetics of the oil palm in 2009, becoming the first company in the world to completely sequence, assemble and annotate the oil palm genome.

INDONESIA

The Indonesian economy was revived from its near-collapse in 1965–1966 by the macro-economic policies of the group of technocrats known as the Berkeley Mafia. Its leader, Professor Widjojo Nitisastro, was installed and supported by President Soeharto.

Within a few years they had put Indonesia on a path of seven per cent annual growth, sustained for 25 years. The proportion of Indonesians in the "very poor" category fell from 52 per cent in the mid-1960s to seven per cent by 1990, as per capita income increased nearly three times. At the same time, however, power and business became steadily concentrated into Soeharto's inner circle of family, relatives, favoured generals and some ethnic Chinese businessmen from his early days, notably Liem Siu Liong (founder of the Salim group) and Bob Hasan.

By the late 1980s the first family's rapacity alarmed even Soeharto supporters. The six Soeharto children had all joined in the fun and members of the family held significant shares in over 1,200 companies. This portfolio yielded an income stream measuring billions of US dollars annually by the time of its heyday in the mid-1990s. However, the end came relatively quickly as the 1997 Asian economic crisis led to riots in Jakarta and students on the streets demanding that Soeharto resign and be brought to justice. In 1998 they got the first of their demands but the second was denied when Soeharto died in 1999.

More than 10 years after the resignation of Soeharto, fewer than five per cent of patents in Indonesia are owned by domestic businesses and the country, which has the good fortune to be blessed with abundant natural resources, punches well below its weight on the intellectual property scene.

Perhaps in an attempt to redress this, much time and effort has been spent by the Indonesian government since 2007 on getting recognition that *batik* is Indonesian and not Malaysian in origin. In September 2009 *The New York Times* carried an article on the latest spat with neighbouring Malaysia. However, although particular *batik* designs may be protected by copyright, *batik* itself remains free for anyone to make. Just like the terracotta warriors and the Egyptian pyramids, it is not protected by any intellectual property right—although, for what it is worth, the United Nations Educational, Scientific and Cultural Organisation (UNESCO) added Indonesian *batik* to its Intangible Cultural Heritage list in 2009.

Indofoods

One company started in the Soeharto era (in 1990) that has developed a formidable array of brands is Indofoods. It is controlled by the Salim family that was close to the former president. Today the company is the largest instant noodle maker in the world, with a capacity of over 15 billion packs. Under its brands Indomie, Supermi and Sarimi, Indofoods dominates the domestic instant noodle market.

The company's 2008 Annual Report notes that the Supermi brand "achieved four consecutive MURI (Museum Rekor Indonesia) records for:

1. the most people eating noodles in an event (34,371 people);
2. the most people cooking noodles in an event (5,388 people);

3. the largest replica of Borobudur constructed using 77,480 packs of instant noodles measuring 15.9 m by 15.9 m by 4.7 m; and
4. the longest noodles, measuring 1,000 m."

Other food product areas in which it has a large presence are dairy products (having acquired Indolakto, with its portfolio of dairy brands including Indomilk, Cap Enaak, Tiga Sapi, Indoeskrim, Nice and Orchid at the end of 2008), wheat flour (with its brands Segitiga Biru, Kunci Biru and Cakra Kembar), cooking oils (Bimoli) and margarine (Simas Palmia).

THE PHILIPPINES

Remarkably, the Philippines enjoys the longest tradition of intellectual property protection in the Southeast Asia region, as the first intellectual property decree was introduced by the Spanish colonial power in the early 19th century. Despite this tradition, it remains on the US government's list of IP transgressor nations because of the weaknesses in its patent protection and failures in addressing digital piracy.

The only way is up

Officials are trying to shore up the number of Filipino inventions being patented, as well as encouraging the registration of designs and trademarks, all of which have declined significantly in recent years.

In 2006 patent applications totalled 4,766—a minimal improvement from a decade earlier when applications hit 4,238. Of the 2006 applications, only three per cent came from Filipinos. This more or less continued the poor performance of domestic applicants during the first four years of the millennium, when 96.4 per cent of Philippines patents were granted to foreigners, although this was a slight improvement on the 1990s when the figure was 98 per cent. Remarkably also, between 1948 and 2006, only 21 patents were granted to universities and research and development institutes.

There can be little surprise that the Director of the Intellectual Property Office Philippines (IP Philippines), Carmen G. Peralta admitted in October 2008 that intellectual property protection remains a second priority among Philippines policy makers.

However, IP Philippines considered that it had a good year in 2009. Figures retrieved for January to November 2009 show that patent and trademark applications increased more than four times. There were 577 patent and trademark applications filed during the 11-month period, compared to 139 in the previous year. IP Philippines attributes the growth to the regional IP satellite offices set up in Cebu, Angeles, Davao, Legazpi and Baguio, which deal with IP applications in the provinces.

Bio-pirates ahoy!

Complaints are often heard in the country about so-called "biopiracy" and "theft" by foreigners of Filipino discoveries. In 2008 the Director-General of IP Philippines noted how many of the Philippines' bio-diversity and genetic resources were being lost to foreign patenting without benefits flowing back to the country.

Dr Lourdes Jansuy Cruz, a Filipino scientist from Diliman, the University of the Philippines, recently won recognition for a discovery that would plug a big gap in the painkiller market, but at the same time she learnt the hard way that the actual discovery is only the first step towards putting a successful drug on the market.

In the 1970s and 1980s, Cruz was involved in discovering Contoxins—toxins from peptides found in the venom of *Conus* snails found in the Philippines—known to be a thousand times more powerful than the drug morphine. Study on the *Conus* snail had begun in the 1970s when Cruz's partner on the project, Dr Baldomero Olivera, discovered from local farmers that some marine snails could kill people. The two doctors worked out that snail venom had many components affecting the nerves and muscles. There are 300 different species of *Conus* snails in the Philippines alone and 700 worldwide, with each species containing 100 to 200 different peptides. Their study would provide a lifetime's research for a number of scientists, observes Cruz.

For her efforts, Cruz was chosen as one of the five winners of the 2010 L'Oréal-UNESCO Women In Science Awards, an award given to one exceptional woman researcher per continent each year and for which there are usually over 1,000 nominees. She received the US$100,000 (PHP4.6 million) prize and the honour of being the first Filipino winner of such an award.

This may seem like a paltry reward for a discovery hailed as an alternative to morphine. And it is. One of the peptides found in the research carried out by Cruz and Olivera was developed by a US biotechnology firm Cognetix Corp, later bought by Elan Pharmaceuticals. The drug Prialt ziconotodine (Prialt) was launched in 2008 and has been a huge commercial success, generating revenues of US$4.7 million in the third quarter of 2009 alone. However, the scientists have received no royalties or indeed anything else for Prialt from Cognetix or Elan. Cruz recalls: "Olivera tried to write to the company, [saying], 'You know, you should at least give [us something].' They didn't want to." Looking back, the Filipino scientists realise that failing to get US patents for the many peptides that were isolated and identified during their 15 years of research may have been a huge mistake, although obviously it would have been very expensive to do so. They are also realistic enough to accept that the costs of the drug development and the testing involved in getting it ready for the market was way beyond their resources and at least they "opened the playing field for the study of snail toxins".

Despite these setbacks, the country does have its IP champions.

Jollibee

From beginnings in 1975 as a two-branch ice-cream parlour, Jollibee has grown to be a fast-food giant with almost 2,000 outlets worldwide. Total sales for the first half of 2009 were PHP29 billion. Its most popular brand, Jollibee, is known all over Asia.

The brand name was chosen by founder Tony Tan Caktiong, after changing his ice-cream parlour name from Magnolia in 1975. The change in the company's focus from ice-cream to hamburgers and fries came in 1978, along with Tan Caktiong's business manager and mentor who changed the brand name first from Jolibe to Jolly Bee, then finally pushed the two words together to form Jollibee—with the connotations of a bee's hard work, honey representing the sweet things in life, and "jolly" obviously meaning happiness and enjoyment.

In the late 1970s Tan Caktiong heard rumours that the most famous burger chain in the world was going to expand into the Philippines. "They will eat you alive," his friends predicted. When they told him that he would either have to sell Jollibee to McDonald's or become one of its franchisees, Tan Caktiong had a third suggestion: "I can fight McDonald's."

He travelled to the home of fast-food and the Golden Arches, the USA, to study how it was done there and, back in the Philippines, transformed Jollibee by adding drive-throughs, colourful uniforms and food adapted to suit Filipino tastes. In 1980 the smiling red bee mascot was born, featuring in Jollibee's first TV commercials. The "Langhap-Sarap" ("smells delicious") advertising slogan, which it still uses today, also helped strengthen Jollibee since it played to the local Filipino view that good food smells good. By the time McDonald's opened its first store in the country, its red-haired clown and hamburgers had nothing new to offer the Filippino people, compared to its local competitor which already had nine stores running and an aggressive marketing strategy.

In 2002 *The Economist* commented: "The Philippines is a huge embarrassment to McDonald's ... In 1981, when the golden arches first went up in Manila, everybody assumed that McDonald's would rule the Filipino market, as so many others ... By the 1990s, Jollibee was trouncing its rival so thoroughly that McDonald's was forced to choose between retreat and imitation. McDonald's denies that it has opted for the latter, but that is how it looks—and tastes—to Filipinos."

A Taylor Nelson Sofres survey conducted in 2001 showed that Jollibee was the most frequently visited hamburger chain, with 69 per cent of the respondents admitting to doing so, compared to 16 per cent saying they visited McDonald's.

By the end of the 1980s Jollibee was in the top 100 companies in the Philippines and was the first Filipino fast-food chain to cross the PHP1 billion sales mark.

Since its massive home-grown success, Jollibee has gone global and expanded into different areas of fast-food. In 1994 it bought an 80 per cent stake in another Filipino-owned chain named Greenwich, a pizza chain started by Cresida Tueres that had 50 branches at the time. Rapid expansion ensued. By 2005 Greenwich had grown to over 240 branches and Jollibee bought the remaining 20 per cent in 2006 for PHP384 million in cash.

In the meantime, the company had diversified again. In January 2000 it acquired an Asian quick-food chain named Chowking. It entered the Chinese market in October 2008, acquiring Hongzhuangyuan, a Beijing porridge store with 38 restaurants throughout China, for PHP2.5 billion.

Along with these acquisitions, Jollibee has invested millions of pesos in its brand, registering its Jollibee trademark and logo around the world. By the end of 2008, the company owned 135 registered trademarks in over 34 countries, from Argentina to Vietnam. Tan Caktiong himself attributes his success to his brand, noting in an interview with WIPO on the importance of IP rights: "It's a very competitive world; you need to create something unique." Clearly the company is doing something right: in 2009 it opened its 27th store in the US, and its second store in Las Vegas, Nevada, moving towards achieving its aim of having 3,000 stores outside the Philippines by 2020.

Nature's Legacy Eximport

One of the most developed provinces in the Philippines, Cebu, is home to Nature's Legacy Eximport, a small-scale home-furnishings business that has transformed itself into an internationally-known company that is one of the Philippines' Invisible Gold success stories.

Founders Catherine and Pedro Delantar, along with other local businesses, had been producing hand-carved natural Mactan stone products from resources found in Cebu. To compete more effectively with more established exporters, the Delantars came up with a new product that simulated the look and feel of Mactan stone but was lighter and more durable. The couple then set up the Nature's Legacy company in 1996 and registered the name as a trademark too. It now has 26 utility model patent registrations to its name in the Philippines and also claims copyright protection for its product designs.

Splash Corporation

Drs Rolando and Rosalinda Hortaleza are in the *Forbes Asia* List of 40 Richest in the Philippines, with a net worth of US$90 million. The couple's business, Splash Corporation, has progressed a long way from their first innovative idea of repackaging hairspray back in 1985.

Under the original company name, RBH Cosmetics, the couple sold hairspray formulations that could be easily transferred from aerosol cans to cheap and reusable plastic squeeze-spray containers. They then developed their own hairspray product that could be sold in this way. Its success earned the couple their first PHP1 million in 1987. By 1989 the re-named Splash had launched a completely different product—the first fruit-based facial cleanser in the Philippines under the trademark, Extract. This product quickly established itself, with sales of PHP40 million and rose to be No. 2 in the cosmetics market.

Twenty years later, the company has grown into the largest Filipino-owned manufacturer of skin-care products with its hugely successful brand Maxipeel™, commanding an 84 per cent share of the Philippines market. Splash generated PHP3.165 billion in revenue in 2008 and has expanded its international presence into more than 30 countries as far apart as the US and Nigeria.

Again, Splash Corporation attributes its worldwide success to its IP strategy of constant innovation and product differentiation. The company owns over 120 trademarks and has more than 200 pending trademark registrations. Its main brands such as Extraderm, Skin White and Biolink are registered in more than

50 countries. Splash also has more than 15 patents granted in the area of skin-care products and medicinal herbal teas, a market it has recently expanded into.

Perhaps Splash learnt an early lesson on the importance of protecting your innovative products. The company launched Extract in 1988. Even though sales reached PHP40 million it was easily copied by competitors because there was no IP protection surrounding the product. As a result, Splash's leadership of the astringent market lasted for only two years, as "me-too" products took away its market share. The company learnt its lesson. When it developed a new product in 1991 called Extraderm, it made sure that was protected by utility model patents as well as the trademark registration. Splash rocketed to the top of the personal care industry when Extraderm was launched and gained its first PHP billion revenues. Now, with every product developed by the company as much IPR protection as possible is secured to keep imitators at bay whilst building brand awareness.

San Miguel

San Miguel is one of the world's best-selling beers and is in the top 10 beer brands in the world. Its parent company, since 1963 named San Miguel Corporation (SMC) after its best-known product, is the largest publicly listed food, beverages and packaging company in Southeast Asia, with over 100 manufacturing facilities in the Philippines, Australia, China, Hong Kong, Indonesia and Vietnam. Because nine out of every 10 bottles of beer consumed in the Philippines is brewed by San Miguel, SMC is rarely known for anything else despite the breadth of its commercial activities.

Enrique Barretto y de Ycaza founded and named his brewery company after Saint Michael the Archangel, the trade name stemming originally from a local brewery in Barcelona, Spain, and the name of a district in Manila where Barretto lived and worked. On 29 September 1890, Barretto received a royal grant from Spain to open Southeast Asia's first brewery in Manila near the Palace of the Governor-General of the Philippines. By 1896 San Miguel was outselling imported beer brands by five to one.

San Miguel's fierce competitive streak and powerful global brand, with its heavy association with beer, has been disadvantageous to the company at times. In the 1970s a Filipino competitor, Asia Brewery, entered the domestic beer market with a bargain-priced beer under the descriptive name Beer (also known as "Beer na Beer"), which looked and tasted very similar to San Miguel's famous product. This clever marketing played on the fact that beer had become synonymous with San Miguel. After the upstart started to take significant market share, SMC retaliated in 1990 by filing a complaint in the Philippine courts against Asia Brewery for trademark infringement and unfair competition. Successful at first, they lost in the Supreme Court.

Not everyone is trying to emulate the San Miguel brand. The Philippines' San Miguel beer brand co-exists with a Spanish counterpart, Cerveza San Miguel beer, often sparking debates about which came first. The brands' logos differ slightly: SMC's trademark consists of "San Miguel" often written horizontally on its bottles and canned beer, with the "S" in San and the "M" in Miguel written in red in gothic letters with fine strokes of serif, and the rest of the lettering in black. SMC also has the Escudo—the official seal of Manila City that was on the document bearing the original royal grant from Spain. On the other hand, Cerveza San Miguel from Spain has a slightly different green and red font (although also written diagonally on products), together with a galleon in full sail on the top of the label.

The Spanish beer's origins date back only to 1946, when Andres Soriano, then-President of SMC, set up a brewery in Spain named La Segarra and gave it a licence to brew San Miguel beer. Seven years later, the La Segarra shareholders signed "the Manila Agreement" with Soriano, cutting ties with the Philippines parent company but retaining the right to produce its own line of San Miguel branded beer. To make it worse for its old parent, La Segarra later changed its company name to San Miguel, Fabricas de Cerveza y Malta S.A. in 1957. In 2000 it was bought by Mahou S.A. and the Mahou-San Miguel Group is now Spain's largest brewer. The two San Miguel Groups now have no connection with one another.

In recent years SMC has fast-tracked its way into the highest beer-consumption market in Asia—Thailand, by purchasing Thai Amarit Brewery's assets for PHP5,459 million (US$97 million) in 2004. SMC went further Down Under, picking up some lucrative and well-established brands on the way. J. Boag & Son Ltd, from Launceston, Tasmania—"a long way from anywhere in 1881", according to its own advertising—became a wholly-owned subsidiary of SMC in 2000 for AU$92 million. Boag is a key player in Australia's premier beer industry. On the non-beer side, SMC also bought Melbourne-based dairy-product maker National Foods in 2004, adding famous brands Pura Milk, Yoplait yoghurt and Berri Juices to its portfolio and expanding its dairy market into Indonesia, New Zealand and Malaysia. However, SMC's foray into the Australian beer market only lasted seven years when it off-loaded J. Boag & Son to Tasman brewer Lion Nathan for AU$325 million in November 2007, two-and-a-half times more than it had paid originally.

In an attempt to leverage the value of its global brand, SMC recently engaged in "brand-splitting", when San Miguel Beverages (SMB) was spun-off from its parent company in July 2007. The company's domestic beer assets were transferred into a wholly-owned subsidiary that would concentrate on its beer empire alone. It is important to realise that although SMB continued to build up the value of the San Miguel brand, it did not own it at that time. The 2007 asset transfer excluded land, income and valuable intellectual property. SMB only had an exclusive licence to use the SMB brand and other IPRs, paying to SMC a monthly royalty fee of two per cent of its sales revenues. Since then, SMB has bought the rights from SMC.

Throughout SMC and SMB's beer domination, they have not been alone. They've had their own bully. Japan's second-largest beer maker, Kirin Holdings, has been in the shadows, pursuing an aggressive strategy to become Asia and Oceania's dominant beer maker. It all started in 2001 when Kirin became a shareholder in SMC, with a 15 per cent stake worth US$536 million. Four years later the Japanese company raised its stake to 19.7 per cent.

Kirin was also involved in SMC's exit from the Australian premium beer and dairy-foods market when Lion Nathan, of which it owns 46 per cent, took Boag off SMC's hands. It also acquired National Foods from SMC for AU$2.8 million.

SMB was not the only one to realise the hidden value in San Miguel; Kirin did too, and was very much interested in San Miguel's Invisible Gold. SMB's recent spin-off from its parent and its buy-back of its property and IPR assets saw Kirin simultaneously selling its 20 per cent stake in SMC and purchasing a huge 43.25 per cent stake in SMB for a whopping ¥100 billion (US$1.06 billion). The deal was completed in May 2009.

Chikka Asia

Started as a dot.com company in 2000 by Denis Mendiola and a group of investors, Manila-headquartered Chikka Asia has created the world's first mobile instant messenger—the Chikka Text Messenger (CTM). Users log on to Chikka by SMS, even receiving messages when offline. Named after Filipino slang for "small-talk", Chikka was designed with its home country in mind as by 2000 the Philippines was called the "Text Capital of the World" because of its high volumes of SMS usage (over 30 million messages sent daily).

Chikka's pioneering SMS features are protected by the largest portfolio of patents for SMS applications worldwide. Bidshot, which was acquired by Chikka in 2002, had obtained patents for the first SMS-enabled auction site, where one is alerted on the status of a bid and is able to then bid via SMS. Features like outbid, sale alerts and wireless message boards are all patent-protected in one country or another, as is the feature that sellers and buyers can interact anonymously whilst bidding. Between 2002 and 2004, a total of 12 patents had been filed by Chikka and its affiliates.

In 2009 a subsidiary of Philippine Long Distance Telephone Co (PDLT), Smart Communication Inc, agreed to purchase Chikka Holdings, the parent company of the group, for an undisclosed sum. At the time, Chikka was reported to have 34 granted patents and over 40 applications pending approval.

Some Filipino companies have also shown that, as an alternative to building their own from scratch, they recognise the importance of acquiring companies that have invested heavily in their IPRs.

Pancake House Inc

Like Jollibee, Pancake House Inc (PHI) made its name supplying the Philippine consumer with something other than rice-based food. Today it has far more than pancakes up its sleeve. Multi-branding is now the name of its game. When consumers grow tired of a brand,

Chairman Martin P. Lorenzo believes in buying a fresh new one to attract them back.

Started in 1970 by Milagros Basa, Leticia Zamora and Carmen Zaragosa, PHI only began to grow when it was bought by Lorenzo and his investor group. Lorenzo originally had his reservations about the venture, telling people that his decision to buy the chain seemed like a "big mistake"; Pancake House was "just losing money". However, he went ahead and bought all the operating assets from Extrovert Corporation (the then-owner of Pancake House outlets), including its trademarks, trade names, service marks and other IPRs such as the secret recipes for food made by the restaurant, along with supplier and customer lists and all the existing franchise agreements. Lorenzo then refreshed the Pancake House brand, refurbishing the restaurants, employing new management and staff and expanding the menus.

He was also careful to prevent competition from the chain's old owners. His investor group also purchased the IPRs, business name and recipes of a separate and distinct corporation called Pancake Connection Inc, in which Basa, one of the founders of Pancake House, was a shareholder.

Under the new owners, the chain grew from 22 outlets in 2000 to triple that figure by the second quarter of 2006, with 66 outlets. By June 2008 it had 81 outlets.

Pancake House invested heavily in franchising its brand, winning awards as well as acquiring add-on brands. Royalties from franchisees in 2008 alone increased by PHP2.19 million to PHP13 million and before that had been growing steadily from year to year as the number of franchises increased. In 2004 Pancake House acquired Dencio Food Specialists (DFSI), particularly for its branded chain of restaurants, Dencio's, and associated IPRs.

In its next venture, Pancake House bought Japanese restaurant chain Teriyaki Boy, paying PHP274.5 million for the trademarks of the Teriyaki Boy alone, worth 82 per cent of the total purchase price. By offering Japanese-style food adapted to Filipino tastes and aiming at the Filipino teen market with Japanese *anime* designs, Teriyaki Boy became the leading Japanese brand in the Philippines in the casual dining industry just two months after acquisition. By the end of 2008, Teriyaki Boy had 35 outlets and revenues of PHP321.17 million.

In 2009 Pancake House showed that its ambitions are not limited to the home market. It purchased the French bakery chain Le Coeur de France for PHP105 million, aiming to establish it in Vietnam, a former French colony. The trademark Le Coeur de France and other related intellectual property rights were valued at PHP53 million, just over half of the entire purchase price of PHP105 million. This acquisition brought Pancake House's group to 150 outlets, generating PHP3 billion in sales—all going to show the value of Pancake House's portfolio of Invisible Gold.

Edgardo Vasquez

On the other hand, an illustration of how difficult it can be for innovators in the country is provided by the experience of engineer and inventor Edgardo Vasquez.

In December 2007, the Regional Trial Court of Quezon City (RTC) found Avida Land Corporation (Avida) liable for patent infringement and ordered it to pay Vasquez and his company, Vasquez Building Systems Corporation (VBSC), PHP96.5 million (around US$2.4 million at the time) in damages and attorney's fees of PHP500,000. Vasquez had started the legal action seven years before in December 1999.

In 1989 Vasquez had applied for a Philippine patent for his invention relating to a prefabricated modular housing unit and the process of using column panels and roofing assembly to build a house. The patent was granted in March 1994 and Vasquez assigned it to VBSC. Between 1992 and 1997, Avida contracted with VBSC to construct modular housing units using Vasquez's invention. VBSC even set up a satellite casting plant on Avida's site to expedite the completion of its mass housing projects.

Some time in 1997, Vasquez discovered that Avida had been using his invention in the construction of additional mass housing projects without his knowledge or consent. In response to Vasquez's complaint about this, Avida said that it was not using his invention but instead was licensed to use the Tex system owned by Tex Holdings Plc, an English company that had its own patent.

Not accepting this, Vasquez sued for patent infringement in 1999. An exhausting seven years later, the Quezon City court decided in his favour. The court held that the Tex patent and even another patent, the Phenix patent, did not help Avida because the Vasquez patent was filed earlier than either of them.

On the issue of damages, the court awarded PHP90 million for income lost by Vasquez, which would have been earned if the business relationship with Avida had continued; PHP5 million to compensate for the irritation and depression suffered; and PHP1 million to teach Avida not to infringe intellectual property rights belonging to others.

Despite the difficulties and official lack of interest in IPRs, WIPO estimated in a 2008 study that copyright-based industries (CBIs) contributed 4.82 per cent or PHP144 billion to the Philippines' GDP from 1999 to 2003. These CBIs employed about

317,000 people, or approximately 11.1 per cent of the total work force of large businesses.

Unsurprisingly, the largest contributors were the core copyright industries, comprising the film, software, publishing and entertainment industries, which accounted for 3.5 per cent of GDP. Among these sectors, publishing was the top contributor, accounting for 2.13 per cent of GDP. However, the study did note that the contribution to exports of the Philippines' copyright-based industries declined from 18.18 per cent in 1999 to 13.34 per cent in 2004. There seems little doubt that the government needs to focus more on encouraging its businesses to develop and exploit their own IPRs.

THAILAND

After Thailand's economic bust following the Southeast Asian crisis in 1997, the country has strived to make progress in its economic development. This has not been easy and the ongoing political turmoil involving supporters of former Prime Minister Thaksin Shinawatra has made it even harder. GDP growth, for example, has been unsteady, at two per cent in 2008, dropping from 3.8 per cent in 2007. This relative lack of growth has been attributed by some to the country's reputation for widespread piracy and counterfeiting. The Obama Administration in its May 2009 US Trade Report contended that the "Thai government has made little progress … in addressing the widespread problems of piracy and counterfeiting" and kept the kingdom on the priority watch list for the US Trade Representative. In 2007 Thailand lost certain trading privileges with the US after overriding patent protection on two HIV drugs and a heart drug, although the country argued that it was entitled to do this by the TRIPs Agreement.

Thai patents

As for recent patent application figures in the country, for reasons not clear only 1,388 patent applications were filed in 2007, with 232 patents being granted. This is a very low figure when compared with the 6,248 patent applications in 2006, and grant of 1,121. Nevertheless, the figures seem to suggest that Thai locals are becoming more innovative. In 2005 and 2006, a mere 14 per cent of patent applications were made whereas in 2007 just under two-thirds (63 per cent) were filed by Thai locals. Unfortunately, it is not really possible to work out the extent to which those "Thais" are in fact the Thai subsidiaries of foreign companies (such as the leading "Thai" design patent owner, Delta Electronics (Thailand), which is a subsidiary of a Taiwanese company) and therefore the IPR is not under the control of Thais. Similarly, there were over 550 US patents granted to Thais between 1976 and 2006 but only around one in five belonged to domestic Thai companies as opposed to Thai subsidiaries of mostly multinationals.

Thailand's recent efforts to strengthen its IP protection must be noted—efforts the Thai government emphasises when trying to persuade foreign investors that it is safer to invest in its country than in China. After many abortive attempts, Thailand has joined the Patent Cooperation Treaty (PCT), becoming its 142nd member with effect from the end of 2009. This gives Thai inventors the opportunity to register patents outside their country more quickly and cheaply. Hopefully it will encourage foreign filings by Thais, which in 2005 numbered only 17 in Japan and 14 at the European Patent Office. In the United States, 37 patents were granted to Thais in 2005—fewer than in 1998—a third of which were in the electronics field.

Recent initiatives

Furthermore, several initiatives have been taken to encourage Thai SMEs to obtain greater IP protection. Thailand's Science and Technology Ministry has teamed up with the Commerce Ministry to launch low-cost licensed software and financial accounting software that will last for a year, to be given to SMEs to improve competitiveness and help those companies develop their business strategy. Similarly, a public-private partnership is planned by the Science and Technology Ministry, to help businesses that struggle with technology absorption. It is hoped that such an initiative will help boost R&D investment in the economy.

An even more ambitious plan is being considered by the Commerce Ministry: to create the world's first IP securities market in Thailand—a stock exchange for IP products. The aim is to facilitate the commercialision of IP and generate higher returns for the economy. In June 2009, Deputy Commerce Minister Alongkon Ponlaboot unveiled the idea, with a finalised plan to be submitted to Prime Minister Abhisit Vejjajiva for consideration: "Innovators with low investment capital would have a chance to trade in the IP securities market … [which would trade] any IP goods, including songs, lyrics, software, books, films and food recipes."

Royal inventions

Thailand is highly unusual in having a head of state who himself is an active user of the IP system. In January 2009, the King of Thailand, King Bhumibol Adulyadej, received from Dr Francis Gurry, Director-General of WIPO, an award for his outstanding commitment to promoting IP rights in Thailand and his outstanding contributions as an inventor. The King has had more than 20 patents granted in his name—one invention being artificial rainmaking technology with practical rural benefits in Thailand—as well as 19 trademarks.

Whilst Thailand still has a very long way to go to make IPRs an integral part of the country's economy, there are interesting examples of Thai businesses creating and innovating while making good use of the IP system. Many of the key players hail from Thailand's richest families. Indeed, in *Forbes* magazine's Thailand's 40 Richest list there is an unusually high number of tycoons with fortunes made in IPR-rich sectors such as food and beverages, broadcasting and media stations, and telecoms, to name a few, as opposed to real estate and services such as hospital operators and insurance, which are key industries in Thailand but not ones which rely on IPRs to any great extent.

Rice production

Thailand is the world's biggest rice exporter, with over 10 million metric tons exported in 2009/10. What is remarkable, however, is how so few of the many fortunes generated in Thailand actually depend on this staple food product.

Despite this, Thailand has big problems looming in its paddy fields. Its well-known Khao Hom-Mali rice, also known as jasmine-scented rice, faces stiff competition from developed countries as they seek to patent strains of the grain. Half of Thailand's rice revenue comes from jasmine rice, which sells for around US$1,000 per tonne, compared to normal white rice at around US$550 to US$580 a tonne, and is largely exported to the USA. However, Louisiana State University Agri-Centre has invented a new variety of aromatic rice (given the quirky name of Jazzman) as an alternative to jasmine rice and has a pending plant variety patent application at the US Department of Agriculture. This has led to protests from the Isarn farmers of north-west Thailand, which have gone all the way to the

Thai government in Bangkok. Even though it is thought that the Jazzman rice strain was actually developed from a Chinese strain of rice, there remain fears that it will still affect sales of Thai-imported rice in the US if it is actively marketed by branding and packaging appearance as an alternative to jasmine rice.

There are mixed feelings also over patent applications that have been made by Thais in Thailand covering the aroma of jasmine rice—in technical terms, "transgenic rice with reduced expression of Os2AP and elevated levels of 2-acetyl-1-pyroline". The King of Thailand has praised the scientists involved in patenting the aroma, but local farmers and legal scholars have questioned whether it is such a good idea. Somchai Ratanachueskul, a lecturer in law at the Thai Chamber of Commerce University, has warned that it may lead to mass patenting by huge agricultural companies of local resources in the country. On the other hand, the National Science and Technology Development Agency (NSDTA) argues that Thai people must themselves act to protect such inventions for fear of other countries acting first. The NSDTA probably had in mind the problems with the patenting of basmati rice strains encountered by India and its neighbouring countries.

Agarwood harvests

Aromatic agarwood is dark, resinous heartwood that forms in *Aqualaria* trees native to Southeast Asia. Known as the "wood of the gods", it was originally found growing in the wilds of the eastern India states, down to Bangladesh, Thailand, Indochina, even in Papua New Guinea. Now it has been over-harvested in the wild and has become such a rarity that it has been listed since 1995 as a potentially threatened species under the Convention on International Trade in Endangered Species of Wild Fauna and Flora. However, the agarwood business has become very lucrative for Thai businesses, with seven of the 17 known species growing in the country. The value lies in the oil that the tree produces, whose market price ranges from US$50,000 to US$80,000 per litre, especially if of high quality.

The story goes that local Thai tycoon Dr Boon Vanasin, when invited to a banquet held by the crown prince of Saudia Arabia, discovered that burning agarwood cost the prince THB10 million. Researching into agarwood's market potential, he found that the agarwood market was estimated at more than THB180 million a year. This led to the formation of Krissana Panasin Company, which deals with agarwood development. The company has developed its own agarwood varieties named Panasin, using seeds from the best agarwood varieties in Thailand. Boon boasts that his company was also the first to bio-engineer agarwood trees to create heartwood that will grow throughout the whole tree.

Despite such success for Krissana, the immense value of agarwood has led to allegations of patent infringement against the company and others. Agarwood Siam Co. launched a lawsuit in July 2007 against Krissana and another agarwood grower, Touchwood Forestry Co, for using Agarwood Siam's 2005 Thai patent covering a "wound-making technique to stimulate *Aquilaria* resin in *Aquilaria* trees". Agarwood Siam asked for damages totalling THB110 million from the two companies. However, in May 2009 the Intellectual Property Court in Bangkok dismissed the Agarwood Siam complaint.

Charoen Pokphand Group

Charoen Pokphand Group (known as Chia Tai Group in China) is Thailand's biggest conglomerate and one of the first Asian multinational companies. It is also probably the world's largest chicken producer and animal feed miller. With over 250 companies in 20 different countries, it reported revenues of US$19 billion in 2008.

Established in 1921, when Chia brothers Ek Chor and Siew Whooy opened a small seed shop in Thailand importing seeds to sell to Thai farmers, its operations now range from food production and agri-business to seeds, telecoms and Internet service providers, retail (bringing 7-Eleven stores to Thailand as franchisee) and real estate, even to financial investment. The group has expanded all around Asia, mostly in the animal feed and livestock farming business, trading primarily under the CP trademark and logo. Within its largest subsidiary, Charoen Pokphand Foods (CPF), it has many brands used under the housemark, Kitchen of the World.

Despite its vast empire, the CP Group narrowly escaped the 1997 Asian financial crisis. A slimmed-down business was restructured from nine business groups into three core areas: food production, telecommunications and services. Spending on R&D was increased, particularly aiming at improving the efficiency of technology in the animal feed businesses and developing proprietary seeds and plants.

For example, CP Crop Integration has made the headlines with its hybrid technology rice, investing about THB30 million per year in R&D on the rice seed. Beginning its project in the early 2000s, it now offers to the world commercial seeds capable of producing up to 20 per cent higher yields than other rice varieties. This area has proved lucrative. Revenues in 2008 were at THB2.2 billion, with customers as far afield as Bangladesh, Nepal and Ukraine.

Seed ownership and plant protection does not stop there. CP Crop Integration has diversified into rubber plantations in the north and northeast of Thailand to tap the China market, where demand is high. The aim here is to develop a new rubber plant variety with increased yields. At the same time, it is developing both new products for use in plantations and an automatic tapping device capable of drawing more latex. It is also working alongside the National Metal and Materials Technology Centre to develop a cheaper and more efficient palm-crushing system suitable for community use.

Where next for the CP Group? Apparently, into software. It has established a technology subsidiary in Shanghai-Zicure Corporation, which will develop proprietary software for use in retailing.

Stars Microelectronics

Stars Microelectronics (SMT) is another Thai company that is neither short of innovative ideas nor profits. The company manufactures microelectronic modules for touch-screen products and integrated circuits (IC), and boasts of being capable of producing 80 million microelectronic pieces a year and 700 million pieces of IC chips to go into products such as bar code scanners, optical mouse sensors and personal multimedia sensors. Described as a world-class electronics company when given the SME Technology runner-up award in Thailand's Innovation Awards in 2003, SMT's net profit has continued to increase despite the economic downturn. Net profit was THB45 million in 2005 and in the following three years increased more than 350 per cent to THB201 million.

To what does SMT attribute its success? According to its co-founder and chief executive Polsak Lertputipinyo, one of the main things is "high technology". With high technology comes innovation and usually innovation protection. The company expresses itself proud of the patents it has received to protect its innovations—for example, for electronic modules for use in agricultural machinery.

SMT also gained recognition for inventing Thailand's first rice colour-sorter, able to separate mixed rice according to grade—a product that is not an obvious one for a leading microelectronics company to come up with. The company adapted technology used elsewhere in building this invention. Using two high-speed cameras to capture the colour of the grain, the engineering team used line-scanning technology to scan the rice from left to right at a speed of 15,000 lines per second. Light that illuminates the rice also captures image data, which is sent to processors that can calculate the position of the contaminants. This information is sent to 86 ejectors, which blow out the targeted contaminants in the rice. A patent was obtained by SMT for the jet technology used in the ejection process, which discards no grain other than that targeted.

Narai Intertrade

Far away from the high-tech patent end of the IPR spectrum, Thai businesses have also succeeded in building successful brands.

Wasna Lathouras is the president of Narai Intertrade, which markets NaRaYa fabrics. When working as a tour guide in Samut Prakan province, she met a Greek businessman by the name of Vassilios Lathouras, who soon became her husband and business partner. Together, they founded Narai Intertrade in 1989 to trade in automotive spare parts and electrical equipment, but quickly expanded into fabric bags and accessories. The Lathouras began to market, under the company's own brand name, fabric bags made by villagers throughout Thailand. The brand they chose for this was NaRaYa—named after the Hindu god Phra Narai and chosen for its easy pronunciation.

By 2008 the company was subcontracting nearly 80 per cent of its production to more than 3,000 families around the country who produced a variety of bags in different designs and fabric patterns. In addition, it had more than 600 staff working at its Bangkok factory.

Narai has shops throughout Thailand, and overseas in countries such as Japan, Taiwan, Singapore, Hungary and Saudi Arabia. The company has also expanded into kitchenware, home décor and children's items. But, a successful business will always attract imitators: by the middle of 2007, Narai was suing a number of traders in China, Taiwan and Vietnam for copying its designs and infringing its trademark. The previous year it was forced to bring a successful legal action against its own sole agent in South Korea for copyright infringement.

As a result of her company's experiences, Khun Wasna told *The Nation* newspaper at this time:

> "Despite the high cost of registering intellectual property rights overseas, it is worth it to ensure long-lasting benefits from a company's creativity."

Thai Union Frozen Foods

Set up in 1988 with initial funding of THB25 million and a joint venture with Mitsubishi Corporation and Hagoromo Food Corporation of Japan, Thai Union Frozen Foods had its origins a decade before when founder Kraisorn Chansiri acquired a failing tuna cannery in Samutsakorn, near Bangkok. Along with his son Thiraphong, he invested in developing technology for processing smaller fish under two kilos.

Today, the group is Thailand's leading producer of frozen and canned seafood. Its third quarter 2009 results saw net profit breaking through the THB1 billion mark, a 12 per cent increase from the same period in 2008.

Thai Union's most profitable activity is the export of frozen and canned food products. Its overseas investments in this area have hit the headlines particularly through its Chicken of the Sea trademark, which is the third largest canned tuna brand on the American market.

The brand, a mermaid with a sceptre, was originally created by the Van Camp Seafood Company from California and first appeared on Chicken of the Sea products in 1952. In 1997 Van Camp Seafood's assets were acquired by Tri Union Seafood, a partnership made up of Thai Union, Tri-Marine International (the leading raw tuna trading company from Singapore) and Edmund Gann, a successful tuna-fishing fleet operator. In 2000 Thai Union became sole owner of Chicken of the Sea International (the new name of Van Camp Seafood Company) when the other partners sold out for US$38.5 million.

Thai Union continues to expand its reserves of Invisible Gold both inside and outside Thailand. For example, one of its subsidiaries, Thai Union Feedmill, manufactures and distributes aquaculture feed under trademarks such as Nanami, EGO Feed and Shobu, along with other products sold under the Fisho and Sealect brands.

When the group tried to expand into the China market, it initially set up its own marketing subsidiaries to help establish its brands. When this turned out to be unsuccessful, the group did not hesitate to change course. The different route was taken of paying US$4 million in 2005 to acquire a 50 per cent stake in Century Union (Shanghai) Foods Co. In this way, the Thai company gained better access to the market through Century's brand, which was already known to local consumers.

Ever acquisitive, Thai Union Foods bought the Ace of Diamonds US trademark from Mitsubishi Corporation for US$200,000 in September 2008. The brand is used on canned tuna, seafood, vegetables and fruit products.

At the end of 2008, Thai Union's intellectual property assets were valued at THB754.4 million.

Osotspa International

In an interview with *USA Today* in July 2008, Osotspa International President Soonthorn Kengvibul boasted that Osotspa is "one of the leading companies in Thailand that invests in branding. Most of the products in Thailand (mainly in exports) don't invest much in branding".

Osotspa's story started almost 120 years ago when a small pharmaceutical company named Teck Heng Yoo opened a little shop based in Yaoawarat, Bangkok's Chinatown. The Pae family developed a pharmaceutical product under the Kilane trademark to respond to a dysentery outbreak suffered by the Thai army. The success of Kilane was followed by that of Krisnaklan, a traditional Chinese medicine for stomach aches. The company continued to prosper, diversifying into medicines, food products, personal care, health and hygiene products and, finally, beverages, where it had its greatest success.

In 1969 Taisho Pharmaceutical from Japan granted Osotspa a licence to make the energy-drink Lipovitan-D in Thailand. Eleven years later, Osotspa started to manufacture its own energy drink under the Magnum brand. Today, Osotspa claims to have around two-thirds of the market for energy drinks in Thailand, more than four times T.C. Pharmaceutical's Krating Daeng (the original Red Bull). The Osotspa portfolio of drinks includes M-150, an electrolyte drink; M-Sport; Hang, a specialty drink claimed to relieve hangovers; and the various Shark products, including variants such as lite, sugar-free and an alcoholic version containing vodka.

Osotspa has been baring its teeth to protect its Shark trademark, trying to prevent rival energy-drink makers from using any aspect of the mark. In August 2004, Osotspa was successful in legal proceedings in Florida to stop Impulse Beverage from selling products bearing a shark logo similar in design to Osotspa's. Impulse was ordered by the court to repackage its cans, redesign its trucks and launch a new ad campaign.

Across the Atlantic at the European Trademark Office in Spain the following year, Osotspa opposed a German company's application to register as a trademark for energy drinks the word "Hai", on the ground that it is the word for "shark" in German and Dutch. The opposition was unsuccessful because the court considered there are obvious visual and aural differences between "Shark" and "Hai" (even though the concepts were similar because of the meaning), especially as energy-boosting drinks are bought on their visual appearance.

Univanich Palm Oil

Univanich Palm Oil is an example of a Thai business that has evolved from being a joint venture with a foreign partner who provided technology and know-how, to an independent business generating its own IPRs.

The company's first plantations were laid down in 1969. These produced crude palm oil and crude palm kernel oil, a useful ingredient in cooking and salad oils, margarines, soaps and shampoos. The company then expanded its activities to include palm fruit processing and a seed business. A joint venture was formed with Unilever PLC between 1983 and 1998, with Unilever holding a 51 per cent stake in Univanich during that period.

In 1998 Unilever sold out and a public company was formed between Thai Oil Palm, Siam Palm Oil and Hup Huat Palm Oil. Total revenues of the company have almost trebled in the last four years, from THB2.5 million in 2004 to THB6.9 million in 2008.

Part of that success is a result of its oil palm research, where the company operates an advanced palm-breeding programme that generates valuable IPRs and produces high-yielding hybrid seeds for sale to Thai oil palm farmers. In addition, an oil palm tissue culture laboratory was established in 2005, the first of its kind in Thailand, aiming to clone elite mother palms and develop high-quality seeds from the more than 60,000 cultures the company has under its management.

Indonesia has recognised Univanich's efforts; Indonesia is the world's largest crude palm oil cultivator, with more than five million hectares in production. However, it has previously been closed to outside seed producers because of its high-standard breeding programmes. Univanich's official seal of approval by Indonesia's Ministry of Agriculture shows the high quality of its planting materials.

Siam Safety Premier

An unusual invention from Thailand that is doing very well all over the world is a fire-extinguisher ball made by Siam Safety Premier (SSP). The product was developed by Woradech Kaimar when assisting the community fire service in Thailand. In 1997 a particularly bad fire destroyed the Royal Jomtien Hotel in Pattaya and took the lives of many tourists. This prompted Kaimar to develop a device to help fight fires in their early stages and stop them from spreading. The resulting ball-shaped fire extinguisher is lighter and more portable than cylindrical extinguishers. When rolled or thrown into a fire, the ball activates within three to 10 seconds to disperse fire-extinguishing chemicals of mono-ammonium phosphate and non-chlorofluorocarbon, which dampen flames and absorb the oxygen. The ball also has an in-built fire alarm that activates upon exploding.

In its first years of production, THB25 million was initially invested in experimentation and IP protection at the USPTO and at WIPO in Geneva. Today, the company owns patents in Thailand, China and the USA. It also has copyright and design protection, as the ball has been designed to be lighter and more fashionable to suit home décor. It is now sold under the Elide Fireball trademark.

By 2009 the ball was sold in more than 50 countries and had an export value of over THB120 million.

Again, where there are inventions, imitators follow in their shadow. In 2007 SSP unsuccessfully requested the National Intellectual Property Office of Vietnam (NOIP) to seize the Auto Fire Extinguish Ball products made by Dai Trien Import Export Trading Co, a Vietnamese company. Unsurprisingly, as SSP's patents were not granted in Vietnam, this was refused. More successfully, in August 2009, the Thai authorities seized a large number of fake fire-extinguisher balls on behalf of SSP. The seized goods—982 balls and 37,469 sheets of wrapping film—were said to have a combined worth of over THB2.25 million.

Kang Yong Electric

As is the case across Asia, many Thai companies do not themselves innovate but prefer to rely on foreign technology. A good example is Kang Yong Electric. Established in 1964 as a joint venture with Mitsubishi Electric of Japan, the company's initial business was to produce parts and assemble refrigerators, electric fans and water pumps under the Mitsubishi trademark.

Today, with total sales revenues in the year to 31 March 2009 of THB6,317 million and a net profit of THB426 million, the company still relies on its former joint-venture partner Mitsubishi, which provides the design technology and know-how. In return,

Kang Yong pays royalties and technical assistance fees, totalling THB39.5 million for the period from April to July 2009. At an audit committee of Kang Yong Electric approving the payment of that amount to Mitsubishi, it was noted pragmatically that "the Company is not ready to develop high technology by [itself], therefore the Company rely for its research and development on MELCO (Mitsubishi Electric Corporation) to develop electric home appliances under the 'Mitsubishi' trademark. As a result, the [payment] to MELCO who owns the technology and trademark is reasonable".

Heritage issues

There has also been controversy in Thailand about Thai traditional knowledge being exploited commercially by others not of Thai descent and this has spilled over into the area of IPRs too.

An example was Rusie Dutton or Hermit Body Twist, a traditional Thai exercise of body-twisting similar to yoga (which India claims as part of its heritage). As long ago as 1808, King Rama I is thought to have ordered the inscriptions and statues teaching Rusie Dutton to be inscribed on the walls of Wat Pho in Bangkok.

In February 2006 a Japanese entrepreneur, Masaki Furuya, submitted two trademark applications to the Japanese Patent Office (JPO) for Rusie Dutton (in both English and Japanese), one for books and magazines, the other as a service mark for teaching Thai body twists. Though Furuya's company was established as a non-profit organisation, the Thai Ministry of Commerce protested strongly to the JPO about its approval of the trademarks. These were revoked in June 2006. At the same time, the Thai government proposed that the 200-year-old Rusie Dutton inscriptions should be included in the UNESCO Memory of the World Programme of 2009 and this was agreed to by UNESCO in March 2008.

A NOTE ON BRUNEI

The oil-rich Brunei's legal system is still based on English common law. It has enacted new laws on copyright, designs and trademarks in the last 10 years still based on the British IP system. As a former British colony—and a country that enjoys close links with neighbouring Malaysia and Singapore—Brunei has a re-registration system that allows patent grantees in the UK, Malaysia or Singapore to apply for re-registration in Brunei within three years of the date of grant. Whilst the supervisory ministry for all intellectual property matters is the Attorney-General's Office there is, however, no independent intellectual property office.

With the exception of the likes of Datastream Technology Group, the main infocomms company in the country and owner of a number of registered trademarks including Fascom, Simpur and Zippi, there are few locally-owned IPRs.

13 Sri Lanka, Pakistan and Vietnam

Sri Lanka, Pakistan and Vietnam are each developing their IP systems in their own ways, distinct from those of their dominant neighbours —India, in the case of the first two, and China, the last.

SRI LANKA

Like other former colonies of Britain, Sri Lanka (or Ceylon as it was known until 1972) has a long history of providing protection for intellectual property rights—ever since the British Inventors' Ordinance of 1859 was extended to the country.

The first Ceylonese patent was granted to a British engineer for a coffee pulping machine in 1861 and the first trademark, Aurora, was registered in 1888. In the following century, only about 9,000 patents were approved. Despite such a long history of IP, piracy and a shortage of home-grown creativity has plagued the country and there is limited awareness of the value of IPRs as commercial assets.

After the first trademark registration in 1888, only about 25,000 were registered in the following century. Though this had increased sharply to 60,000 by 1996, annual registrations at the Sri Lanka Intellectual Property Office are low, with only 1,908 trademarks registered in 2008, although that was a significant increase on the paltry 711 registered in 2007. Trademarks granted to local resident companies are around the 35 per cent level.

Ravi Fernando, CEO of the Sri Lanka Institute of Nanotechnology (SLINTEC), attributes the low numbers to the fact that Sri Lanka's economy is still based upon exported commodities, rather than creative and innovative products that can both benefit from premium pricing and royalty streams if licensed to others. This is an issue that affects not only Sri Lanka but most less developed economies in the world.

Over recent years there has been the occasional welcome initiative in Sri Lanka to encourage more use of the IP system to protect creativity and innovation. SLINTEC was established in 2008 and opened its doors in May 2009 as a partnership between the National Science Foundation and five high-profile companies from Sri Lanka's private sector—Brandix, Dialog, Hayleys, Loadstar and MAS—to boost R&D. The institute is focusing on generating IPRs for its partners and aims to have patents in the nanotechnology field by 2012, if not before.

Furthermore, some Sri Lankan inventors are gaining recognition on the world stage. For example, at the 37th International Exhibition of Inventions, Techniques and Products organised by WIPO in Geneva in April 2009, the prestigious International Press Prize was awarded to M.A. Prince Chandrasena for a computer mouse operated using the head and mouth, designed for use by disabled people. The WIPO Award—the only cash prize awarded in the competition—was given to Dammika Sujith for his coir fibre extracting machine.

The youth of the country seem to be getting involved too. An 'O'-level student, E. Chandula Padmasiri, came third in the Intel International Science & Engineering exhibition, held in the USA, for inventing a mobile phone-associated microscope, a lightweight portable microscope device that can be used in a camera phone.

As would be expected, patents are pending in Padmasiri's name to protect the device.

Also, to show that it is not only India that can succeed in the software area, in October 2009 the London Stock Exchange bought Colombo-based MillenniumIT for US$30 million. The company was set up in 1996 by Tony Weerasinghe, a former country manager of US software giant Oracle, to develop ultra-fast trading systems needed by stock exchanges.

Tea production

Sri Lanka is the third largest producer of tea in the world. In 2008 US$1.3 billion in revenue was generated by its tea industry, one of the largest export earners for the country. It is no surprise, then, that some Sri Lankan tea companies are trying to stand out from the crowd through the use of IPRs.

One tea company in particular claims to have changed the profile of Sri Lanka's tea industry away from a mass-produced commodity exporter of tea. Merrill Fernando was determined to create a business that was more than just a supplier of tea to overseas companies who would put their own brands on. He created his own tea brand, controlling everything from garden to cup. In the early 1980s he registered his own tea trademark, Dilmah—derived from the first syllables of his sons' names, Dilhan and Malik. He also imported the first tea-bagging machine into Sri Lanka, despite discouragement and opposition from local tea boards and customers. By 1988 Fernando was selling Dilmah tea—packed at source—directly to consumers, cutting out the middleman and saving costs while still being able to charge premium prices. About his determination to decommoditise tea and establish his own brand, he told *The Hindu Business Line* in 2003: "Economic colonisation has taken over from where political colonisation has left off and producers remain mere suppliers to the western branding companies." Dilmah is now recognised to be the world's third largest tea brand, as famous as its nearby competitor Tetley Tea, owned by India's Tata Group. It has even diversified into T-bars—trendy tea-boutiques in places like the Colombo Hilton.

Such pride in local Sri Lankan-branded tea has now led to the national tea board registering as trademarks in over 60 countries the Ceylon Tea mark itself, the green lion logo, its Pure Ceylon Tea slogan and, as Geographical Indications (GIs), the names of seven growing areas in the country. The Tea Board, despite being very careful as to who is authorised to use its brands, faces the problem of counterfeit Ceylon Tea in markets such as the Middle East.

But, whatever you do, do not to call it Sri Lankan tea. Though the country changed its name from Ceylon in 1972, there has been promotion and marketing of Ceylon Tea by various businesses since the 1920s and it continues today. The country's Tea Board did consider changing the brand from Ceylon Tea to Sri Lankan Tea, but met with huge opposition from the country's leading tea producers, who argued that it would cost too much to rebrand. In addition, many felt that, prior to the end of the long-running civil war in May 2009, Sri Lanka was too associated with strife.

Rileys

Rileys, a subsidiary company of the largest Sri Lankan conglomerate Hayleys Group and whose motto is "Innovation: our way of life", is a pioneering manufacturer of floor mats using coir fibre and rubber. It exports to over 20 countries, and its products are protected by more than 400 registered designs and patents around the world.

Following closely behind success often are copycats, and so a need to sue to protect the innovation. Rileys has shown itself unafraid to use legal proceedings to stop copycat competitors. It has litigated in Asia and Europe, and even in the US, to stop infringement of its designs—particularly of its leading product, the Bootscraper, a flocked and spiked mat made with coir fibre rods. It doubles up as a shoe scraper and comes in different designs. Even in the high-cost English courts, Rileys succeeded in a legal action to stop a British supermarket chain from selling look-alike products.

Sometimes it is hard work and very expensive litigating against the copiers; it seems as if there is a never-ending stream. Despite the stern warning on Rileys' website against infringing its intellectual property rights, Chrishan Mendis, inventor of the Bootscraper and company chairman, acknowledges that there are many cheap imitations on the nearby Indian market. He also noted that China is a major problem for his company since its laws require compelling evidence of copying to be produced and that is often very difficult and time consuming to find.

PAKISTAN

As the United States Trade Representative marked in 2009 the 20th anniversary of its Special 301 Report on IP protection by US trading partners, Pakistan remains—as it was in 1989—on the Special Watch List for inadequate protection of IPRs.

Although the Pakistan government contests its inclusion on the list, it is clear that the country has a long way to go in the IP field. Amjun Nisar, President of the Karachi Chamber of Commerce and Industry (KCCI), spoke in July 2009 of the importance of improving the IP system to protect brands made in Pakistan and to attract FDI to the country. Piracy is still a major issue. Kamal Ahmad, manager of Microsoft Pakistan, claimed in 2008 that roughly 84 per cent of software used in the country was pirated, which he argued has deterred both foreign investors from undertaking research work in the country and individual entrepreneurship from locals.

Despite many Pakistani companies becoming aware of the importance of IPRs to their businesses, remarkably few have taken the step of developing their own. An unusually large proportion of companies are licensees of IPRs belonging to foreign businesses. Even in Pakistan's main exporting industries, such as textiles, companies have been very slow to develop their own Invisible Gold, preferring to enter into agreements to use those developed and owned by others outside the country.

Nevertheless, to try and secure a competitive edge, some Pakistani companies have bought IPRs from foreign businesses outside the country. For example, in 2004 Bashir Janmohammad, chairman of Westbury Group, the leading palm oil importer in Pakistan, purchased for PKR1.4 billion the ghee and oils business, together with its Dalda trademark, of Unilever Pakistan, paying PKR30 million (US$356,000) for the trademark alone. The trademark dated from the days of the British Raj and was a combination of the name of the Dutch manufacturer, Dada Limited, which first imported hydrogenated vegetable products in 1930, and Hindustan Lever Limited, the company to first brand the product. The letter "L" placed in the middle represents "Lever". (Westbury's attempt to exclude Unilever from competing for five years after the purchase was struck down by the Pakistani competition authorities as an unreasonable restraint of trade.)

Lahore-based Highnoon Laboratories, a pharmaceutical company with a turnover of almost US$23 million in 2008, describes itself as a company that has made the transition from making generic off-patent pharmaceuticals to one that has its own extensive brand portfolio focusing on cardiology, gastroenterology and psychiatry drugs. However, in its 2008 annual report, the company's intangible assets were limited to only two trademarks, Tres Orix Forte and Skilax drops, bought from Spanish pharma companies Almiral Prodesfarma and Laboratiorios Almiral for €500,000 and €290,000, respectively.

VIETNAM

Vietnam has a large (87 million) and very young population: 60 per cent are under 30, born after the war that, with the victory of the North Vietnamese in 1975, resulted in the northern and southern parts of their country being united again a year later. Unfortunately, its economy was ravaged by the war years and made little progress in the following decade of international isolation and rigid communist rule. In the period from 1975 to 1990 there was an annual average of two patent applications by non-residents, whereas there were an average of 27,114 such filings a year between 1990 and 2001.

This increase in interest in the Vietnamese market arose after the Sixth Congress of the Vietnamese Communist Party in 1986. Reformers led by Nguyen Van Linh took control and implemented economic reforms known as Doi Moi ("renovation"), with the aim of replacing the command economy with a socialist-oriented market economy on the lines of that in next-door China. Part of those reforms involved attracting FDI to the country, which had gone on to fight with both Cambodia and China since its reunification.

In the 1990s Vietnam achieved around seven per cent average GDP growth and continued at the same rate after the Asian financial crisis of the late 1990s from 2000 to 2005, making it the world's fastest-growing economy after China, especially after a Bilateral Trade Agreement with the USA came into force in 2001. Over the same five-year period, FDI increased by 300 per cent, with the likes of Panasonic, Yamaha, Canon and Intel setting up plants. Manufacturing (including textiles and furniture), IT and other high-tech industries now form a large and fast-growing portion of GDP. Agriculture accounts for only 20 per cent compared to 42 per cent in 1989, although the economy has doubled in size over the period. Having joined the WTO in January 2007, the country ranked 75th out of 133 in the WEF *Global Competitiveness Report 2009–10.*

Local companies such as Saigon Cosmetics Corporation (SCC) have had to fight against a preference on the part of domestic consumers for foreign brands. Established as long ago as 1976 as a state-owned cosmetics workshop, SCC was incorporated in 1987 although still state-owned, and became private in 2000. Since then, it has been built into a successful business employing more than 350 people and turning over in excess of US$10 million a year. Its three business segments are contract manufacture for foreign brands, distribution of foreign brands in Vietnam and its in-house portfolio of products. Its own perfume brands today include Miss Saigon Elegance, DeAndre, Anderman, SC, Cindy and Essy, as well as Aroma Link, which it makes and sells under a licence from Laura Beaumont Inc in France. In 2007 SCC became the first Vietnamese company to receive a WIPO Award for Scientific & Industrial Innovation.

With its success have come counterfeits, and over the past 10 years SCC has had to fight legal actions in the Philippines, Cambodia and China, as well as its domestic market.

As the government continues with its programme of privatisation, so will the importance of IPRs increase. In August 2009 Prime Minister Nguyen Tan Dung called on the Vietnam Development Bank to increase its lending to key projects in which IPRs play an important role.

14 Bangladesh, Laos and Cambodia

Categorised by the WTO as Least Developed Countries (LDCs), Bangladesh, Laos and Cambodia have the furthest to go in developing a fully-functioning IP infrastructure.

BANGLADESH

As a result of political volatility since independence from Pakistan in 1971, the People's Republic of Bangladesh has attracted relatively low levels of FDI. In 2008, it was approximately US$1 billion. On a visit to New York in 2009, Prime Minister Sheikh Hasina, who took power for the second time after the December 2008 elections, announced that her aim is to grow this to US$7 billion by 2015. (Hasina's father, Sheikh Mujibur Rahman, was the country's first Prime Minister after separation. Along with his wife and three sons he was assassinated in 1975; Hasina was abroad in Germany at the time.)

Despite GDP growth of around six per cent in recent years, Bangladesh remains a LDC, with a per capita income of US$520, compared to the global average of US$10,200. In the past, jute was the economic engine of the country but its share of the world export market peaked in the 1940s at 80 per cent, although it still accounted for 70 per cent of export earnings at the time of separation from Pakistan. Today, Bangladesh grows significant quantities of rice, tea and mustard. Although two-thirds of Bangladeshis are farmers, more than three-quarters of Bangladesh's export earnings now come from the clothes industry, which supplies the likes of H&M. This sector employs more than three million workers, 90 per cent of whom are women. As most of the work is outsourced production for European and American companies, there are few domestically-owned intellectual property rights.

Since the amendment of India's patent laws to provide protection for pharmaceutical products, the domestic Bangladesh pharmaceutical industry has expanded and there has been a marked increase in the number of patent applications in Bangladesh. After Independence it adopted Pakistan's patent law, which dated back to the colonial 1911 British Act and includes protection for product patents. Despite this, few patents were filed in Bangladesh until recently and the vast majority were to protect processes rather than products.

LAOS

Laos is rich in medicinal plant resources. In an effort to promote the use throughout the country of traditional medicines and healing remedies, the government set up the Traditional Medicine Research Centre (TMRC) in the Ministry of Public Health to document details of all traditional medicines. The TMRC has also been collaborating with an international body, the International Cooperative Biodiversity Group, in its efforts to discover medicinal products. Any benefits, profits or royalties arising from the medicines and knowledge would be shared with all the local communities involved. Studies produced by the TMRC have noted that the number of traditional medicine products produced by the Pharmaceutical Factory No. 2 of the Ministry of Public Health has increased significantly in recent years. This growing demand, particularly from China, Thailand and Vietnam, led to the identification of this sector in the *National Export Strategy 2006–2008* as a key growth sector for trade.

Laos is not a member of the WTO.

CAMBODIA

As long ago as 1996, Cambodia entered into a bilateral trade agreement with the United States committing the country to introducing a system to protect IPRs that went further than the minimum provisions of TRIPs. Notwithstanding this, in a 2006 report on "The Current Situation of IPR Protection in Cambodia", Thouk Much Theary and Lao Reasey from Cambodia's Ministry of Commerce were probably speaking of their own country's IP situation when they made the comment: "In developing Asian countries, they have just begun to take their first steps in terms of IPR protection, and in some cases, there has been no solid policy of why, when, how, and by whom IPR protection should be enforced or realised."

Cambodia has taken its first steps in IPR protection only within the last 10 years, enacting a full set of IP laws in 2002 and 2003, with sub-decrees for implementation of its trademark and copyright laws following in 2005 and 2006, respectively. The country does, however, have an effective trademark registration system with more than 30,000 trademarks on the register.

Nevertheless, Cambodia continues to have major problems with enforcing and protecting IPRs. Thouk Much and Lao's report acknowledged that officials lack the know-how and knowledge to deal with enforcement issues.

A NOTE ON MYANMAR

Myanmar, another LDC, does not have a modern IP system to speak of. Its laws are based broadly on British legislation from the colonial era. The country has been unable to keep up with the rapid developments and reforms in IPR protection. It was said to be drafting new IP laws back in 2005 to bring its IP system up to speed but these are yet to be seen. In addition, most industries remain state-controlled, with any profits gleaned being kept largely in the hands of the ruling junta.

15 Buying and selling IPRs

Just like any other property, IPRs can be bought and sold, traded and swapped. Although the usual way of building up a portfolio of IPRs is to create and to innovate, many Asian businesses have turned to the market to acquire patents, know-how, brands and copyrights belonging to others—either the rights themselves or as an important part of a corporate merger, acquisition or joint venture.

"Our goal is to acquire technology, management, and most important, to get access to overseas markets"—to use the words of Lu Guanqiu, the Chairman of Wanxiang Group, a Hangzhou-based conglomerate that supplies GM, Ford, Volkswagen and many other car companies and since 1995 has acquired more than a dozen US auto-parts makers. Along with that access comes the need to know how to play the IPR game there.

The commercial reasons for buying IPRs are many and varied, and include the following:

1. to take over a competitor;
2. to specialise in what you are good at;
3. to take a leap up the technology curve; and
4. to buy a bit of history.

We will look at each of these in turn.

TO TAKE OVER A COMPETITOR

Creative Technology

Buying a competitor who has sued you is what Singapore's Creative Technology, inventor of the Sound Blaster sound card, did to resolve patent disputes with Aureal Semiconductor when, in the late 1990s, Creative broke into the ultra-litigious California market where suing for patent infringement is a sport. Aureal alleged infringement of various technology patents such as those covering PCI (peripheral component interconnect) audio and 2D/3D positional sound APIs (application programming interfaces). Creative counter-sued, and the situation was resolved when Creative acquired Aureal's assets in September 2000 for US$32 million.

AAPICO Hitech

Founded as Able Autoparts Industries in 1985 by a Malaysian engineer, Yeap Swee Chuan, AAPICO Hitech Public Co Ltd went public in Thailand in 2002. Today the company is known as one of the leading designers and manufacturers of automotive assembly jigs, dies and OEM parts in Southeast Asia. It is a first-tier supplier to Toyota, Isuzu, Daimler and other leading carmakers.

Acquiring competitive technologies through acquisition is also the company's top priority. In 2003 AAPICO (based in Ayutthaya, north of Bangkok) bought the local parts business of the Dana Corporation of Toledo, Ohio, for US$50 million. In February 2006, it also bought a 20 per cent stake in Jackspeed Corp, a maker and exporter of car parts and accessories in Singapore, to help it expand its product line and increase sales in Southeast Asia, as well as in China and India. The company's 2009 annual report shows Intangible Assets (rights in its sophisticated CAD/CAM software) valued at THB89 million, of which THB38 million consisted of product development. In March 2009, AAPICO launched a new generation of its Powermap product, Thailand's first car navigation system to display real-time 3D landmarks and junctions with a choice of voice navigation in Thai, English, Malay, Cantonese, Mandarin, Japanese and Korean.

United Phosphorus

Making 26 acquisitions of companies and products in 15 years puts India's United Phosphorus Ltd, led by Rajju Shroff, in the top category for success in international expansion. Revenues in the five years up to 2009 (during which time it made 16 acquisitions) increased by over four times and net profit over six-and-a-half times.

Punj Lloyd

When India's Punj Lloyd engineering and construction company acquired the English Simon Carves company in 2006 (by buying its Singaporean parent Sembawang Engineering), it was getting not only one of the oldest names in petrochemical engineering but a lot of know-how and other intellectual property valuable for its major projects around the globe. One of Simon Carves' specialities, in which it had a number of patents, is cryogenic tanks. Punj Lloyd built the cryogenic storage tank package at the Reliance Jamnagar refinery. As CEO Atul Punj (whose family holds 44 per cent of the shares) knew, the IP capabilities acquired with Sembawang and Simon Carves now allow his Bombay stock exchange-listed group to provide end-to-end solutions for complete delivery of complex cryogenic, high pressure LNG, LPG, ethylene, ammonia and other similar storage tanks—a major growth area in the oil and gas sector.

TO SPECIALISE IN WHAT YOU ARE GOOD AT

NTT DoCoMo

Perhaps the strength of your business lies in marketing, not in innovation or creativity, or vice versa. Also, the development of many products requires varying skill sets you may not have in your own company. When Japan's NTT DoCoMo was looking at the various vertical markets for its mobile telecom products, it linked up with the likes of Coca-Cola Japan and C. Itoh (Itohchu) to develop a product linking mobile phones with vending machines; Sony and SEGA for mobile games to be played on its mobile phones; and Mitsui, NEC and Nissan for car navigation systems.

Daiichi Sankyo

As Takashi Shoda, the CEO of Japanese pharmaceuticals company Daiichi Sankyo, admitted to the *Financial Times* in November 2009: "The era of trying to do everything in-house is gone. Innovation means open innovation, partnership, networking, relationships with academics. There used to be an NIH—not invented here—syndrome. If a drug project did not begin in-house, we were not interested. That is changing now. Management is constantly encouraging outsiders."

To support Shoda's contentions: Daiichi Sankyo itself is a merger of two well-established but medium-sized Japanese companies. Since the completion of the merger in 2007 it has acquired Indian generic drug company Ranbaxy and the privately-owned U3 Pharma in Germany (founded by a professor from the Max Planck Institute of Biochemistry), as well as expanded its research collaboration in the antibodies field with another German company, MorphoSys.

TO TAKE A LEAP UP THE TECHNOLOGY CURVE

Lenovo

When China's Lenovo Group paid an eye-watering US$1.75 billion to acquire IBM's PC business, it also gained entry into a treasure trove of technology—to over 1,000 granted patents (a huge leap for a company which had one granted patent in 1996, just before it overhauled IBM to become the largest seller of PCs in the Chinese market)—and in Thinkpad bought one of the best-known global brands for computer notebooks. It also bought IBM's joint venture in Shenzhen (excluding the X-series production line), a research and development centre in Japan and the Raleigh Research and Development centre in North Carolina, together with sales offices in more than 160 countries throughout the world.

To illustrate the importance of the acquisition to the Chinese company's Invisible Gold hoard, in March 2009 Lenovo announced that it had sued Taiwanese rival Clevo Computer Co in New York, claiming the Taiwanese company infringed two patents for PC functions it had acquired from IBM. The lawsuit claimed that Clevo also owed millions of dollars in licensing royalties under a 1999 agreement with IBM, which Lenovo had taken over and didn't expire until the end of 2009. Taipei-based Clevo, which owns the Buynow retail outlet chain in China selling PCs and other electronic products, was due to pay US$3 million on 31 August 2006 and another US$3 million by 31 August 2009.

Tata Group

When India's Tata Group shocked the world early in 2008 by spending US$2.3 billion to acquire the iconic car brands Jaguar and Land Rover from Ford—right under the noses of US private equity houses—it was the intellectual property in the business that provided much of its value. The brands, copyrights, patents (including one for a new engine that complies with Euro IV emission norms) and know-how in its R&D labs could all be combined with Tata's value engineering, management expertise and manufacturing efficiency.

As part of the acquisition, Tata had to take over an estimated 40 contracts, ranging from engine production to the operation of information technology systems. The two brands also gave Tata access to a large number of suppliers and vendors, who supply them with often sophisticated technology not just for the cars but also manufacturing, such as former Xerox-owned Chrystal Software, which supplies product design and application solutions to Jaguar.

According to an article by Nirmalya Kumar in the *Harvard Business Review*, companies from India deal with their foreign acquisitions more tenderly than do those from other countries. He contends that this is because usually they are seeking know-how and technology in their forays abroad and don't want to frighten off, or get rid of, the incumbent management in whose minds much of that know-how and technology resides. When Tata Tea bought the venerable Tetley Tea company for US$435 million in 2000, it left the British managers in place, so their expertise and knowledge of the markets could be used.

Back in India, Tata Motors itself stated that at the end of March 2008 it owned 20 patents and had 183 patent applications in India. It had also filed patent applications in the UK, USA and the European Patent Office and had filed 29 applications under the Patent Corporation Treaty—which would later enter the national phase, when they may result in the grant of national patents. In addition, they had filed 83 design applications in India for aesthetic features of products and components.

TO BUY A BIT OF HISTORY

Renown

When Japan's Renown paid ¥20 billion to buy the British brand Aquascutum in 1990, it was hoping to acquire some of the glitter attached to a trademark first used by tailor John Emary in London in 1851, the year of the Great Exhibition. Aquascutum had also been used on clothes worn by the British Queen and Winston Churchill, among many other celebrities.

By June 2009 Renown had lost faith and tried to sell the business to its Asian distributor, Hong Kong-based clothing retailer and wholesaler YGM Trading, which already owned well-known French clothing brand Guy Laroche and American brand Hang Ten (named after the number of toes it takes to stay on a surf board). This attempt failed and later in the year, the brand was sold to a British consortium.

VIP Industries

In 2004 India's VIP Industries, the second-largest luggage manufacturer in the world after the mighty Samsonite, bought Carlton, a family-run business in England that had hit hard times and gone bankrupt. Dilip Piramal, chairman of VIP, explained why this was such a wonderful opportunity:

> "Successful acquisition of a well-known international brand offers significant synergies as well as a much-desired gateway to the world market."

To put it in the words of Nirmalya Kumar in his 2009 study of *India's Global Powerhouses*: "It was a powerful one-two punch—

Carlton had the brand name and the heritage; VIP had the manufacturing muscle and hard-side [luggage] design capability."

Others

Asian businesses that have bought a bit of history by acquiring European businesses with a rich heritage, or perhaps even only the trademarks, include:

- India's **Eicher Motors,** which is the proud owner of the Royal Enfield brand for motorcycles—its logo featuring a cannon and the motto, "Made like a gun, goes like a bullet". Using technology from the UK, Japan and Italy, the company launched two new retro models in November 2009, the Classic 500 and Classic 350. The company's CEO, R.L. Ravichandran, reminisces about the era when British motorcycles "ruled the world", although his brand's UK parent died long ago. Royal Enfield was the brand of the Enfield Cycle Company, an English engineering company producing motorcycles that also made rifle parts for the Royal Small Arms Factory at Enfield Lock in Middlesex; hence, the use of Royal Enfield since 1890. The company itself adopted the name Royal Enfield in 1893, when it also started using the trademark Made Like a Gun. In 1955, a joint venture between the English company and majority shareholder Madras Motors called Enfield of India was formed and started assembling Bullet motorcycles under licence. By 1962 it was manufacturing complete bikes. When the English company succumbed to international (particularly Japanese) competition in the 1960s and was dissolved in 1971, the Chennai-based Enfield of India continued. In 1994 it was acquired by Eicher Motors.
- Hong Kong's **May Cheong** die-cast toy company which at the beginning of 2006 went to the bankruptcy court in Milan to

buy the trademarks, tools, moulds and inventory of the respected Italian die-cast toy maker Bburago, founded by toymaker Mario Besna in 1974.

- Hong Kong's **Dickson Poon,** who bought the French maker of luxury pens and lighters S.T. Dupont for US$52 million in 1987 (a month before the stock market crashed).
- Malaysia's **MUI** which, for US$73 million, bought a 40 per cent stake in the Laura Ashley business in 1998, 30 years after the first shop selling its famous floral dresses opened in Chelsea. Since acquiring control of the iconic but troubled brand (long after the death of Laura Ashley herself on her 60th birthday in 1985), Khoo Kay Peng's MUI has repositioned Laura Ashley as primarily a home furnishings brand, although in February 2010 fellow MUI subsidiary Metrojaya, with design approval from the British company, launched a less expensive and more local Laura Ashley fashion range at its department stores in Malaysia's Klang Valley.
- Singapore's **Aussino Group** which, along with its chairman Anthony Lim, bought a minority stake in venerable Savile Row couture brand Hardy Amies in 2003 and has subsequently set up a joint venture to open retail outlets in China.
- **Wang Xiao Lan**, head of Taiwan's biggest publishing company, United Daily News Group, who bought Lanvin, France's oldest fashion house, in September 2001.
- In July 2005 **Nanjing Automobile Group** (NAG) bought the assets of MG Rover, including the iconic MG trade name. This deal with the bankruptcy administrator of the English company did not include the Rover name, which was later sold to Ford, at which point Shanghai Automotive (SAIC)—which had failed in its attempt to buy MG Rover—set up the Roewe company to

manufacture cars based on the Rover 25 and Rover 75 models. In 2004 SAIC had bought the IP rights, excluding the trademark Rover, for these two models and the Powertrain K-Series engine for £67 million. At the end of 2007, SAIC took over NAG to reunite MG with Rover—or, rather, its Chinese incarnation, Roewe. If SAIC were to sell Roewe cars outside the Chinese market it is very likely that Tata Motors, who bought the Jaguar and Land Rover business from Ford for US$2.3 billion in 2008, would sue for infringement of its Rover trademarks—which it acquired as part of the package, along with two other iconic British auto brands no longer in use, Daimler and Lanchester.

16 You can't do it all yourself: licensing of IPRs

Many businesses fail to play the IP game effectively because they are scared of cooperation—of collaborating with others who are good at things they are not. All too frequently, the inventor of the new product or the creator of the new programme is afraid of involving others for fear of being ripped off or exploited. What they need to realise is that it is better to have 50 per cent, or even five per cent, of something than to have 100 per cent of nothing. It's the failure to recognise and act on this truth that lies behind the multitude of great products that never make it out of the garage or the inventor's workshop.

Some people are very good in certain aspects of the long journey from mind to market; others are very good at other aspects. There is no point in having the best product idea since the wheel if nobody knows about it, if nobody makes it, if nobody markets it, or if nobody has it for sale in their shop. This is where one-plus-one is usually far more than two. In a study of biotechnology inventions in China that was published in 2010, Chen Qiongdi describes the huge increase in the level of patenting in this area but warns that the leading owners of invention patents are universities "and the rates of patent transfer and patent license are very low at present". In other words, it's one thing to get a patent but quite another to actually make money from it.

LOVE TO LICENCE

This is where the legal device of the licence is a critical part of the IP game. A **licence** is a permission to do something: to make, to sell, to do those things you can't do yourself. It's basically the same as taking or granting a lease of a building: the person taking the lease has the right to use the building, sometimes to the exclusion of his landlord, sometimes not.

A licence of IPRs is a lease to use those IPRs in return for a fee (or, as it is usually called, a **royalty**). There is a temporary sharing of your IPRs, so that the licensee (the tenant, the other person or business) can use the brand, the design or software (for example), for a specified period of time, without infringing the rights of the licensor (the landlord, you, the owner of the rights). Sometimes the landlord agrees not to use the rights himself; sometimes he reserves the right to do so.

With IPRs, you also have the international aspect: trademarks, copyrights and know-how all transcend national boundaries and very few businesses are as strong in foreign markets as they are at home. An IPR owner may want to exploit its trademark/patent/copyright itself in Singapore but is happy to grant a local company a licence for use in Thailand or in Indonesia where they don't have the same knowledge of how the market works.

> "A licence of IPRs is a lease to use those IPRs in return for a fee ... a royalty. There is a temporary sharing of your IPRs."

Just as a lease need not be in writing, a licence of IPRs need not in most cases. But it's usually much better for both sides if it is. The rights and obligations are set out clearly then, plus there's a document that can be filed with the authorities if required (as it is in Thailand or in China, as Danone found to its cost in its dispute with Wahaha).

On the other hand, there is a need to be culturally sensitive. In some countries many take the pragmatic view that if the parties intend to honour an agreement, there is no need to sign a written document.

PLAIN SAILING

"The person who would not honour it probably would sign it," the Managing Director of AFAI High Performance Ships (AFAI), a Hong Kong partner in a successful Gaungdong licensing and joint venture arrangement to make high-speed ferries in Panyu, has commented. The catamaran ferries were designed by Tasmanian shipbuilder Incat (company motto: "Think fast, think light"), whose earlier arrangement with AFAI to build Incat's high-speed ferries in Hong Kong, which lasted from 1982 to 1989, was also not documented but based on trust.

When AFAI proposed to Incat that they move into the Pearl River Delta market by setting up a joint venture with a local shipbuilder connected with the Guangzhou Maritime Shipping Bureau, which would be licensed by Incat, the Australian company was happy to do so. Incat had decided early on in its corporate life that the global demand for ferries meant it should not rely solely on its Tasmanian shipyard, with its limited production capacity. In addition, it needed to internationalise through licensing its designs and know-how (or frequently, show-how).

In the words of Incat's legal director: "To some extent you can't get into a local market unless you know someone locally. Having the boat built in China with a Chinese family-operated company opens up the whole market to us." But trust in the Hong Kong company only went so far. Incat was required by its (unsigned) arrangement with AFAI to provide a significant amount of data and technical information to its Hong Kong partner. It undertook to allow AFAI full and unfettered access to any part of Incat's shipyard in Tasmania for the purpose of ensuring effective technology transfer. However, in practice, Incat's disclosure of its real technology secrets was limited as it wasn't expected to provide AFAI with the background research on which the data and technical information was based (and without which the Hong Kong business needed to keep Incat involved on an ongoing basis).

As the Managing Director of Incat explained: "Just having a set of plans, although it might look valuable, is not of great value without having all the back-up information. You can build the ship but then you can't sell it [on the international market] unless you have all the information." Also, the ships built in China were not Incat's market-leading large, wave-piercing catamarans but rather its older K Class catamaran, so the commercial risk of technology and know-how leakage was reduced.

For the owner of IPRs, licences can provide the opportunity to expand their use beyond what your own resources allow—perhaps to another country where you don't have operations yourself—and to generate new (and usually incremental) revenue streams.

CHOOSE WISELY

Don't forget that to a large extent you are putting in the hands of others the future value of your IPRs. If they succeed, so do you. But if they fail, you fail. That means finding the right licensee is critical, in the same way as is finding a reliable tenant for your apartment—one who pays on time and looks after it. Take references, check out the market, before choosing a potential licensee. If you feel unhappy with them during the negotiations, drop them. A good licensee is like a partner; a bad licensee is like a nightmare tenant.

One area where IPR licensing plays a huge role is in character merchandising, which is based on brands, designs and copyrights. The "daddy" of this area in Asia is Hello Kitty, a character created by Ikuko Shimizu for his then-employer Sanrio Co as long ago as 1974. Sanrio founder Shintaro Tsuji had originally gone to freelance designers for his characters but disliked having to pay them royalties on use of the characters, so he started to have all his character design done by his own employees such as Shimuzu. That meant that Sanrio owned the IP rights and could license their use by others. A wise decision: royalties for use of the Hello Kitty character still account for around half of Sanrio's US$1 billion-plus turnover, with the cat appearing on over 50,000 products in over 60 countries.

"A good licensee is like a partner; a bad licensee is like a nightmare tenant."

BULL'S EYE!

In the early 1980s Krating Daeng (which means "red water buffalo") was a successful local Thai product, a tonic drink keeping Thai truck drivers awake on their long drives from the northern city of Chiang Rai to Bangkok in the south. Its popularity was noted by a visiting Austrian toothpaste salesman by the name of Dietrich Mateschitz, who decided to track down its maker.

After a bit of research Mateschitz found that the drink was made by T.C. Pharmaceutical Co, a firm set up in 1962 by Chaleo Yoovidhya, which fortuitously happened to be the Thai licensee of the Austrian's then-employer. This made it easier for Mateschitz to approach Yoovidhya to suggest launching the drink outside Thailand.

The Thai was realistic enough to see that he didn't know the market outside his own country well enough, and in 1984 Mateschitz and he each invested US$500,000 in a new company, taking a 49 per cent share each, with Yoovidhya's son Chelerm given the remainder. The Thai contributed his product and manufacturing know-how to the new venture, the Austrian his marketing knowledge.

Three years later, the newly-carbonated version of the Thai product was launched on the Austrian market, still containing taurine amino-acid, caffeine and glucuronolactone from the original recipe but repackaged in a sleak blue-and-silver can and called Red Bull. Helped by viral marketing to enhance its underground cachet, it spread rapidly around the globe (except to France where it remains banned) to keep millions of people awake and dancing, totally unaware of its Thai origins.

In the process, Yoovidhya made it onto the *Forbes Billionaires List* in 2003. By 2008, he was Thailand's richest man. Why? Because back in 1984 he realised, as many business people don't, that it's better to have 49 per cent of what might be a lot, than to keep 100 per cent of nothing. It's all about playing to your strengths and recognising the strengths of others, as he did the marketing genius of Dietrich Mateschitz.

"It's better to have 49 per cent of what might be a lot, than to keep 100 per cent of nothing."

REJECTING THE 'NOT INVENTED HERE' SYNDROME

Taking a licence of technology you don't have can form the basis for long-term technological success. An excellent example is provided by Tokyo Tsuchin Kogyo. This later became Sony Corporation, because that name was easier on the Western tongue. In return for a US$25,000 upfront fee, Sony licensed its transistor technology from

Western Electric, the manufacturing arm of American Telephone & Telegraph (AT&T), which had made its patents available for licensing a couple of years earlier in 1951. The fact that the co-founder of Sony, Akio Morita, had done this without their approval so irritated the bureaucrats at the Ministry of International Trade & Industry (MITI) that they resorted to the bureaucrat's greatest weapon—foot dragging. When Morita's partner Masaru Ibuka asked MITI to approve the US$25,000 foreign exchange that he needed to deliver on the deal, it took more than three months to get permission to proceed.

Sony did not just sit back and rely on the technology licensed by Western Electric. It improved and adapted it. So, even though researchers at Bell Labs had tried—and failed—to add phosphorous instead of antimony so as to "dope" (add extra electrons to) transistors to improve their conductivity, Ibuka and his team at Sony tried, again and again and again. Eventually one of the team, Tetsuo Tsukamoto, succeeded in getting a phosphorous-doped transistor to work, improving the high frequency characteristics of the transistor by more than 50 times. In doing so, he laid the foundations for Sony's astonishing success in TVs and other electronic products—and led also to the work on tunnel diodes for which another Sony researcher, Leona Esaki, won the Nobel Prize in 1973.

COMBINING RESOURCES

In 2004, after reviewing his company's product offerings in the competitive field of commercial vehicles, the new Chief Operating Officer of India's Eicher Motors, Siddhartha Lal, realised they were just not good enough to make headway against the industry giants Tata Motors and Ashok Leyland. He started looking around for partners with skills to complement those of his own company. After negotiating for over two years with the likes of Mercedes and Volvo, Eicher threw in its lot with Volvo in a 50:50 joint venture.

To best exploit the potential of the new venture, Volvo and Eicher transferred their respective Indian Commercial Vehicles operations to a new company, VE Commercial Vehicles (VECV). In May 2008 Eicher transferred its entire truck and bus operations, together with its components and engineering design services divisions. Volvo did the same with its existing Indian truck sales and distribution operations. Volvo also invested INR1,082 crore in VECV for a 45.6 per cent stake. The balance 54.4 per cent is held by Eicher. However, Volvo also bought 8.1 per cent in Eicher, which meant that its effective holding in VECV was 50 per cent.

Siddharta Lal explained: "If either had a majority shareholding, the level of trust would not be there. They would have hesitated in transferring technology and expertise; we would have been conservative, living in the constant fear of being kicked out."

The tie-up fills crucial missing links for both players—technology and expertise for Eicher, production at emerging-market costs and a 300-strong sales and support network for Volvo.

RIDE THE WIND

In a similar way, India's Suzlon Energy became the fifth-largest wind turbine manufacturer in the world through a judicious use of licences followed by acquisitions. Set up by Tulsi Tanti in 1995 to provide power to his textile business, the company went public only 10 years later. Realising early on that he should not reinvent the wheel, Tanti entered into a know-how licence with a German business, Sudwind GmbH Windkraftanlagen, which, in return for royalties, provided his new company with the technical knowledge it needed. When the German licensor went bankrupt, Suzlon jumped in to hire its engineers and set up a turbines R&D centre in Germany.

Another acquisition followed, this time a bankrupt Dutch company that made and had the technology for the rotor blades used in wind turbines. In 2004 Tanti took the bold step of establishing his international headquarters in wind power-friendly Denmark, where two competitors Vestas and NEG Micon had just merged so there were unemployed engineers looking for jobs. Hardly pausing for breath, two years later Suzlon acquired the Belgian company Hansen Transmissions, the world's second-largest maker of wind turbine gearboxes. Expanding its technology base a year later it bought a Dutch company, Repower, which made turbines larger than those made by Suzlon previously. From scratch, Tanti had built in a hectic 13 years one of the world's leading players in the growing field of wind power.

GOOD THINGS CAN COME TO AN END ...

Of course, building a business up based on a licence from somebody else can be dangerous. What happens when the licence is ended, perhaps without warning? As usual, the answer depends on how well-drafted the licence is to protect the interests of the licensee, and how much the licensee has avoided being dependant on the revenue stream from just one licence.

So, when it was announced in February 2009 that at the beginning of 2010 Dickson Concepts in Hong Kong would lose its more than 20-year-old licence from Polo Ralph Lauren Corporation to make and sell Polo and Ralph Lauren products in Southeast Asia and China, investors held their breaths for a while. Polo had decided to take back the wholesale and retail distribution of its products in Southeast Asia as part of its worldwide strategy to revamp the tired brand.

But all was not lost for Dickson. Thanks to a well-drafted contract, the company was paid US$18.2 million for the loss of its import, manufacturing and sales rights in Hong Kong, Indonesia, Malaysia, the Philippines, Singapore, Taiwan, Thailand and China.

... OR PERHAPS NOT

Hong Kong also provides an unusual example of the child swallowing the mother. In 2003 Esprit Holdings of Hong Hong, originally an Asian afterthought of US retailer Esprit de Corp, purchased for US$150 million from two private equity firms the Esprit brand in those areas it didn't already own it. This move led the Hong Kong company to become the owner of a truly global brand. Michael Ying, who had founded the Asian company, had already bought a one-third interest in the global brand back in 1994 and then, Esprit Europe in 1997. In the logical next step, full ownership of the global brand came under one Hong Kong roof in 2003.

Taking or granting a licence of IPRs is a commercial practice likely to become of increasing economic importance as economies in Asia develop and grow. Frequently, the quickest way to access technology or expertise is to take a licence to use it, rather than to try to re-invent the wheel. Conversely, the most effective way of commercialising IPRs a business has developed is often to licence others to use them in return for payment, especially in unfamiliar markets. For these reasons alone, both licensing in and out should become essential tools for Asian businesses in the never-ending fight for competitive advantage.

17 The dark side: counterfeiting and piracy

No book on the business of IPRs can be complete without describing the massively important nether world of counterfeiting and piracy. In the words of a South African judge: "Like a mongrel attracts ticks, so does success in selling products attract counterfeiting."

With music and films, piracy (or blatant infringement of copyright) is rife and becomes easier with every advance in digital copying technology. This has led *Wired* magazine's Chris Anderson to conclude in his recent provocatively titled bestseller, *Free*, that "China is a country where piracy has won. Years of half-hearted crackdowns under diplomatic pressure from the West have had no apparent effect on the street vendors or countless sites that host MP3 for downloads. Every year there are some ceremonial piracy busts, and some of the bigger Web sites occasionally have to pay fines, but none of this has stopped average Chinese music consumers from finding pretty much everything they want for free."

This market reality leads Anderson in quite a different direction to that of the music and film companies on whose behalf the governments of the USA and the UK, in particular, continually put whatever pressure they can on Beijing to enforce its copyright laws. Rightly or wrongly, Anderson puts forward the radical view that what is needed are new business models that reflect, rather than ignore, the digital reality that "piracy is zero-cost marketing" and make money in other ways.

LIFE AND DEATH

This is not a view with which the successful Chinese film director Lu Chuan agrees. Appointed in 2009 by the General Administration of Press and Publication (GAPP) and the National Copyright Administration (NCA) as one of their "Anti-Piracy Image Ambassadors", Lu Chuan told *China Intellectual Property* magazine:

> "The film market is much like a garden, where vegetables should belong to the planters. However, piracy makes it impossible for planters to get their harvest, because 'thieves' have stolen the vegetables. Therefore, creators become the bottom species in the 'food chain', followed by investors, while the pirates move to the top of the chain. I think this is rather a dark fact …
>
> Take the film *City of Life and Death* for example: after the film was released, cinema chains got their part of the proceeds, and then issuers got their income. After that, investors reclaimed their portion of the sums, and finally creators got their part. As a matter of fact, film creators are also the creators of wealth. In the absence of their labour and hard work, there would be no film or copyright and copyright transactions would become impossible. To be blunt, I am the core of a creative team, but still I have not gotten my pay yet [for four years' work]. A significant portion of the proceeds is ... grabbed by the pirates. One pirated disk may edge out one or even dozens of movie tickets."

The film director bemoaned the fact that within five days of the nationwide release of his film *City of Life and Death* on 22 April 2009, pirated copies were being found. But, he continued more optimistically, strong enforcement measures taken in Beijing, Shanghai and Guangzhou meant that the film managed to earn over RMB180 million at the box office, although none of the producers and promoters had yet been paid. He noted pragmatically that most of those who go to watch a film at the cinema would not buy a pirated DVD: "They will always go to the [cinema]."

"China, along with India, is responsible for the vast majority of the fakes making it to the international market," says Roger Bate, an economist who researches health policy and is the author of *Making a Killing: The Deadly Implications of the Counterfeit Drug Trade*.

COUNTERFEIT? THINK AGAIN

What exactly is counterfeiting, except an over-used and much-misused description of something generally accepted to be wrong? It is where someone tries to copy as closely as possible a successful product protected by IPRs, perhaps by trademarks, sometimes by copyright or a right similar to it, and occasionally by patents—sometimes, all three.

So, when pharmaceutical giant Pfizer has a counterfeiting problem with one of its blockbuster drugs (and the World Health Organisation estimates that six per cent of all pharmaceutical products are counterfeit), it will certainly involve infringement of its trademarks—say, Viagra—but probably also the copyright in the packaging of the drug and in the patient information leaflet in the pack, although the counterfeiters may not bother with such niceties as informing the patient about how to take the drug safely. It may also involve an infringement of a patent or patents but usually the counterfeiter doesn't even make the effort to try and copy the formulation on which so much R&D money was spent. For the counterfeiter, chalk will do, regardless of the consequences for the poor patient whose illness continues unabated if he is lucky and worsens if he is not.

POTENTIALLY LETHAL

Far worse can happen with counterfeited products than that they are not effective or don't work:

- In 1984 the cloth covering of some counterfeit Cabbage Patch dolls were treated with such toxic chemicals that when a child in California tried to restuff her doll she had to have her hands treated for burns.
- In 2005, 19 people died in Turkey after drinking counterfeit raki, the country's most popular drink. The manufacturer of the genuine product had to recall and destroy all stocks in the affected bottle size because through the counterfeiters' actions they had become unsaleable.
- In October 2006 it was reported by a Moscow radio station that over 1,000 people had been hospitalised in the previous two months and more than 50 had died from drinking counterfeit vodka selling for as little as 70 roubles (US$2.50) a bottle. Ingredients used included brake fluid, eau de cologne, cigarette-lighter fluid and de-icer.
- In 2008 *The New York Times* reported that Chinese suppliers were being blamed for the contamination of Baxter Labs' blood-thinner heparin in the United States after reports of deaths (as many as 81) and hundreds of allergic reactions.

- In early 2009 a diabetes drug was withdrawn from the market in China after samples showed the medicine, which killed two people in the western region of Xinjiang, was six times as potent as it should have been.

And so on and so on, the examples are endless. Along with other counterfeits of safety-critical products such as plane parts, the huge trade in counterfeit products is an active target for worldwide police and intelligence services' attention, especially given the persuasive and pervasive evidence of the involvement of organised crime syndicates. In one review of Chinese pharmaceutical counterfeiting operations, profits of 5,000 per cent were quoted, leading to the question posed by one participant: "Why bother with currency counterfeiting or narcotics, where the profit margins are much lower?"

PRETEND LUXURY

Bundled together with the horrible counterfeiting of medicines and the like is the copying of luxury brands. It is here that the arguments get blurred, especially the moral ones.

When Rolex tries to clamp down on the huge business of fake watches, or Chanel tries to stop wholesale counterfeiting of its handbags, it will usually be on the basis of their registered trademarks alone because the counterfeiter doesn't even try to make them look slightly different; they try to get as close as possible to a perfect-looking copy. Some succeed and the copies infiltrate the genuine distribution chains where the potential purchaser (and sometimes the brand owner itself) can't tell them apart. Others sell their cheap look-alikes in market stalls in Bangkok where nobody thinks they are genuine but the people who pay THB500 fancy wearing a chunky bracelet watch with the Rolex trademark on the face ... even if it stops or falls apart in days or weeks.

What's wrong with that, say the man and woman in the street? Rolex doesn't lose a sale because the Bangkok buyer wouldn't dream of paying and probably doesn't have hundreds of thousands of RMB or HK$ for a real Rolex Oyster, so why does it matter? Isn't imitation the sincerest form of flattery and wouldn't Rolex executives be slightly worried if their watches weren't being ripped off? Isn't counterfeiting a sign of true brand strength, of true cult status? Such a view is heresy to the guardians of the luxury brands who, with shrill voices and deep pockets, stride around the world buttonholing and haranguing the politicians who can introduce ever more draconian penalties for the heinous crime of counterfeiting Louis Vuitton branded luggage or a Longines watch.

A TOUCH OF HYPOCRISY

But, whisper it quietly, hypocrisy rears its ugly head here as it does in so many other fields of human endeavour.

The luxury brand owners know that the desperately poor peasant arriving in Shanghai from the agricultural provinces today who buys the fake Gucci wants to buy the genuine bag tomorrow once he or she has made it big. Many have in the past decade and are the staple customers of the Chanel and other luxury brand boutiques in Hong Kong. Indeed, Canadian author and activist Naomi Klein alleges that designers—and she mentions Stussy, Hilfiger, Nike, Polo and DKNY—deliberately turn a blind eye to the piracy of their logos on T-shirts and baseball caps in inner city areas. In response to that, some people might say, so what? It is of course a brand-owner's right to choose when and if to try to stop others' unauthorised use; many brand owners would bankrupt themselves if they tried to stop each and every infringement. (More absurdly, Klein claims also that they don't make serious attempts to stop shoplifting because presumably they would prefer the street cred generated by "cool people" wearing stolen designer goods.)

SOFT TARGETS

And then there is software. So easy to copy it's almost embarrassing. But it's still counterfeiting, and raises the hackles of trade negotiators from Washington to Brussels.

It has been estimated that 90 per cent of Microsoft Windows programs running on PCs in China are fake, or rather haven't been authorised by Microsoft. Many are bought at street markets or even in swanky shops throughout China in boxes identical to those sold in PC warehouses across the US and Europe. But they are counterfeits, cost a fraction of the genuine programs, and not a penny flows back into the Microsoft HQ coffers at Redmond, Washington.

THAT'S INCREDIBLE!

Although the scale of illegal copying is massive, the credibility of the IP owners' case isn't helped by their inflation of revenues lost.

In a typical headline, Singapore's *Business Times* announced on 16 August 2005, "IT Fakes Cost US$100b a Year in Lost Revenue: KPMG", reporting on a study which actually stated that global tech groups lost *up to* US$100 billion. That's not a difficult conclusion to come to; after all, US$1 billion or even US$1 million would be included in the description "up to US$100 billion"!

Similarly, in July 2007 *The New York Times* business section carried an article with the headline, "FBI and Chinese Seize $500 Million of Counterfeit Software", reporting on the seizure in China of 290,000 counterfeit Microsoft and Symantec disks and certificates of authenticity after a joint operation by the FBI and the Chinese government. Certainly a good haul, but the headline's US$500 million would have meant that each disk was worth US$1,724, rather than the actual average cost at the full retail price of around eight per cent of that, at about US$120.

WHOLE LOT OF HYPE

Hype and hysteria in this area have a long history. In an early example of the hyperbole which plagues the whole area of counterfeiting, in September 1912 Anthony Gref, an attorney for German pharmaceutical company Bayer, and Herman Metz, a sales agent for another German company, Hoechst, announced a war on infringers. Metz told reporters: "Frauds are practiced on such an extensive scale that the lives of at least 100 million people in the United States are placed in jeopardy month in and month out."

But the total population of the United States at that time in 1912 was about 95 million.

More recently, in January 2006 the *Financial Times* carried the trenchant views of Guy de Jonquieres, its World Trade Editor, on a report that a French-based association of luxury goods manufacturers claimed that fake products were costing its members US$4.3 billion a year in lost sales in Japan.

> "The figure turns out to be, if not fake, somewhat contrived. It was arrived at by multiplying the estimated unit sales of counterfeit products by the price of genuine ones.

The calculation assumed that, if brand-conscious Japanese consumers could not buy pirated copies, they would all buy the real thing.

"Does anyone really believe that? In fact, international studies have found that the overwhelming majority of sales of counterfeit products are to people who would never have bought genuine ones, because they could not afford them. In China, where incomes are very low, that proportion must be particularly large. So the wages—and the costs—of piratical sin are rather smaller than they may seem.

"Moreover, at least some of the retail business that brand owners do forfeit to fakes could arguably be considered long-term marketing investment. Just as owning a Picasso reproduction does not reduce the desire to possess an original, today's buyers of fakes are often tomorrow's eager customers.

"All this would be just shop talk if luxury goods makers were not also lobbying hard to get governments and law-enforcement agencies to step up the fight against piracy. Central to their campaigning is the contention that counterfeit goods are bad, not just for their businesses, but for society as a whole. It is true that fake product sales often escape tax and help fund organised crime. But when producers also insist that their self-interest is identical to that of consumers, scepticism is in order.

"There is a clear social gain from banning counterfeits that pose health and safety risks, but which consumers cannot easily identify as such. Pharmaceuticals are a case in point, although for cigarette companies to shelter behind the same argument makes nonsense of it.

"But I have never heard of anyone being killed or maimed by a fake handbag. In any case, most shoppers know that if a product bearing a familiar brand name is unusually cheap, it is unlikely to be authentic. And if a fake is indistinguishable in quality and appearance from the real thing, some are, where is the consumer harm?

"Claims that piracy deters innovation by reducing the incentive to invent are also sometimes overstated. That may be true of products such as computers and software—although, even here, Linux and growth of 'free ware' tell a different story. However, relatively few luxury goods take much research or capital to produce. Those that sell on 'heritage' values require almost none. Most of the investment is in advertising and marketing.

"I am not condoning intellectual property violations: free and prosperous economies require private property rights that are clear-cut and effectively enforced—even if producers have sometimes sought unreasonably to expand the limits of the monopolies that those rights confer on them.

"However, if they want to rally the rest of society to the defence of their interests, they should do so with arguments that are as genuine and reputable as their products. After all, playing straight with the public is supposed to be what good branding is about."

Counterfeiting is a very serious problem, and it should be treated as such, but exaggerating its size doesn't help. For example, to value the amount of pirated Microsoft software in China or music downloads at the unit prices paid in, say, the USA is just nonsense aimed at grabbing airtime and newspaper headlines.

It is important to remember in the hysteria that sometimes surrounds counterfeiting and piracy that only a relatively small proportion of the trademark, copyright and patent infringement cases that reach the courts involve piracy or counterfeits. Most IPR infringements around the world that end up before courts involve either innocent adoption of another's IPRs or the deliberate use of what turns out to be somebody else's IPR, which the infringer either didn't know about or took the view, wrongly, that it wasn't infringed.

A few email websites with useful information on the counterfeiting scourge (although, don't believe everything you read):

- www.iipa.com: International Intellectual Property Alliance, an American association of copyright-based industries;
- www.iacc.com: International Anti-Counterfeiting Coalition, a US-based group of mainly US companies; and
- www.qbpc.org.cn: Quality Brands Protection Committee, which represents foreign companies on IPR issues in China (but is dominated by the luxury brands).

Microsoft in China

Unlike many companies whose only response is to reach for the telephone number of the US State Department or the US Trade Representative when counterfeiting rears its ugly head in China, Microsoft has refined its strategy and recognised that more subtle and longer-term measures are needed (perhaps combined with the telephone call). In the late 1990s the software giant attacked counterfeiters in the law courts and attracted unwelcome publicity as a big bully. In 1999 it was described by its former country manager as "arrogant and selfish" and an "enemy of Chinese consumers". As a result,

the Chinese government actively promoted the development and use of a Chinese version of Linux (and early in 2003 the China-IBM Linux Solution Cooperation Center was set up in Beijing), with the post office and the National Statistics Bureau buying Linux software. In a further slap in the face in December 2001, the Beijing municipal government awarded six software supply contracts to local vendors including Red Flag, the Chinese Linux developer. Microsoft was left out in the cold.

Microsoft reacted positively, however, and engaged with the government in constructive discussions about how it could contribute to the development of China as a software research and production base, rather than merely a source of licensing revenue. In June 2002 it agreed to contribute US$750 million over three years to assist in the development of China's software industry through such measures as research programmes and education, investments in joint ventures and university laboratories, and hardware purchases from Chinese factories. In addition, in February 2002 in an attempt to assuage Chinese concerns about software security issues, Microsoft agreed to give government officials controlled access to the source code for Windows® and certain technical information. The strategy is long-term but so is China as a market for software. At the very least, Microsoft must be given credit for being quick to realise that in China the stick is often less effective than the carrot and that mutually beneficial relationships are likely to succeed far more than adversarial ones.

18 What next in Asia?

There is a need to build innovation and creativity into the DNA of more of Asia's businesses. This requires a change of their short-term trading mentality to one that encourages R&D, product development and brand creation in the interests of developing a sustainable and long-term competitive edge. Industries as diverse as cars and cellphones are starting to learn this and the need to build up their own Invisible Gold portfolios.

The ownership of, and access to, IPRs was one of the chief stumbling blocks to the takeover of Ford's Volvo business by China's Geely (and actually stopped Beijing Automotive's bid to buy Opel from Ford succeeding in July 2009). Even some of the "bandit" handset makers in Shenzhen—where IPRs have for long been someone else's problem and blatant copying was the name of the game—have started to realise that competing on price alone is a business strategy with a limited shelf-life. As Jin Hongxiang, president of SOP that owns Shenzhen Xinghuabao Electronics, told the *Financial Times* in February 2010: "We are legitimate handset makers now. We are building our own brand" [instead of copying others' branded devices and making a margin of less than two per cent in markets such as Dubai].

That change in mindset also makes it easier for businesses to bridge the gap from the low-value Original Equipment Manufacturer

(OEM) model to the more lucrative and sustainable Original Design Manufacturer (ODM) model. After that, comes the stage where the business develops its own products and brands, and sometimes retail outlets.

> "Competing on price alone is a business strategy with a limited shelf-life."

An example of a business that has made the transition successfully is Hangzhou-based China Ting Group, which is listed in Hong Kong. As well as supplying the likes of US clothing retailers Guess and Macy's (originally just manufacturing the clothes from the US companies' designs but then moving on to designing in-house), China Ting has developed five brands of its own: Finity, Maxstudio, Elanie Riese, Riverstone and Dbni. It has over 450 retail outlets, which generated sales of HK$286 million in 2008 (with profit up 5.7 per cent on the previous year, compared with a 18.2 per cent decline in profits from its work for others), focused on second- and third-tier cities in China.

COLLABORATE OR PERISH

There is little or no doubt that IPRs will become more important in Asia in the coming years, even though much of the hype behind the rise of China and India ignores the fact that American, European and Japanese corporations still dominate many areas of business through the ownership of copyrights, brands and genuinely innovative patents.

Similarly, the relentless shift of manufacturing to lower cost countries in Asia and elsewhere means that other countries must concentrate on adding value to products and services through innovation and creativity. As K. Ramasamy, founder in 1970 of Roots

Industries that today is India's largest hornmaker, told the *Financial Times* in April 2009, it was a "great joy" when he succeeded after many attempts in persuading Germany's Bosch to enter into a long-term technical collaboration agreement. At present the United States, Japan and European countries have the lion's share of Invisible Gold reserves and that will not change soon or with their agreement.

Asian economies are changing, however, as the mantra of "going up the learning curve" reaches the farthest recesses of the region, and there is much to be confident about. What will not help is either an inferiority complex or a superior attitude towards cooperation and collaboration between countries, businesses and people. Brand building, creativity and innovation all require the optimal use of available resources, and Asian business needs to become more flexible and open to working together with outsiders. The isolationist mindset of many Japanese corporations about which Kikkoman's Yuzaburo Mogi has expressed so much concern should not be repeated elswhere in Asia. Instead, the lesson from Red Bull—the globally-successful product that resulted from a marriage of Thai ingenuity with Austrian marketing genius—should be taken to heart: it's far better to have half of a lot than to keep all of nothing.

In today's globalised world, brands, design and technology are developed (and frequently discarded) at breakneck speed. Before it can blink, a business that tries to do everything itself is often left behind with an un-cool brand, old-fashioned design and obsolete technology. The "not invented here" and "I know best" syndromes should be consigned to the waste basket. Instead, the Asian business should identify and concentrate on its strengths and get help with its weaknesses.

At government level there needs to be concentration on the building of the "soft" infrastructure to support the IP laws that have been introduced all around Asia over recent years. Those laws are not enough on their own. What is now important is to ensure those laws are implemented and enforced in an efficient and effective way. Both businesses and investors must be confident of protection for the results of their investments of time and money to nurture the creativity and innovation from which we all benefit.

> "The 'not invented here' and 'I know best' syndromes should be consigned to the waste basket. Instead, the Asian business should identify and concentrate on its strengths and get help with its weakenesses."

Although much progress has been made in the first decade of the 21st century, there is a long way for Asia to go in the Invisible Gold field. But the signs are encouraging that throughout the region both governments and businesses are starting to recognise how IPRs are at the heart of much of today's Knowledge Economy and, as such, demand attention.

Glossary
Appendices
Sources
Index

GLOSSARY

APEC the Asia-Pacific Economic Cooperation forum; formed in 1989 and has 21 member economies (of which 12 are Asian): Australia, Brunei Darussalam, Canada, Chile, People's Republic of China, Hong Kong China, Indonesia, Japan, Republic of Korea, Malaysia, Mexico, New Zealand, Papua New Guinea, Peru, the Philippines, Russia, Singapore, Taiwan China, Thailand, the United States of America and Vietnam

ASEAN the Association of Southeast Asian Nations; member countries are Brunei Darussalam, Cambodia, Indonesia, Laos, Malaysia, Myanmar, the Philippines, Singapore, Thailand and Vietnam

CSIR the Council for Scientific and Industrial Research, India

EPO the European Patent Office

EU the European Union; the 27 member states comprise Austria, Belgium, Bulgaria, Cyprus, the Czech Republic, Denmark, Estonia, Finland, France, Germany, Greece, Hungary, Ireland, Italy, Latvia, Lithuania, Luxembourg, Malta, the Netherlands, Poland, Portugal, Romania, Slovakia, Slovenia, Spain, Sweden and the United Kingdom

FDI Foreign Direct Investment

FTA Free Trade Agreement

GATT the General Agreement on Tariffs and Trade; signed in 1947 and replaced by the World Trade Organisation Agreement in 1994

IPOS the IP Office of Singapore

IPRs or **IP RIGHTS** intellectual property rights

KIPO the Korean IP Office

JPO the Japanese Patent Office

MYIPO the Malaysia Intellectual Property Office

ODM Original Design Manufacturer

OEM Original Equipment Manufacturer

PCT the Patent Cooperation Treaty. The Treaty provides a mechanism, administered centrally by WIPO in Geneva, to make a single patent application and search, and in some cases a single preliminary examination. After that stage the applications (for the countries designated by the applicant) are sent to national patent offices for them to decide on the grant of a patent in their territories.

SAIC the State Administration for Industry and Commerce, China, which is responsible for trademark matters in that country

SIPO the State Intellectual Property Office, China

SMEs Small- and Medium-Sized Enterprises

TRIPs the 1994 Agreement on Trade-Related Aspects of Intellectual Property Rights, which sets out the minimum standards on IPRs which member countries of the WTO must provide. Non-compliance with TRIPs can lead to a complaint to the WTO, by a member country of WTO only, which may result in reference to the dispute settlement procedure laid down in the WTO Agreement.

USPTO the United States Patent and Trademark Office

USTR the United States Trade Representative

WIPO the World Intellectual Property Organisation, the United Nations agency responsible for 24 multilateral treaties in the area of IPR and which administers the Patent Cooperation Treaty (PCT), Madrid trademark and Hague design systems, as well as operating an Arbitration and Mediation Centre that also resolves Internet domain name disputes. The Organisation has 184 member countries.

WTO the World Trade Organisation, which came into existence on 1 January 1995 and replaced the GATT (although in fact this was a treaty rather than an organisation). There are now a total of 153 member countries in the WTO.

APPENDIX 1:
Asia's largest companies with IP exposure[1]

Table 1

Company	Country	Sector	Global Rank 2000
NTT DoCoMo	Japan	Wireless telecoms services	3
NTT	Japan	Telecoms	7
Toyota Motor	Japan	Automobiles	15
Seven Eleven Japan	Japan	Food & drug retailers	33
Sony	Japan	Household appliances & electronics	35
Softbank	Japan	Software	44
China Telecom (HK)	Hong Kong	Telecoms	51
Fujitsu	Japan	Computer hardware	53
NTT Data	Japan	Computer services	78
Matsushita Electrical Industrial	Japan	Electronic equipment	87
Hutchison Whampoa	Hong Kong	Diversified industrials	90
Hikari Tsushin	Japan	Telecoms	92

[1] Data is taken from the FT.Com website. Companies are ranked by market capitalisation using the share price recorded on the end of each financial year multiplied by the number of shares issued. Yahoo! Japan has been excluded from the 2009 list as it is an associate company of Yahoo Inc (US).

Company	Country	Sector	Global Rank 2000
Hitachi	Japan	Telecoms equipment	97
Murata Mfg	Japan	Semiconductors	104
Matsushita Com. Industrial	Japan	Telecoms equipment	108
Korea Telecom	South Korea	Telecoms	115
Kyocera Corp	Japan	Telecoms equipment	122
Rohm	Japan	Computer hardware	123
Taiwan Semiconductor	Taiwan	Semiconductors	125
Ito-Yokado	Japan	Retailers (soft goods)	129
Oracle Corporation Japan	Japan	Software	141
Samsung Electronics	South Korea	Semiconductors	146
NEC Corp	Japan	Software & computer services	148
Takeda Chemical Industrial	Japan	Pharmaceuticals	149
Honda Motor	Japan	Automobiles	159
United Micro Electronics	Taiwan	Semiconductors	166
Cable & Wireless HKT	Hong Kong	Telecoms	168
Canon	Japan	Electronic equipment	170
Singapore Telecom	Singapore	Telecoms	176
DDI	Japan	Telecoms	186
Sharp Corporation	Japan	Electronic equipment	206
SK Telecom	South Korea	Telecoms	217
Fanuc	Japan	Electronic equipment	223
Japan Telecom	Japan	Telecoms services	232
Secom	Japan	Security & alarm services	234

Company	Country	Sector	Global Rank 2000
Toshiba	Japan	Computer hardware	235
Advantest	Japan	Semiconductors	240
Tokyo Electron	Japan	Semiconductors	260
Pacific Century Cyberworks	Hong Kong	Internet	261
Nintendo	Japan	Home entertainment	262
East Japan Railway	Japan	Rail, road & freight	267
Denso	Japan	Auto parts	271
TDK	Japan	Household appliances & housewares	288
Bridgestone	Japan	Tyres & rubber	300
Shin-Etsu Chemical	Japan	Chemicals (specialty)	306
Fuji Photo Film	Japan	Photography	319
Kao	Japan	Personal products	323
Yamato Transport	Japan	Rail, road & freight	325
Wipro	India	Software	352
Singapore Airlines	Singapore	Airlines & airports	355
Nippon Steel	Japan	Chemicals (specialty)	362
Nissan Motor	Japan	Automobiles	363
Trend Micro	Japan	Software	364
SMC	Japan	Engineering (general)	372
Fuji Television Network	Japan	Broadcasting contractors	383
Japan Tobacco	Japan	Tobacco	384
Mitsubishi Electric	Japan	Computer hardware	388
Fsas	Japan	Computer services	389
Keyence	Japan	Electronic equipment	395
Nippon Television Network	Japan	Broadcasting contractors	402

Company	Country	Sector	Global Rank 2000
Central Japan Railway	Japan	Rail, road & freight	407
Ricoh	Japan	Electronic equipment	412
Asustek Computer	Taiwan	Electronic equipment	433
Benesse	Japan	Publishing & printing	437
Infosys Technologies	India	Software	450
Mitsubishi Corp	Japan	Distribution (other)	457
POSCO	South Korea	Steel	461
Itochu Techno-Science	Japan	Software	467
Telekom Malaysia	Malaysia	Telecoms	474
Yamanouchi Pharmaceuticals	Japan	Pharmaceuticals	479
Dai Nippon Printing	Japan	Publishing & printing	486
Hindustan Lever	India	Personal goods	497

Table 2

Company	Country	Sector	Global Rank 2009	Global Rank 2008	Global Rank 2007
China Mobile	Hong Kong	Telecoms	5	5	16
Toyota Motor	Japan	Motor vehicles & parts	22	22	7
Samsung Electronics	South Korea	Technology hardware & equipment	51	58	56
NNT DoCoMo	Japan	Telecoms	56	92	77
Nippon Telegraph & Telephone	Japan	Telecoms	57	95	81
Honda Motor	Japan	Motor vehicles & parts	86	147	119

Company	Country	Sector	Global Rank 2009	Global Rank 2008	Global Rank 2007
Nintendo	Japan	Leisure goods	92	90	200
Taiwan Semiconductor Manufacturing	Taiwan	Technology hardware & equipment	99	146	145
Canon	Japan	Technology hardware & equipment	104	110	100
Takeda Pharmaceutical	Japan	Pharmaceuticals & biotechnology	150	184	130
Panasonic[2]	Japan	Leisure goods	156	145	158
Japan Tobacco	Japan	Tobacco	157	159	160
Singapore Telecom	Singapore	Telecoms	158	178	249
China Unicom	Hong Kong	Telecoms	165	314	N/L
Bharti Airtel	India	Telecoms	188	218	256
POSCO	South Korea	Industrial metals & mining	193	198	230
Mitsubishi Corp	Japan	Support services	202	151	212
KKDI	Japan	Telecoms	216	330	236
Hutchison Whampoa	Hong Kong	General (industrials)	218	208	202
Shin-Etsu Chemical	Japan	Chemicals	219	412	338
East Japan Railway	Japan	Travel & leisure	220	263	273
Sony	Japan	Leisure goods	231	210	154
Seven & I Holdings	Japan	General retailers	239	381	300
Mitsui	Japan	Support services	265	231	261

[2] Matsushita Electric Industrial changed its company name to Panasonic Corporation on 1 October 2008 and consolidated all its brands under the Panasonic name.

Company	Country	Sector	Global Rank 2009	Global Rank 2008	Global Rank 2007
Nippon Steel	Japan	Industrial metals & mining	270	250	164
Chunghwa Telecom	Taiwan	Telecoms	280	366	499
Denso	Japan	Motor vehicles & parts	283	315	260
China Railway Construction	China	Construction & materials	289	N/L	N/L
Aluminium Corp of China	China	Industrial metals & mining	293	273	N/L
Hon Hai Precision Industries	Taiwan	Electronic & electrical equipment	294	238	245
Fanuc	Japan	Industrial engineering	308	405	403
China Railway Group	China	Industrial engineering	309	433	N/L
Nissan Motor	Japan	Motor vehicles & parts	311	227	162
Kweichow Moutai	China	Beverages	314	363	N/L
Astellas Pharma	Japan	Pharmaceuticals & biotechnology	322	472	374
Infosys Technologies	India	Software & computer services	330	465	334
China Cosco	China	Industrial transportation	337	242	N/L
Baoshan Iron & Steel	China	Industrial metals & mining	340	288	N/L
Bharat Heavy Electricals	India	Industrial engineering	345	367	N/L
ITC	India	Tobacco	362	497	N/L

Company	Country	Sector	Global Rank 2009	Global Rank 2008	Global Rank 2007
Softbank	Japan	Telecoms	363	486	327
JFE Holdings	Japan	Industrial metals & mining	373	331	238
Tencent Holdings	Hong Kong	Software & computer services	375	N/L	N/L
Wilmar International	Singapore	Food producers	376	498	N/L
Telekomunikasi Indonesia	Indonesia	Telecoms	381	439	413
Central Japan Railway	Japan	Travel & leisure	400	398	354
Kyocera	Japan	Electronic & electrical equipment	403	N/L	N/L
Fast Retailing	Japan	General retailers	418	N/L	N/L
Daiichi Sankyo	Japan	Pharmaceuticals & biotechnology	423	425	399
Shanghai Electric Group	China	Industrial engineering	427	N/L	N/L
Bridgestone	Japan	Motor vehicles & parts	433	N/L	N/L
Jardine Matheson	Hong Kong	General (industrials)	441	487	N/L
SK Telecom	South Korea	Telecoms	449	N/L	N/L
Fujifilm	Japan	Technology hardware & equipment	452	N/L	434
Komatsu	Japan	Industrial engineering	461	326	436
Hyundai Heavy Industries	South Korea	Industrial engineering	466	319	N/L

Company	Country	Sector	Global Rank 2009	Global Rank 2008	Global Rank 2007
Sumitomo	Japan	Support services	470	N/L	400
Kao	Japan	Personal goods	478	N/L	N/L
Tata Consultancy Services	India	Software & computer services	483	481	318
Kirin Holdings	Japan	Beverages	485	N/L	N/L
Keyence	Japan	Electronic & electrical equipment	487	N/L	N/L
Hindustan Unilever	India	Personal goods	495	N/L	N/L
Mitsubishi Heavy Industries	Japan	Industrial engineering	497	N/L	412
Larsen & Toubro	India	Construction & materials	N/L	421	N/L
Angang Steel	China	Industrial metals & mining	N/L	490	N/L
Sumitomo Metal Industries	Japan	Industrial metals	N/L	N/L	366
Foxconn International[3]	Hong Kong	Technology, hardware & equipment	N/L	N/L	424
Wipro	India	Software & computer services	N/L	N/L	500

[3] Foxconn International is a company related to Hon Hai Precision Industries.

APPENDIX 2:
Asian brands in the Brand Finance Global 500 List

Asian brands included in Brand Finance's Global 500 List

Rank 2010	Rank 2009	Brand	Country	Industry Group	Brand Value 2010 (in US$m)	Brand Value 2009 (in US$m)
10	10	Toyota	Japan	Automobile manufacturer	27,319	21,995
23	16	China Mobile	Hong Kong	Telecoms	18,673	17,196
25	220	Mitsubishi	Japan	Distribution/ wholesale	17,805	3,002
45	35	Honda	Japan	Automobile manufacturer	13,083	11,461
51	34	Sony	Japan	Electronics	12,648	11,597
53	48	ICBC	China	Banks	12,083	10,031
54	62	China Construction Bank	China	Banks	10,276	9,024
63	56	NTT DOCOMO	Japan	Telecoms	11,247	9,649
64	51	Tata	India	Miscellaneous manufacturer	11,216	9,921
67	73	Nissan	Japan	Automobile manufacturer	10,412	7,742

Rank 2010	Rank 2009	Brand	Country	Industry Group	Brand Value 2010 (in US$m)	Brand Value 2009 (in US$m)
77	84	Bank of China	China	Banks	9,615	7,053
81	46	Hitachi	Japan	Electrical computer & equipment	9,095	10,139
82	88	Toshiba	Japan	Electronics	8,949	6,804
107	93	Reliance	India	Oil & gas	7,250	6,604
114	129	China Telecom	China	Telecoms	7,027	5,195
118	105	TEPCO	Japan	Electric	6,653	6,031
119	55	Nintendo	Japan	Toys/games	6,585	9,674
124	n/a	China United Network	China	Telecoms	6,444	n/a
125	110	Canon	Japan	Office equipment	6,421	5,919
126	124	MUFG	Japan	Banks	6,393	5,445
137	n/a	Agricultural Bank of China	China	Banks	6,032	n/a
142	188	China Unicom	Hong Kong	Telecoms	5,704	3,585
154	153	Fujitsu	Japan	Computers	5,497	4,447
157	114	Panasonic	Japan	Electronics	5,438	5,818
166	162	NEC	Japan	Electronics	5,129	4,257
174	209	Petro China	China	Oil & gas	4,879	3,168
176	158	Sharp	Japan	Electronics	4,805	4,352
187	253	Softbank	Japan	Telecoms	4,539	2,723
200	176	Aeon	Japan	Retail	4,153	3,873
201	185	Sinopec	China	Oil & gas	4,152	3,671
202	186	LG Electronics	South Korea	Electrical/ computers	4,149	3,648

Rank 2010	Rank 2009	Brand	Country	Industry Group	Brand Value 2010 (in US$m)	Brand Value 2009 (in US$m)
213	226	KDDI	Japan	Telecoms	3,871	2,918
220	252	Asahi	Japan	Beverages	3,734	2,725
221	391	China Life Insurance	China	Insurance	3,714	1,692
224	246	Singapore Airlines	Singapore	Airline	3,654	2,776
225	n/a	SAIC	China	Automotive	3,651	n/a
229	n/a	Jardines	Hong Kong	Holding company (diverse)	3,594	n/a
230	n/a	Petronas	Malaysia	Oil & gas	3,578	n/a
233	121	Lexus	Japan	Automotive	3,554	5,531
238	n/a	TSMC	Taiwan	Semiconductors	3,499	n/a
245	192	SMFG	Japan	Bank	3,462	3,428
246	n/a	China State Construction	China	Engineering & construction	3,459	n/a
254	n/a	MOL	Japan	Transport	3,402	n/a
255	271	Sanyo	Japan	Electrical/ computers	3,402	2,538
266	217	Bridgestone	Japan	Automobile	3,325	3,020
268	194	Tokio Marine	Japan	Insurance	3,304	3,377
270	234	JR-East	Japan	Transportation	3,292	2,854
272	297	Bank of Communica-tions	China	Banks	3,269	2,297
275	389	Ping An	China	Insurance	3,237	1,712
281	331	Suzuki	Japan	Automobile manufacturer	3,211	2,060
292	232	Espirit	Hong Kong	Apparel	3,057	2,869

Rank 2010	Rank 2009	Brand	Country	Industry Group	Brand Value 2010 (in US$m)	Brand Value 2009 (in US$m)
305	n/a	Bharat Petroleum	India	Oil & gas	2,945	n/a
330	424	Acer	Taiwan	Computers	2,795	1,529
332	305	Yamaha	Japan	Leisure time	2,774	2,169
334	266	Kirin	Japan	Beverages	2,765	2,619
342	n/a	POSCO	South Korea	Iron/steel	2,659	n/a
344	n/a	Mazda	Japan	Automotive	2,654	n/a
345	353	Ricoh	Japan	Office/business equipment	2,651	1,894
363	n/a	Camel	Japan	Tobacco	2,574	n/a
374	214	Mizuho	Japan	Banks	2,508	3,065
377	449	Wilmar	Singapore	Agriculture	2,498	1,432
379	370	Wipro	India	Software		1,819
398	145	Winston	Japan	Tobacco	2,378	2,084
409	90	7-Eleven	Japan	Retail	2,302	6,743
410	126	Mild Seven	Japan	Tobacco	2,301	5,399
413	199	Chubu Electric Power	Japan	Electric	2,285	3,331
415	310	SK Telecom	South Korea	Telecoms	2,282	2,139
416	n/a	Nippon Steel	Japan	Iron/steel	2,269	n/a
417	455	Kia	South Korea	Automobile manufacturer	2,264	1,414
422	241	Japan Airlines	Japan	Airline	2,247	2,813
423	n/a	Infosys	India	Software	2,246	n/a
431	470	China Merchants Bank	China	Banks	2,212	1,362

Rank 2010	Rank 2009	Brand	Country	Industry Group	Brand Value 2010 (in US$m)	Brand Value 2009 (in US$m)
432	n/a	JR West	Japan	Transport	2,210	n/a
439	n/a	ICICI Bank	India	Banks	2,164	n/a
440	399	Kyocera	Japan	Electronics	2,162	1,662
445	362	Shinsegae	South Korea	Retail	2,148	1,859
447	n/a	Toray	Japan	Textiles	2,136	n/a
448	328	Fujifilm	Japan	Miscellaneous manufacturer	2,131	2,074
449	335	Shiseido	Japan	Cosmetics/ personal care	2,130	2,044
450	476	Yamato	Japan	Transportation		1,343
457	n/a	Aisin	Japan	Auto parts & equipment	2,080	n/a
461	n/a	BYD	China	Electrical components & equipment	2,065	n/a
471	n/a	Tokya	Japan	Transport	2,005	n/a
473	n/a	Midea	China	Home furnishings	1,992	n/a
476	n/a	CSR	China	Transport	1,987	n/a
480	n/a	NTT DATA	Japan	Computers	1,967	n/a
484	n/a	Shanghai Pudong Development Bank	China	Banks	1,962	n/a
485	n/a	KEPCO	Japan	Electric	1,956	n/a
492	352	UNIQLO	Japan	Retail	1,929	1,904
495	n/a	Sumitomo	Japan	Auto parts & equipment	1,925	n/a
497	n/a	Yamada	Japan	Retail	1,909	n/a
499	481	Komatsu	Japan	Machinery/ construction & mining	1,898	1,329

APPENDIX 3:
Timeline of significant events in Asia's Invisible Gold story

1856 The first patent law was enacted in **India**, based on the British Patents Act 1852, giving protection for 14 years.

1858 In **Japan**, the Tokugawa Shogunate government opened the country to foreign trade.

1868 In **Japan**, the Meiji Restoration returning power to the Imperial House started the process of modernising the country.

1883–1884 The **Paris Convention** for the protection of industrial property was signed, and came into force in 1894 with 14 member states. Most countries in the world are now members.

1885 Japan introduced the *Tokkyo Senbai Jorei*, its first effective patent law.

1886 The **Berne Convention** was passed to protect literary and artistic works through copyright law.

1891 The **Madrid Convention** was established, providing for international registration of trademarks in multiple jurisdictions around the world.

1899 **Japan** joined the Paris and Berne Convention, and also changed its patent law to allow applications from foreign applicants.

1910 **Thailand** established its first trademark registration unit under the Thailand Ministry of Agriculture.

1912 The UK's Imperial Copyright Act 1911 came into force in **Singapore** (replacing the Imperial Copyright Act 1842).

1928 **India** joined the Berne Convention.

1931 **Thailand** joined the Berne Convention.

1937 The first patent, covering "Mountings for Electric Lamps", was registered in **Singapore** under a new procedure allowing patents granted in the UK to be registered in the then-Crown Colony.

1947 **The Philippines** introduced a patent system and set up a Patent Office, as well as passing an "Act to Provide for the Registration and Protection of Trademarks, Trade Names and Service Marks, Defining Unfair Competition and False Marking and Providing Remedies Against the Same."

1948 **Pakistan** joined the Berne Convention.

1949 **Vietnam** joined the Paris Convention and Madrid Agreement.

1950 **Indonesia** joined the Paris Convention.

1951 **The Philippines** joined the Berne Convention.

1952 **Sri Lanka** joined the Paris Convention.

1959 **Sri Lanka** joined the Berne Convention.

1961 **Korea** introduced its first modern patent system covering invention patents, utility models and design patents.

1962 The Universal Copyright Convention was adopted in Geneva, Switzerland, making it one of the two principal international conventions protecting copyright.

1965 **The Philippines** joined the Paris Convention.

1967 The World Intellectual Property Organization (WIPO) Convention was signed in Geneva, creating WIPO.

1975 **Japan** and **India** joined WIPO.

1976 **Vietnam** joined WIPO.

1977 **Pakistan** joined WIPO.

1978 **Sri Lanka** joined WIPO.

1979 **The Republic of Korea** and **Indonesia** joined WIPO.

1980 The **Republic of Korea** joined the Paris Convention. **China** and the **Philippines** joined WIPO.

1982 **China** introduced its first modern IP law, the Copyright Law, and passed the Trademark Law (which came into force in March 1983). **Indonesia** replaced the colonial Auterswet with a national Copyright Act.

1985 **Japan** celebrated 100 years of its IPR system. **China** joined the Paris Convention. **Bangladesh** joined WIPO.

1986 **Malaysia** permitted local patent applications under the Patents Act 1983. The Act also introduced 'utility innovation' protection (lasting 15 years maximum) for minor inventions. (In 1995, the test for 'novelty' of such inventions was changed from a local one to a global standard and since then the number of applications has been small, averaging around 75 a year since 2000.)

1989 A Protocol to the Madrid Agreement of 1891 ("Madrid Protocol") was concluded to make the Madrid trademark system more compatible with the domestic laws of countries which had not joined the Madrid Agreement. **Malaysia** joined WIPO and the Paris Convention. **China** joined the Madrid Agreement. **Thailand** joined the WIPO Convention.

1990 **China** enacted its first Copyright Law. **Malaysia** joined the Berne Convention. **Singapore** joined the WIPO Convention.

1991 After a financial crisis, **India** started to dismantle the Licence Raj and liberalise its economy. **Bangladesh** joined the Paris Convention.

1992 **China** joined the Berne Convention.

1994 The TRIPs Agreement was signed in Marrakesh, Morocco.

1995 The World Trade Organisation took over from the GATT the job of managing world trade. **Japan** issued its two millionth patent. **Korea** extended its patent protection from 15 years from date of publication to 20 years from date of patent filing, bringing its system into line with international standards. **Singapore** joined the Paris Convention and became an independent patent-granting country on 23 February with the coming into force of the Patents Act 1994. **Laos** and **Cambodia** joined WIPO. **China** joined the Madrid Protocol.

1996 The WIPO Copyright Treaty was signed in Geneva. The **Republic of Korea** joined the Berne Convention.

1997 **Indonesia** joined the Berne Convention.

1998 **Cambodia, India** and **Laos** joined the Paris Convention. **Singapore** joined the Berne Convention.

1999 **Japan** opened the Industrial Property Digital Library (IPDL). **Bangladesh** joined the Berne Convention.

2000 **China** and **Japan** joined the Madrid Protocol.

2001 **China** joined the WTO. The first World Intellectual Property Day took place on 26 April.

2002 **India** extended patent protection from 14 to 20 years. **Japan, Indonesia** and **the Philippines** joined the WIPO Copyright Treaty,

2003 The **Singapore**-USA Free Trade Agreement was signed; since then—in the words of Associate Professor Ng Loy Wee Loon—"the name of the IP game in Singapore has been Expansion". The **Republic of Korea** joined the Madrid Protocol.

2004 **Pakistan** joined the Paris Convention. **Vietnam** joined the Berne Convention. **Republic of Korea** joined the WIPO Copyright Treaty.

2005 **Vietnam** enacted its Intellectual Property Law, which includes provisions on circuit layouts, geographical indications, unfair competition, trade names and trade secrets. **Japan** established the IP High Court: Judge Masami Ichikawa stated that "… its implications are considerable. The law proclaims that Japan makes much of Intellectual Property, and announces that the Japanese judiciary is ready to better protect intellectual property." **India** introduced protection for pharmaceutical product patents. **Singapore** joined the WIPO Copyright Treaty.

2006 **India** granted its first pharmaceutical product patent to a life sciences company Roche India Pvt Ltd, for its biotech drug 'Pegasys'. **Vietnam** joined the Madrid Protocol (on trademarks) and introduced a new and detailed Intellectual Property Law to replace the relevant provisions of the Civil Code, which had applied since 1996.

2007 **China** joined the WIPO Copyright Treaty.

2008 **Thailand** joined the Paris Convention.

2009 In March the five millionth patent application was filed in **China**.

2010 The China-ASEAN FTA came into force.

SOURCES

Regular reading of newspapers and journals from around the world, but particularly the *Financial Times*, *Wall Street Journal Asia*, *Business Times* (Singapore), *China International Business*, *China Daily*, *China Economic Review*, *South China Morning Post* (Hong Kong), *Bangkok Post*, *The Independent* (UK), *The Economist*, *Business Week*, *Fortune*, *Forbes Asia*, *TIME*, *Intellectual Asset Management*, *Managing Intellectual Property*, *Trademark World*, *Copyright World*, *Patent World*, *China Intellectual Property*, has provided leads to many of the examples mentioned. The excellent blogs *ipdragon* and *spicyipindia* have also been very useful.

In addition, I have used the following specific sources for either background or foreground:

Agtmael, Antoine van *The Emerging Markets Century: How a New Breed of World Class Companies is Overtaking the World* (Simon & Schuster, 2007).

Alford, William P. *To Steal a Book is an Elegant Offense: Intellectual Property Law in Chinese Civilization* (Stanford University Press, 1995).

Anderson, Chris *Free: The Future of a Radical Price* (Hyperion, 2009).

Bell, Sandra *International Brand Management of Chinese Companies* (Physica-Verlag, 2008).

Ben-Atar, Doron S. *Trade Secrets: Intellectual Piracy and the Origins of American Industrial Power* (Yale University Press, 2004).

Bhandari, Bhupesh *The Ranbaxy Story* (Penguin India, 2005).

Bridges, Jon & Downs, David *No 8 Wire: The Best of Kiwi Ingenuity* (Hodder Moa Beckett, 2000).

Chadha, Parmit & Chadha, Radhika *Innovative India* (Penguin Portfolio, 2007).

Chang, Ha-Joon *Kicking Away the Ladder-Development Strategy in Historical Perspective* (Anthem Press, 2002).

Chang, Ha-Joon *Bad Samaritans: The Guilty Secrets of Rich Nations & The Threat to Global Prosperity* (Random House Business, 2007).

Chang, Sea-Jin *Sony vs. Samsung: The Inside Story of the Electronics Giants' Battle for Global Supremacy* (Wiley Asia, 2008).

Chen, Qiongdi *Patent Biotechnology Invention in China* [2010] European Intellectual Property Review 9.

Cheong, Sally *Corporate Groupings in the KLSE* (Modern Law Publishers).

Chong, Seung *The Law and Practice of Mergers and Acquisitions in the People's Republic of China* (Oxford University Press, 2007).

Cornish, William & Llewelyn, David *Intellectual Property: Patents, Copyright, Trademarks and Allied Rights* (Sweet & Maxwell, 6th ed., 2007).

Dyson, James *Against the Odds* (Orion Business Books, 1997).

Emmott, Bill *Rivals: How the Struggle Between China, India and Japan will Shape our Next Decade* (Allen Lane, 2008).

Engardio, Pete (ed.) *Chindia: How China and India Are Revolutionizing Global Business* (McGraw-Hill, 2007).

Ernst, Dieter *A New Geography of Knowledge in the Electronics Industry? Asia's Role in Global Innovation Networks* (East-West Center, 2009).

Fisher, Matthew *Fundamentals of Patent Law: Interpretation and Scope of Protection* (Hart Publishing, 2007).

Gomez, Edmund Terence *Chinese Business in Malaysia: Accumulation, Accommodation and Ascendance* (Curzon Press, 1999).

Grenville Smith, R. & Barrie, Alexander *ASPRO: How a Family Business Grew Up* (Nicholas International Ltd, 1976).

Heller, Michael *The Gridlock Economy: How Too Much Ownership Wrecks Markets, Stops Innovation, and Costs Lives* (Basic Books, 2008).

Hong, Jun & Wu, Hao *Enterprise Patent Strategy and Development of Guangxi Sugar Industry* (2008) 3 International Journal of Business and Management 78.

Hutton, Will *The Writing on the Wall: China and the West in the 21st Century* (Little, Brown, 2006).

Johnstone, Bob *We Were Burning: Japanese Entrepreneurs and the Forging of the Electronic Age* (Basic Books, 1999).

Kamioka, Kazuyoshi *Japanese Business Pioneers* (Times Books International, 1986).

Kawai, Masahiro & Wignaraja, Ganeshan *Asian FTAs: Trends and Challenges* (ADB Institute Working Paper Series, August 2009).

Keen, Andrew *The Cult of the Amateur: How Today's Internet is Killing Our Culture and Assaulting Our Economy* (Nicholas Brealey Publishing, 2007).

Kumar, Nirmalya *India's Global Powerhouses: How They Are Taking On the World* (Harvard Business Press, 2009).

Larçon, Jean-Paul *Chinese Multinationals* (World Scientific, 2009).

Lim, Gerrie *Idol to Icon. The Creation of Celebrity Brands* (Marshall Cavendish Business, 2005.)

Ling, Zhijun *The Lenovo Affair: The Growth of China's Computer Giant and its Takeover of IBM-PC* (Wiley Asia, 2006).

Lo, Chi *When Asia Meets China in the New Millennium: China's Role in Shaping Asia's Post-Crisis Economic Transformation* (Pearson Education Asia, 2003).

Lo, Chi *Phantom of the China Economic Threat: Shadow of the Next Asian Crisis* (Palgrave Macmillan, 2007).

Lopes, Teresa da Silva *Global Brands: The Evolution of Multinationals in Alcoholic Beverages* (Cambridge University Press, 2007).

Mahbubani, Kishore *The* New *Asian Hemisphere: The Irresistible Shift of Global Power to the East* (Public Affairs, 2008).

Morita, Akio *Made in Japan: Akio Morita and Sony* (Collins, 1987).

Matsushita, Konosuke *Quest for Prosperity: The Life of a Japanese Industrialist* (PHP, 1988).

McCartney, Sarah *The Fake Factor: Why we Love Brands but Buy Fakes* (Marshall Cavendish Business, 2006).

McMillan, John *Reinventing the Bazaar: A Natural History of Markets* (W.W. Norton, 2002).

Mertha, Andrew C. *The Politics of Piracy: Intellectual Property in Contemporary China* (Cornell University Press, 2005).

Naim, Moises *Illicit: How Smugglers, Traffickers and Copycats are Hijacking the Global Economy* (Arrow Books, 2007).

Nie, Winter & Xin, Katherine (with Lily Zhang) *Made in China: Secrets of China's Dynamic Entrepreneurs* (Wiley, 2009).

Nilekani, Nandan *Imagining India: Ideas for the New Century* (Allen Lane, 2008).

Pasuk Phongpaichit & Baker, Chris *Thailand's Boom and Bust* (Silkworm Books, 1998).

Pasuk Phongpaichit & Baker, Chris *Thaksin* (Silkworm Books, 2009).

Pike, Francis *Empires at War. A Short History of Modern Asia since World War II* (IB Tauris, 2010).

Piramal, Gita *Business Maharajas* (Penguin Books India, 1996).

Porter, Michael E., Takeuchi, Hirotaka & Sakakibara, Mariko. *Can Japan Compete?* (Macmillan Press, 2000).

Robertson, Jill *MacPherson: The Chocolate King* (Lothian Books, 2004).

Rogers, Jim *A Bull in China* (Wiley, 2008).

Roy, Subir *Made in India: A Study of Emerging Competitiveness* (Tata McGraw-Hill, 2005).

Sakakibara, Mariko & Branstetter, Lee *Do Stronger Patents Induce More Innovation? Evidence from the 1988 Japanese Patent Law Reforms* 32 RAND Journal of Economics 77.

Schaub, Mark E. *China: The Art of Law* (CCH Hong Kong, 2007).

Schein, Edgar *Strategic Pragmatism: The Culture of Singapore's Economic Development Board* (MIT, 1997).

Schuman, Michael *The Miracle: The Epic Story of Asia's Quest for Wealth* (Harper Business, 2009).

Schwartz, Evan *Juice: The Creative Fuel that Drives World-Class Inventors* (Harvard Business School Press, 2004).

Shimizu, Hiroshi *Japanese Firms in Contemporary Singapore* (NUS Press, 2008).

Shiva, Vandana *Monocultures of the Mind: Understanding the Threats to Biological and Cultural Diversity*, inaugural Hooper Lecture, Centre of International Programs, University of Guelph, 21 September 1993.

Sim, Wong Hoo *Chaotic Thoughts from the Old Millennium* (Cruxible, 2003).

Smith, David *The Dragon and the Elephant: China, India and the New World Order* (Profile Books, 2008).

Tan, Loke Khoon *Pirates of the Middle Kingdom: The Art of Trademark War* (Sweet & Maxwell Asia, 2004).

Wee, Chow-Hou & Combe, Fred *Business Journey to the East: An East-West Perspective on Global-is-Asian* (McGraw-Hill, 2009).

Wei, George *Some Thoughts on Intellectual Property Rights in Singapore: A Monograph for Gerald Dworkin* (2009).

Williamson, Peter J. *Winning in Asia: Strategies for Competing in the New Millennium* (Harvard Business School Press, 2004).

Yates, Ronald E. *The Kikkoman Chronicles: A Global Company with a Japanese Soul* (McGraw-Hill, 1998).

INDEX

ABOUT THE AUTHOR

David Llewelyn is Professor of Intellectual Property (IP) Law at King's College London; Visiting Professor at Singapore Management University; and External Director and Deputy Chairman of the IP Academy, Singapore. He is also Of Counsel at international law firm White & Case, based in its Singapore office; Chairman of IP investment and strategy firm, IPR-X Asia-Pacific; and Honorary Professor at the University of Hong Kong.

Involved in the field for more than 30 years, David is recognised as one of the world's leading experts on the protection and commercialisation of IP. He is co-author of *Kerly's Law of Trade Marks and Trade Names* (14th ed. 2005) and the leading student textbook *Cornish, Llewelyn and Aplin on Intellectual Property: Patents, Copyright, Trade Marks and Allied Rights* (7th ed. 2010).